Comparing the Policy of
Aboriginal Assimilation

Andrew Armitage

Comparing the Policy of Aboriginal Assimilation: Australia, Canada, and New Zealand

UBCPress / Vancouver

© UBC Press 1995

Reprinted 1998

All rights reserved. No part of this publication may be reproduced, stored in a retrieval system, or transmitted, in any form or by any means, without prior written permission of the publisher.

Printed in Canada on acid-free paper ∞

ISBN 0-7748-0458-0 (hardcover)
ISBN 0-7748-0459-9 (paperback)

Canadian Cataloguing in Publication Data

Armitage, Andrew
　Comparing the policy of aboriginal assimilation

　Includes bibliographical references and index.
　ISBN 0-7748-0458-0 (bound). – ISBN 0-7748-0459-9 (pbk.)

　　1. Native peoples – Canada – Government relations.* 2. Australian aborigines – Government relations. 3. Maori (New Zealand people) – Government relations. 4. Assimilation (Sociology). I. Title.

GN367.A75 1994　　303.48'2　　C94-910877-4

This book has been published with the help of a grant from the Social Science Federation of Canada, using funds provided by the Social Sciences and Humanities Research Council of Canada.

UBC Press also gratefully acknowledges the ongoing support to its publishing program from the Canada Council, the Province of British Columbia Cultural Services Branch, and the Department of Communications of the Government of Canada.

UBC Press
University of British Columbia
6344 Memorial Road
Vancouver, BC V6T 1Z2
(604) 822-3259
Fax: 1-800-668-0821

Contents

Maps and Tables / vii

Preface / ix

Acknowledgments / xiv

1 Introduction / 3

2 Australia: The General Structure of Aboriginal Policy / 14

3 Australia: Aboriginal Peoples and Child Welfare Policy / 41

4 Canada: The General Structure of Canadian Indian Policy / 70

5 Canada: First Nations Family and Child Welfare Policy / 100

6 New Zealand: The General Structure of Maori Policy / 136

7 New Zealand: Maori People and Child Welfare Policy / 160

8 Similarities and Differences among Australia, Canada, and New Zealand / 185

9 Understanding the Policy of Aboriginal Assimilation / 220

Notes / 243

Bibliography / 261

Index / 277

Maps and Tables

Maps
1 Australian Research Sites and Relevant Place Names / 15
2 Western Canadian Research Sites and Relevant Place Names / 71
3 New Zealand Research Sites and Relevant Place Names / 137

Tables
2.1 Australian and Aboriginal population and proportion of children, 1881-1986 / 28
2.2 Aboriginal population as a proportion of state populations, Australia, by census year / 30
2.3 Aboriginal population by urbanization, Australia, 1961-81 / 32
3.1 New South Wales Aboriginal children and the welfare board, 1940 / 45
3.2 New South Wales Aboriginal children in departmental care, 1966, 1969, 1976, and 1980 / 48
3.3 Aboriginal and Torres Strait Islander children, under orders, Queensland, by type of order, 1987 / 55
3.4 Northern Territory welfare administration, 1952-72 / 61
4.1 Indian people by province, Canada, 1871-1986 / 90
4.2 Children, aged 0-16, in the Canadian and status Indian populations / 92
4.3 Indian and Inuit in urban centres, Canada, 1951-81 / 93
5.1 Status Indian children in school, Canada, 1901-61 / 107
5.2 Residential and day school enrolment by province, Canada, 1936 / 109
5.3 Status Indian children in care, Canada, 1966-7 to 1988-9 / 116
5.4 Adoption of status Indian children, Canada, 1964-5 to 1985-6 / 116
5.5 Indian children in care by province, Canada / 118
5.6 Status Indian and non-Indian children in care, Canada, 1978-9 / 119

5.7 Agencies (bands) administering child welfare programs, Canada, 1981-91 / 124
5.8 Staff employed by Indian child welfare agencies, Canada, 1981-8 / 125
5.9 Federal expenditures on Indian child welfare, Canada, 1981-8 / 125
5.10 Status Indian children in care, Manitoba, agreements, 1981-9 / 125
6.1 Maori and non-Maori population and children aged 0-14, 1891-1986 / 127
6.2 Maori and Maori descent populations, 1961-86 / 153
6.3 Rural, urban, and metropolitan distribution of Maori, 1926-61 / 154
6.4 Percentage of Maori and Non-Maori population in centres under and over 1,000, 1961-81 / 154
7.1 Children in care and under supervision, New Zealand, 1921-86 / 163
7.2 Adoption orders, New Zealand, 1956-86 / 165
7.3 Juvenile offences, total and Maori cases, 1956-86 / 170
7.4 Estimate of Maori and non-Maori children in care, per 1,000, 1981 / 171
7.5 Numbers of Te Kohanga Reo by Maori Affairs district, 1982-8 / 175
7.6 Child welfare protection complaints, total and Maori, 1981-6 / 183
8.1 Aboriginal populations, Australia, Canada, and New Zealand, pre-contact to 1986 / 191
8.2 Definitions of aboriginality, Australia, Canada, and New Zealand / 196
8.3 Government of aboriginal land, Australia, Canada, and New Zealand / 200
8.4 Government of financial affairs and daily life, Australia, Canada, and New Zealand / 202
8.5 Separation of aboriginal children from their parents, Australia, Canada, and New Zealand / 206
8.6 Children as a proportion of the aboriginal and general population, Australia, Canada, and New Zealand / 211
8.7 Urbanized aboriginal populations, Australia, Canada, and New Zealand / 214
8.8 Modifications of child welfare systems, Australia, Canada, and New Zealand / 218

Preface

I am a social worker, and this book has its origins in personal reflections on what I observed to be child welfare policy and practice towards First Nations families and children in Canada during two periods of my career. My first experience was in 1963, when I was a social worker for the Department of Social Welfare in the province of British Columbia (BC), Canada. The regional director asked me to undertake a year-long special project, during which I would be based in the department's Fort St John office. The project consisted of taking responsibility for some forty children, mostly First Nations, who had been apprehended from their families and who were staying in foster homes in Fort St John. This was, in today's terminology, an exercise in 'permanency planning.' The children came principally from isolated reserve communities in northern BC along the Alaska Highway, which extended for 600 miles from Fort St John to the Yukon border. A few were from a series of even more isolated communities in northwestern BC, so that the total area from which the children came covered approximately 30,000 square miles. The permanent population of the area was less than 5,000 people, half of whom lived in one settlement – Fort Nelson. Map 2 (p. 71) shows the communities in which these first encounters took place.

The children had been taken from their parents by social workers primarily because of what were considered to be serious cases of neglect, severe risks of injury to children left unattended by their parents, and parental alcoholism. I cannot recall a case that would today be classed as physical or sexual abuse, but it is certainly true that social workers were much less attentive to the occurrence of sexual abuse in 1962 than they are now. The typical pattern of removal was that there would be an allegation of risk to the child from a third party living near the community, often a school teacher or a police officer. The social worker would arrive and make limited inquiries before deciding that the safety of the child required that alternative parenting be found. The children were then moved to Fort St John, some 300 or more miles from their homes (there were no closer foster home resources). Once in Fort St John, it was difficult if not impossible for the overworked social workers to plan for the return of the children to their parents. As a result, the children often languished in foster homes for up to three years without any plan being made for their future. In some cases they were receiving reasonable care by dedicated foster parents and were well settled in their homes; in other cases they had had a sequence of placements, as no home could be found where they could continue to stay. None of the foster parents of these children was First Nations, and neither First Nations language nor culture was considered in making placements.

My task was to make permanent arrangements for the children, including establishing which of them could be returned to their parents. Contacting the families from which these children came was not easy. Many were frightened, and some had moved and were living in either the Yukon or Alberta, placing them outside provincial jurisdiction. Formal communication had to be channelled through Victoria, 800 miles to the south, and then through Whitehorse, 900 miles to the northwest, or through Edmonton, 400 miles to the east. Nevertheless, with persistence, most parents could be contacted. In the end, about half the children were returned to their parents; a quarter were either adopted or arrangements were made for a long-term foster parenting plan; and the remainder were still in an uncertain condition when, a year later, the project ended. I have often wondered what happened to them.

My second experience was in 1986, when I was appointed superintendent of family and child service in BC. In the intervening years, the child welfare of First Nations peoples had become a major issue for provincial social policy. There were many interrelated problems. In BC as a whole, First Nations children made up more than 30 per cent of all children in care, even though they made up only 4 per cent of all children in the province. Furthermore, the evidence of severe family disorganization among First Nations peoples was overwhelming. Professional journals and media reports included evidence, often gathered through the courts, of First Nations peoples being regularly convicted for both physical and sexual abuse. Research reports confirmed that sexual abuse was a frequent feature of the lives of First Nations children living in northern Canada.

At the working level, most social workers knew that problems of this scale exceeded their knowledge and resources, but this was not officially recognized by the government. The official policy with respect to sexual and physical abuse was clear but unenforceable. The social worker's duty was to ensure that the child was protected from abuse. Any sexual behaviour towards a child constituted abuse, as did any physical behaviour resulting in harm. However, at a practical level, apprehending large numbers of children would have received little political support, nor was it possible to find or pay for the requisite child care resources. On the other hand, apprehending a few children seemed discriminatory, inequitable, and token. The result was that social workers in the field were not acting on reports of abuse and neglect but, instead, were seeking alternative ways of working with First Nations peoples to ensure that their children were protected. At head office, there was little information as to the extent of the problem. The minister and senior staff knew that social workers could not follow written policy, but no alternative was formulated.

The time was also one of change, with First Nations peoples increasingly taking responsibility for First Nations child welfare. The Spallumcheen people, in the Okanagan area of BC, had conducted a successful political campaign in 1982 and had obtained an agreement that allowed them to manage their own affairs. The Nuu-chah-nulth people on Vancouver Island had also negotiated a formal agreement with the province – an agreement which gave them the right to act as the child protection authority on their reserve lands; and the Carrier-Sekani people in the central interior of BC had a service agreement with the province which stipulated that support services would be provided to them by First Nations peoples. The location of these initiatives is also shown on Map 2 (p. 71). Across Canada, there were signs of major changes, with 184 out of 592 bands having similar agreements with provincial authorities by 1987-8, as opposed to only 11 in 1981-2.

It appeared that my direct career experience with First Nations child welfare spanned both the beginning and the end of twenty-five years of provincial jurisdiction for child welfare. This book is devoted to understanding the policies – past and present – which have been and are directed towards aboriginal children and families. My search for understanding expanded as I became aware of similar policies in other countries. It expanded again as I came to see these policies as expressions of a general social policy of aboriginal assimilation. As a result, about half of this book deals with the general features of aboriginal social policy, which provides the context for the child welfare policies that were followed. Child welfare policies serve as a detailed examples of how general policies of assimilation have been pursued. This book describes, compares, and discusses the policies of settler populations towards aboriginal peoples, the reasons that have been given for these policies, and the ways that they have been carried out. It provides data on such matters as the extent of, and the trauma due to, aboriginal child adoption by non-aboriginal peoples. However, I chose not to deal with the full impact of these policies on aboriginal peoples, for, in each country, there is a growing literature on this subject – a literature which contains many contributions from aboriginal people.

This book is concerned with why one culture imposed itself on others. The intentions were usually based on a European view of the aboriginal populations' 'best interests', but the results were always disappointing and often disastrous.

Naming Aboriginal and Non-Aboriginal Peoples
The naming of the peoples referred to in this book is a particularly sensitive matter, as in most cases they were named by colonial governments – their own names being disregarded. Although aboriginal peoples' names should, of course, be respected, much of written history does not do so. And, as this account deals with that history, the names used to refer to aboriginal peoples are often of colonial derivation. A few terms require definition:
- 'aboriginal' is used as a generic term to refer to people living on the land at the time of colonial settlement.
- 'Aboriginal' refers to the Australian Aborigines.
- 'First Nations' is used as the collective name for Canadian aboriginal Indian peoples.
- 'Indian' refers to a person with legal Indian status as defined in the Indian Act of Canada.
- 'Maori' refers to the Maori tribes of New Zealand.
- Specific names for aboriginal peoples are capitalized.

Selecting terms to use for the non-aboriginal, immigrant peoples of Australia, Canada, and New Zealand has also been difficult. To call them simply Australians, Canadians, and New Zealanders suggests that these national names are more appropriate for them than they are for aboriginal peoples. 'British' was used in some earlier periods, but, although many settlers have British origins, there are many more who have European, African, and Asian origins. In any case, nearly all would now reject being called British. 'European,' 'settler,' 'immigrant,' 'non-Native,' and 'non-aboriginal' have all been used. In the New Zealand section, the Maori word 'Pakeha' is also used. My use of these collective terms is not meant to imply that these varied peoples have or had a unified identity or set of views. When public policy is attributed to them, it is because it was the official policy of the day. In all periods, there have been many who have dissented from the official view and many more who knew nothing about it.

Acknowledgments

During the time I have been working on this book I have incurred many debts. The first is to my wife Molly for her constant encouragement, companionship, and support. The second is to Professor Roy Parker of the University of Bristol for his knowledge, interest, and advice. Visits to both Australia and New Zealand were essential to gathering data and conducting interviews. These were made possible by the understanding of my colleagues in the School of Social Work at the University of Victoria and through the financial support of the Laidlaw Foundation of Ontario.

Throughout my travels, data gathering, and interviews I have been received with unfailing courtesy and interest from representatives of aboriginal peoples, government departments of social welfare, and universities. I particularly appreciated the opportunity to visit the University of Queensland in Brisbane and Massey University in New Zealand. In the text I have identified the names of those who were particularly helpful to me in my inquiries, but two people deserve special mention for the unique contribution they made to my thinking. They are Vapi Kupenga (Massey University), a member of the Ngati Porou (Maori) people of New Zealand, and my late colleague Elizabeth Hill (University of Victoria), a member of the Anishinaabe (First Nations) people of Canada. Both contributed deeply to my understanding of my subject and left me with a profound respect for their people.

This book has been published with the help of a grant from the Social Science and Humanities Research Council of Canada.

Comparing the Policy of Aboriginal Assimilation

1
Introduction

> It is not to be doubted that this country has been invested with wealth and power, with arts and knowledge, with the sway of distant lands and the mastery of restless waters for some great purpose in the government of the world. Can we suppose otherwise than that it is our office to carry civilization and humanity, peace and good government, and above all the knowledge of the true God, to the uttermost ends of the earth?
>
> – British Parliamentary Papers, *Report of the Select Committee on Aborigines*, 1837

The process of European colonization of the Americas could be said to have begun with Viking settlements. However, the major European invasion began in the late fifteenth century, with the voyage of Columbus to the West Indies in 1492 and with the establishment of semi-permanent Grand Banks fishing settlements. By the early 1500s, the European visitors had decided to establish small permanent settlements to secure safe harbours and to provide established bases for the extraction of natural resources and for trade with aboriginal peoples. Initially, the intrusion into aboriginal life was limited. However, given the competitive and acquisitive nature of European culture, growth and ever-deeper intrusions into aboriginal culture were inevitable.

Contact with Australia and New Zealand began in the seventeenth century, and, by the early nineteenth century, the process of colonization and expansion was worldwide. Although all the European powers participated, Britain succeeded in dominating the most territory. This process of expansion was opposed by aboriginal peoples throughout the world, but they lacked both the military technology to defeat the invaders and a system of communication which would have enabled them to unify their interests.

The early nineteenth century was not only a period of major colonial expansion for Britain, it was also a period of major social reform. The ideals of both processes were interrelated, and common features are apparent in the social policy documents of the time. In 1834 the House of Commons received the royal commission report on the Poor Law.[1] The report provided fundamental principles of British policy and practice in relation to the indigent. In 1835 the House of Commons appointed a select committee on Aborigines, whose 1837 report shared ideals and methods with that which had been produced on the Poor Law.[2] Both reports dealt with policies concerning the 'correct' way to deal with a population that operated outside the accepted economic structure and which was, or could become, a source of disorder. These policies included:

- the assertion of control, that is to say, the assumption that an orderly, managed world was needed and that Britain was to provide it – both at home and overseas
- an assumption that the purpose of policy was to bring 'outsiders,' whether the poor or aboriginals, within the established institutions of British society and, particularly, the wage economy (albeit at the level of the lowest paid independent labourer)
- a commitment to a legal and regulatory process anchored in a separate law for those outside the mainstream of society, pending their full citizenship
- appointment of 'protectors' (who could provide aboriginal peoples with a restricted status under the law and subject them to summary discipline) and of 'overseers' (who could do the same for paupers)
- special recognition for the situation of children, who were considered particularly open to change, education, and salvation
- special recognition for the elderly, for whom change seemed unlikely
- a recognized place for organized Christianity as an essential element in the process of producing citizens
- an obligation to provide orderly reports on the progress of the administration and the welfare of aboriginal peoples and/or paupers.[3]

These principles were introduced more gradually into aboriginal administration than into Poor Law administration, but they nevertheless provided a common framework that has persisted over a long period. Whereas the Poor Law administration was formally ended by the reforms initiated following the Beveridge Report (1941),[4] the framework of aboriginal social policy persisted unchanged until the second half of the twentieth century – and it has not yet been totally relinquished.

The policies set out in the select committee's report were believed to combine virtue with economy:

> One of the two systems we must have to preserve our own security, and the peace of our colonial borders; either overwhelming military force with all its attendant expense, or a line of temperate conduct and of justice towards our neighbours ... The main point I would have in view would be trade, commerce, peace and civilization. The other alternative is extermination.[5]

The reference to extermination referred to the killing of aboriginal men, women, and children that had occurred in many parts of the British Empire. In the Caribbean, Newfoundland, and Tasmania all but a remnant of the resident aboriginal peoples had been murdered. In practice, the choice between killing and 'a temperate line of conduct' was often beyond the control of colonial administrators. As settlement expanded, aboriginal peoples were deprived of their lands and conflict was inevitable. However, once a sufficient number of aboriginal peoples had been killed (i.e., enough to ensure British dominance), a set of policies based on a 'temperate line of conduct' frequently became possible. These policies relied upon a dominant military or civil police force for their ultimate enforcement and were aimed at managing aboriginal peoples by controlling their land use, settlements, government, and daily life. They also called for introducing aboriginal peoples to missionaries.

General aboriginal policy is discussed in Chapters 2, 4, and 6. Each of these chapters also provides the context for a description and discussion of each country's respective aboriginal child welfare policy. Child welfare policy was seen as one of the 'softer' tools used to obtain compliance and, ultimately, to ensure the universal acceptance of British rule. In Britain, the Poor Law was already using child welfare policy as a means of managing families by separating the children of paupers from their parents. Two results were intended: (1) discouragement of the use of the Poor Law; and (2) the provision of children for domestic service and trade apprenticeship. In the mid-nineteenth century, reformatory and industrial school legislation made these objectives more explicit, and the state obtained legal authority to separate a child from his or her parents and to make new provisions for his or her discipline. The power to make care orders for children was subsequently extended to caring for orphans, dealing with truancy, protecting the health of the child and the health of the community, and caring for the child of an unmarried mother (thus freeing her for domestic service). Finally, the state gave itself the power to protect children from parents whom the authorities considered to be abusive or negligent.[6] If the parents were considered to be totally unsuited to the task of raising their children responsibly, guardianship was transferred to other 'fit persons.' For the child, these measures meant a childhood and adolescence in either residential care, a foster home(s), or as an adoptee in Britain or one of its colonies. In addition to these 'normal' reasons for state intervention into parenting, the aboriginal peoples of the settled territories of the former British Empire had their children removed from them so that the dominant culture could pursue its objective of carrying 'civilization and humanity, peace and good government, and above all the knowledge of the true God, to the uttermost ends of the earth.'

In the second half of the twentieth century, removing children from their parents in order to change a people and a culture came to be recognized as an act of oppression, formally considered by the United Nations (UN) to be a type of genocide. According to the 1948 UN Convention on the Prevention and Punishment of the Crime of Genocide:

> In the present Convention, genocide means any of the following acts committed with intent to destroy, in whole or part, a national, ethnical, racial or religious group, as such:
> (a) Killing members of the group;
> (b) Causing serious bodily or mental harm to members of the group;
> (c) Deliberately inflicting on the group conditions of life calculated to bring about its physical destruction in whole or part;
> (d) Imposing measures intended to prevent births within the group;
> (e) Forcibly transferring children of the group to another group.[7]

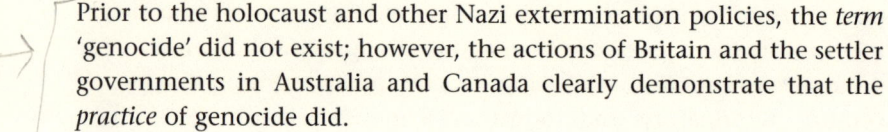

Prior to the holocaust and other Nazi extermination policies, the *term* 'genocide' did not exist; however, the actions of Britain and the settler governments in Australia and Canada clearly demonstrate that the *practice* of genocide did.

In Australia, Canada, and New Zealand there have been periods in which the children of aboriginal minorities have been removed from their parents at rates that were many times greater than the rates at which children of the majority culture were so removed. This practice began in the early days of settlement, was carried out vigorously as late as the 1970s, and still continues, in modified form, in the 1990s. Throughout this book, the extent of separation of aboriginal children from their parents is used as an indicator of important policy differences from decade to decade, country to country, and region to region.

The aboriginal child welfare policies of each country, and the extent to which children were separated from their parents, are described and discussed in Chapters 3, 5, and 7. The comparison of general aboriginal policy with aboriginal child welfare policy, which forms the heart of this book, begs the question: Why compare the policies of different countries? And, specifically, why compare Australia, Canada, and New Zealand?

Reasons for Using the Comparative Method
The first reason for using the comparative method is to address the problem of perspective. The origins, purposes, and effects of a country's social policies have a complexity that defies simple description. It is easy to confuse the effects of a particular policy with changes taking place in demography, economics, or culture, and so to ascribe to it either undue efficacy or undeserved failure. The student is also frequently too close to the policies to be studied to be able to have sufficient perspective on them. He or she is often a member of the society whose policies are being studied and, in addition, has particular views and/or favours particular reforms.

Social policies are difficult to study, as each is in some ways a unique creation. Although there have been attempts to develop demonstration and evaluation models for social programs, the results of such experiments have often been irrelevant to actual changes in policy.[8] The student cannot expect to use experimental designs to test the effects of differing policies.

The comparative method provides a partial solution to the problem of perspective in that it presents one set of actions alongside another set, thus enabling one to ascertain similarities and differences between the two. If the similarities are sufficiently confirmed, then it begins to be possible to ascribe some of the differences to conditions that are unique to a particular society. Joan Higgins, in her discussion of the comparative method, writes, 'Probably the most important reason for engaging in comparative research is that it encourages a distinction between the general and the specific.'[9]

The second reason to use the comparative method is that it assists in the search for new ways to conduct social policy. Change begins in many ways – sometimes through limited and local actions,[10] often through state or national initiatives, and sometimes through international action. Regardless of the origins of change, the practical conduct of social policy is determined by the interface between client groups and those who work with them (i.e., the police, social workers, teachers, clergy, volunteers, etc.). These people, both clients and helpers, can, in practical ways, change their own situations and develop new ways of working together. Often these changes are suppressed in the name of existing policies, good order, and stable government; but sometimes they are allowed to grow and to receive the formal endorsement of social policy authorities. These 'mutations' of social policy occur at different rates in different countries, depending on local conditions. Not all succeed; indeed, many can be expected to fail. However, all are of interest to the student of social policy.

Reasons for Comparing Aboriginal Policy in Australia, Canada, and New Zealand

Australia, Canada, and New Zealand were chosen for study because they each have an aboriginal social policy which is a major subject of current debate. In each country, the aboriginal minority is challenging the fundamental assimilationist objectives of social policy – objectives which have been the cornerstone of government and popular thinking for 150 years. Furthermore, in each of the three countries family and child welfare measures are a major subject in the social policy challenge that aboriginal peoples are posing.

These three countries share a common colonial heritage, and the origins of the aboriginal social policy which each has followed can be traced to the thinking of the 1837 House of Commons Select Committee on Aborigines. Each of the countries has a similar legal base derived from British common law, and each has a minority aboriginal population whose interests do not provide a fundamental threat to state power.

Because all three countries are developed welfare states, their principal assumptions with respect to social policy, and the principal measures which each support, are very similar. These include programs for income security along with universal access to health care and primary and secondary education (all of which are supported by a network of family and child welfare services). These common provisions permit comparisons between the mainstream and aboriginal services of each country. In each country, child welfare policy has been and remains a deliberate part of the general framework of aboriginal social policy.

Australia, Canada, and New Zealand are also developed market economies which place a major emphasis on natural resource extraction, management, and development. This has led each country to take control of the land away from aboriginal peoples. It has also provided the basis for good general living standards for the immigrant populations – living standards which, in each case, are higher than those of the resident aboriginal peoples. The aboriginal peoples in each country see themselves as having been robbed of their resources and confined to those marginal areas that were of little use to the settlers. Today they are seeking a review of, and redress for, this process of dispossession.

Although each of the countries has non-aboriginal minority groups, some of which have also been the focus of ethnically specific family and child welfare policy, this book is concerned entirely with aboriginal peoples. There are important differences between the situations of aboriginal and non-aboriginal minorities:

- As aboriginal peoples were owners, occupiers, and users of the land before European settlement, the natural environment is relevant to their religions, cultures, and social lives in ways which it could not possibly be for any immigrant group.
- Aboriginal peoples were, and in many cases still are, rural peoples, while immigrants are typically urban dwellers.
- Aboriginal peoples did not choose to live as a minority within an alien culture, while immigrant groups came to new countries either through choice or to escape more serious difficulties in their countries of origin.
- In each country there are some laws that only apply to aboriginal peoples.

This is not to deny that there are similarities between the treatment of aboriginal and non-aboriginal minority groups. However, the similarities are recent and occur most often in urban areas. Although urban aboriginal policies are discussed, the primary focus of this book is on the long-term policies which have been directed towards the traditional rural roots of aboriginal family life.

In all three countries, aboriginal peoples were in a colonial relationship to settlers and, for long periods, had little influence on the policies which were applied to them. Australia, Canada, and New Zealand were preoccupied with nation-building, immigration, and the affairs of the British Commonwealth. The task of working directly with aboriginal peoples was usually entrusted to those with a general reputation for good works (e.g., missionaries, educators, and social workers). These representatives of the settler society were also the primary advisors to government on policy matters (although the resources provided for this minor function of government were slim). Their advice was all the more influential as public interest and debate regarding aboriginal peoples was often low, and the views of the latter were consistently disregarded.

Sources
Legal, administrative, statistical, and critical secondary sources, along with direct inquiry and scholarly review, were used in preparing this book.

Legal Sources
The principal legal sources were the laws of each particular country as they related to aboriginal peoples (with particular reference to alternative child care arrangements). One of the distinct indicators of a separate social policy towards aboriginal peoples is the existence of laws that differentiate between the treatment received by them and that received by settlers. The law is also expressed through the actions of the courts. With the establishment of human rights legislation in Canada, and through the interpretation of the Charter of Rights and Freedoms, the courts are playing an increasing role in the establishment of social policy. This is particularly relevant to the situation of aboriginal peoples and has led to the removal of statutory legal provisions which have been judged to be discriminatory.

At the international level, there is the UN Declaration of Human Rights. Although this declaration does not have legal force within member countries, it nevertheless provides a standard for the recognition and protection of minority rights.

Policy and Administrative Sources
Most general social policy is to be found in annual reports, conference proceedings, policy manuals, and similar documents. Royal

commissions, government 'white papers,' and similar statements are of particular importance when policy is being reconsidered and when change may be imminent.

Statistical Sources
Statistics are reviewed in order to contextualize aboriginal peoples and their demographic and geographic distribution; provide data on the extent of alternative compulsory child care arrangements for both aboriginal and non-aboriginal peoples; provide data on the extent of intercultural adoption practice; and compare the countries and their respective arrangements for aboriginal peoples.

This data is used with caution, as it was typically not available in a form that permitted ready comparison between historic periods (and for certain periods, it was not available at all). As a consequence, definitional problems abound. For example, at different times and in different jurisdictions the definition of 'aboriginal' has varied widely. Sometimes the use has been restricted to those persons who have a distinct legal status, as in the Canadian use of the term 'status Indian.'[11] In New Zealand, the status of being Maori has usually been a matter of self-definition. In Australia, the status of being Aboriginal was often a matter of who was recognized as such by police and other local authorities. Estimates of aboriginal populations vary according to the definitions used. For example, Frideres estimates that in Canada the list of status Indians contains only about half the people who could be considered to be aboriginal,[12] while the 1986 Census of New Zealand adopts a definition of Maori which includes any person who can identify Maori descent (as there have been at least four generations born in New Zealand since colonial settlement, this definition extends the name Maori to people who may be as little as one-sixteenth Maori). The problem of defining aboriginal populations affects all the data that purport to show an incidence figure (e.g., the number of children in care/1000) because it either deflates or inflates the base figure used to establish it.

There are also problems with the data on children who are being cared for by the state outside their homes. These data are typically assembled as a by-product of the administrative actions of government agencies. They are collected not to show the impact of such actions on aboriginal peoples but the output of the agency involved. Thus a child welfare agency will record the number of children in care, a corrections agency will record the number of juveniles in confinement, and a school will record the number of pupils in attendance. None of these agencies records the overlap that occurs when a child is simultaneously in more than one system. The numbers cannot be added, and the true total of institutionalized children cannot be deduced.

Major policy shifts can result in further statistical confusion as the correctional, educational, and health and welfare organizations change functions. For example, the definition of 'child' has changed. In the nineteenth century, childhood was limited to the pre-teen years, and entry into the workforce began at thirteen or fourteen. In more recent years, there has been a general tendency to extend childhood through youth, so that child welfare authorities concern themselves with the welfare of young people until they are seventeen or eighteen. To give another example, children who are beyond the control of parents, community members, or informal local processes can enter official statistics in many ways. If they are convicted of an offence, they can be confined by a correctional authority; if their parents or the local welfare department considers that they need alternative parenting, they can become children in care; if a psychiatrist considers them to be mentally ill, they can be admitted to a treatment resource; and if a school considers them to require special attention, they can be sent to a special residential school. The total number of children in alternative parenting arrangements can thus be more meaningful than the number in any one system, particularly from the perspective of aboriginal peoples.

In using statistical data, I record caveats either in the text or endnotes. In addition, all statistics are treated with great caution, and the occurrence of policy differences/changes is only deduced when it is corroborated by major statistical evidence.

Critical Sources
Critical sources include academic/scholarly literature. Each of the countries has an extensive literature which was divided into the following principal categories: international comparative sources; general social policy and administration; aboriginal history, culture, and affairs; and aboriginal peoples and social administration. These categories are used to organize the bibliography.

Direct Inquiry
Direct inquiries (i.e., observation and interviews) were carried out in

travel periods of seven to ten weeks in New Zealand and Australia, respectively. In the case of Canada, they have accumulated over twenty-five years of social work. I do not claim that these observations and interviews are either systematic or representative of any of these countries. However, they were very important in two ways. First, it was not possible to assemble child welfare data on the individual countries without visiting their government agencies, as even officially published statistics were often only available in their respective libraries (most of which also had unpublished data on ethnicity and aboriginal status). Second, interviews with government officials, academics, and aboriginal people served as a way to cross-check conclusions tentatively drawn from the legal, statistical, and critical literature. Government officials represented the position of authorities; academics represented the public systems of debate, discourse, and opinion; and aboriginal people represented those who constituted the objects of policy. Each of these groups had internal differences with respect to opinion and politics. In the end, I made my own decisions on what views to include and on what views to exclude.

Review
When the chapters on each of the countries were drafted, each was reviewed by a senior academic from each country. Professor Peter Read of the Australian National University read the Australian chapters, and Dr. Mason Durie of Massey University read the New Zealand chapters. The Canadian chapters were shared with my colleagues at the University of Victoria. Finally, UBC Press arranged for pre-publication reviews. Each chapter has been strengthened by feedback from these various sources.

2
Australia: The General Structure of Aboriginal Policy

British imperial policy towards Australia was established in the eighteenth century when the continent was claimed for Britain as vacant land, and the first convict settlement was founded at Botany Bay. The Aboriginal inhabitants of Australia appeared to be a strange and incomprehensible people to the British colonists (as, indeed, did the colonists to the Aboriginals). Aboriginal peoples had no settled villages, no agriculture which Europeans could recognize, and seemed to have no political organization. However, Britain wanted nothing from them except their land. This could be taken as needed, for, officially, Aboriginal peoples did not exist. Aboriginal policy was not a priority for either the imperial or the local authorities. There were no Crown treaties with the Aboriginal peoples of Australia, and the conduct of Aboriginal policy was considered to be a local matter. In the nineteenth century, each Australian state developed its own policy. Commonwealth authority for Aboriginal policy and administration was restricted to the Northern Territory until 1967, at which time it acquired concurrent powers with the states to legislate for Aboriginals. This early lack of official attention placed Aboriginal peoples on the margins of Australian society.

History of Aboriginal Policy
The history of Australian policy towards Aboriginal peoples can be divided into four principal periods: (1) initial contact, 1788-1930; (2) protected status, 1860-1930; (3) assimilation, 1930-70; and (4) integration with limited self-management, 1967- . The dates for these periods are not clearly defined, as policy has changed at different times in different Australian states. The time periods for each major policy phase overlap, reflecting the complexity of the process.

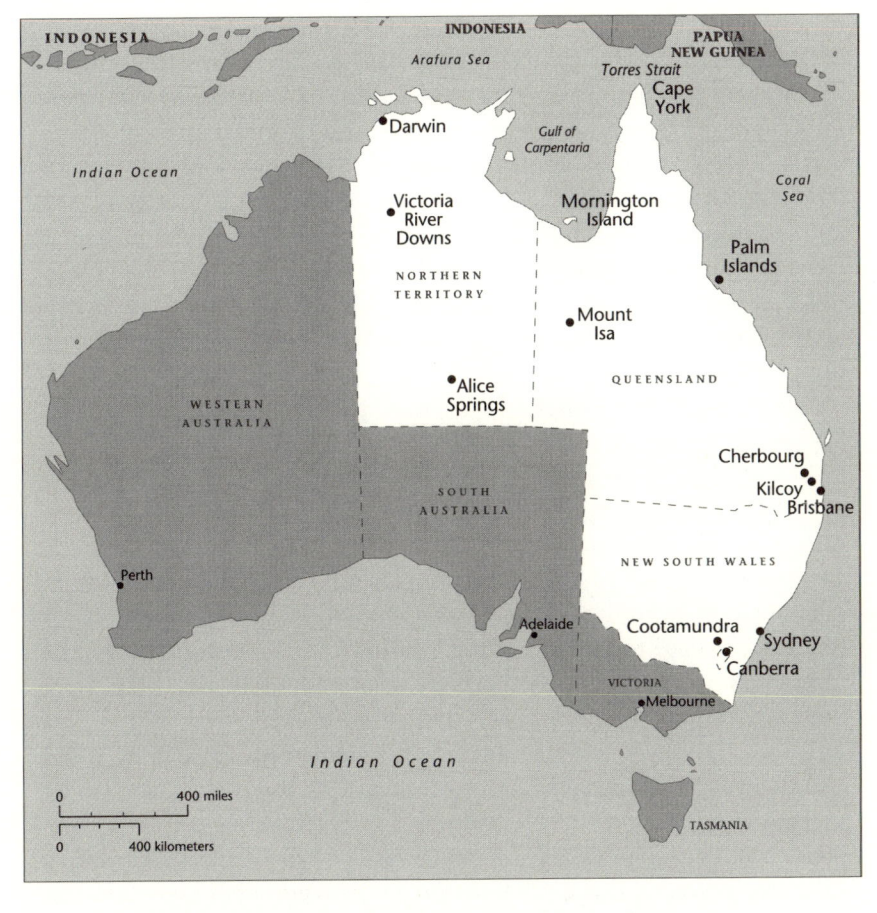

Map 1 Australian research sites and relevant place names

Initial Contact, 1788-1930

For an indefinite period prior to Captain Cook's 1770 exploration of its east coast, the many different Aboriginal peoples had had exclusive possession of Australia. In Britain, Cook's account of the continental coast was not of great interest, but from a military perspective there was a case for establishing a settlement. The settlement was seen both as providing a way to limit the expansionist interests of the Dutch and French and as providing a base for the repair of ships. Coincidentally, Britain was deeply concerned with the problem of crime in its cities, particularly London. The jails were packed, and flogging and capital punishment did not seem to be acting as effective deterrents. In addition, the American colonies (to which, formerly, prisoners had been transported) were no longer available.

The solution to this problem was to be an experiment in criminology and colonialism. In 1787, a fleet set sail to establish a penal exile settlement on the east coast of Australia. The fleet consisted of eleven vessels carrying 1,030 people, including 548 male and 188 female convicts. The fleet carried with it all the implements, materials, and animals necessary to establish a self-sustaining colony, including sufficient supplies for the first two years.[1] The land needed for the colony was obtained by an act of dispossession, assisted in British law by the convenient assumption that Australia was 'terra nullius' (vacant, unoccupied land).

At the local level there was, from the beginning, determined Aboriginal resistance to the loss of their land. The land was the whole basis of Aboriginal life and culture. Although Aboriginal peoples appeared to be without settlements, they were not without territory. All Aboriginals possessed and used their territory to sustain life; and all Aboriginals treasured the land, as its features had been part of their religions and cultures since time immemorial. When the whites took the land, they took everything. Early journal notes show that Aboriginal peoples recognized exactly what had happened. 'They were poor now. White men had taken their good country, they said, no ask for it but took it. Black man show white man plenty grass and water and then white man say come be off and drive them away and no let them stop.'[2] This pattern of dispossession without negotiation, compensation, or recognition was characteristic of the Australian frontier. Land was taken, and the relationship of the Aboriginal owners of the land to the European settlers was defined in terms of the right of the latter to defend his or her property and the duty of civil government to protect property rights. As a consequence, violence was common.[3] On the island of Tasmania, nearly all the Aboriginal inhabitants were hunted and shot. The few who remained were confined to a small island in the Tasman Strait, and, within a generation, the Tasmanian Aboriginal people had died out.

These events, and similar accounts of the effects of European-Aboriginal contact, were the principal arguments used by the 1837 House of Commons Select Committee on Aborigines to make a case for a more managed policy towards aboriginal peoples generally. Australia provided a few examples of such policies. Some early governors of Australia, notably Governor MacQuarrie (1810-21), extended the protection of British law to Aboriginals, particularly in matters of violence. Governor MacQuarrie also experimented with the 'civilization' of these peoples, establishing an educational institution for them at Paramatta and reserving some land for them on the shore of Port Jackson.[4] These early attempts to protect and 'civilize' the Aboriginals were not successful. Aboriginal peoples held to their own beliefs and lifestyles and only stayed in the vicinity of Paramatta and similar institutions to receive rations, blankets, or other benefits.

In the dry interior areas of Australia, although Aboriginal peoples were dispossessed of their land by the development of extensive pastoral cattle ranches, they also frequently remained in the same vicinity and became pastoral station workers. As Aboriginals, they were outside Australia's labour legislation and were employed for rations and accommodation rather than for wages. Nevertheless, the cattle station relationship between Aboriginal peoples and Europeans was based more on mutual benefit than were relationships elsewhere in Australia. The strength of this relationship was that it left Aboriginal peoples in contact with the land that was sacred to them and 'with sufficient resources to carry on their own ceremonial life.' It was characterized by the Australian scholar, Robert Elkin, as constituting a form of 'intelligent parasitism.'[5] However, it was not a stepping-stone to the wage system, as the station economy was a company-store economy based on credit and was not far removed from feudalism.

The frontier contact experience was of extended duration in Australia because of distance and because of the inhospitable nature (to Europeans) of much of the continent. In the north of Queensland and Western Australia and in the Northern Territory, frontier contact continued into the 1920s, 30s, and 40s. However, in the settled areas of Australia, the period of initial contact and dispossession ended in the nineteenth century, when Europeans had acquired all the good land which they could use, and when Aboriginal peoples had been reduced to a small minority.

Protected Status, 1860-1930
The effect of the views of the 1837 House of Commons Select Committee on Aborigines can be seen in several early attempts to protect Aboriginal peoples from some of the problems of the British colony. Early legislation provides examples of attempts to control alcohol use and sexual exploitation.[6] However, the first comprehensive statute to reflect most of the principles espoused by the House of Commons select committee was enacted in Victoria in 1869 and entitled the Aborigines Protection Act, thereby establishing a 'Board for the Protection of Aborigines.' Similar legislation was introduced in Western Australia in 1886 and was also entitled the Aborigines Protection Act; in Queensland, the Aboriginals Protection and Restriction of the Sale of Opium Act was established in 1901; in New South Wales, the Aborigines Protection Act was created in 1909; and in South Australia (which then included the Northern Territory), the Northern Territory Aborigines Act was established in 1910. Each of these acts was a control measure regulating all aspects of an Aboriginal person's life. The board and, through it, officials called protectors and subprotectors were in a position to control the everyday life of all Aboriginal peoples. This included where they could live, where their children could live, where they had to work, what funds they could have as an allowance, and who was and who was not an Aboriginal person.

The settlements created through this legislation were administered, rather than free, communities. The manager of the settlement had all the power of a Poor Law overseer or jail warden. Aboriginals were brought to, and effectively confined in, these settlements because they had no other place to live. The expectation of the time was that the original Aboriginal population would eventually die out, and that these settlements would provide a 'pillow for a dying race.' In time they, too, would be closed.

Through experience and amendment, the detail and complexity of state Aboriginal protection statutes grew. When the Commonwealth of Australia was established in 1900, the obligation of states to legislate for Aboriginal peoples was an accepted part of existing arrangements. The Census of Australia specifically excluded Aboriginal peoples until 1967, and the Commonwealth electoral rolls excluded them until 1962.

However, Aboriginal peoples proved to be more durable than had been assumed in the early protection statutes, and they showed a continued resistance to the loss of their land and way of life. Peter Read, in his study of the Wiradjuri people of New South Wales,[7] documents the resistance shown in two distinct cycles – each of which began with white administrators hoping to produce change through education and example, and each of which ended in the oppressive assertion of white power over Aboriginal lives.[8] However, in spite of this resistance, the continuing official effort to civilize them resulted in the ending of Aboriginal initiation ceremonies, the disruption of Aboriginal families, and the loss of Aboriginal languages.

Assimilation, 1930-70

The policy of assimilation was initiated because the earlier policy of protection had failed to operate in the intended manner. Aboriginal peoples had not disappeared, although it was noted that the number of 'full-blood' Aboriginals was now, in many areas, less than the number of 'mixed-blood' Aboriginals. This was seen as a sign that Aboriginal identity could be destroyed through a process of absorption. In the 1930s, the policy of assimilation was meant to absorb Aboriginal peoples, particularly those of 'light caste,' into the white population. Peter Read writes:

> Aboriginal people were to be brought to live amongst white people. They would proceed to act and think like them as they became progressively europeanised. In successive generations the 'Aboriginal strain' would become less prominent until no one would be distinguished – or would want to be distinguished – as being of Aboriginal descent. Within a few generations the former Aborigines would actually *be* white people.
>
> There remained two practical problems ... : how to get the Aborigines from their homes on the reserves into the towns and how, once they were there, could they be made to *want* to be Europeans?[9]

Policies based on incentive as well as those based on coercion were used to achieve these objectives. Incentives included the process of 'exemption.' An Aboriginal could become an Australian through a process of being exempted from the authority of the board and the protector. This required an application and a review of the person's lifestyle, usually conducted by the local police. If successful, a permit was issued which exempted the Aboriginal person from the provisions of the protection act and, hence, from the authority of the board and director. Coercive policies included not maintaining reserve buildings, closing stores, and ceasing to provide services. Children and youth were prepared for assimilation by being separated from their parents and raised in institutions.

The different Australian states pursued variations of the assimilation policy, depending on what was most suitable to their regional situations. In the Northern Territory, the application of the policy to the whole Aboriginal population, which, in the 1930s, greatly outnumbered the white population, was not practical. As a result, in that state the application of the policy of assimilation was limited to Aboriginal peoples of European-Aboriginal descent. The policy of assimilation was confirmed as official policy as late as 1963 at a meeting of state and Commonwealth ministers in Darwin. By this time, the objectives of the policy included ensuring that 'all Aborigines and part-Aborigines ... attain the same manner of living as other Australians.'[10]

In his examination of Aboriginal policy in New South Wales, Peter Read uses the year 1967 to mark the conclusion of the policy of assimilation. In 1967, the Constitution Act of Australia was amended, following a referendum (5,183,113 in favour; 527,007 opposed) to decide on whether to give the Commonwealth authority to legislate for Aboriginals and to include them in reckoning the population of Australia. The Commonwealth Electoral Act had already been amended in 1962 to give Aboriginals the right to enrol as electors for federal elections. Between 1967 and 1972, all states except Queensland repealed their 'protection statutes' as well as similar statutes which had emphasized the wardship of Aboriginal peoples. In 1967, Victoria introduced an Aboriginal Affairs Act, abolishing the existing welfare board and repealing earlier 'protection' legislation. The Aboriginal Affairs Act established an advisory body (with Aboriginal participation) and provided funding authority for programs for Aboriginals. In 1969, New South Wales dissolved the Aborigines Welfare Board and repealed the Aborigines Protection Act. In 1972, Western Australia established the Aboriginal Affairs Planning and Authority Act, repealing the previous Native Welfare Act. In Queensland, the policy of assimilation was formally continued for a further decade; but even there, by the end of the 1970s there had been a major easing of the control of Aboriginal community life, and Aboriginal peoples were free to take up residence wherever they wished.

Integration with Limited Self-Management, 1967-
The current period of integration with limited 'self-management' has been characterized by the extension to Aboriginal peoples of general social services and by the development of measures designed to permit Aboriginal communities some control over their own affairs.

Following the amendment to the Australian Constitution in 1967, Commonwealth legislation was introduced and has most often consisted of enabling and funding measures such as the 1980 establishment of the Aboriginal Development Commission and of the Commonwealth Department of Aboriginal Affairs. Commonwealth legislation has provided Aboriginal peoples with the means to develop their own organizations and services, which, in turn, has contributed to the growth of Aboriginal pride and self-confidence.

At the state level, the policy of integration has extended all normal state services to Aboriginal peoples (previously, Aboriginal peoples were invisible, as no records of descent or race were kept). The extension of general legislation to Aboriginal peoples also had the effect of bringing them within Australia's labour laws. In pastoral areas, this meant that the cattle stations had to pay them a basic wage. As a result, they drastically reduced their use of Aboriginal station-hands and, in many cases, evicted them. This change, which occurred in the 1970s, destroyed a way of life that had partially accommodated both Aboriginals and Europeans and which had lasted for three generations. In many cases, Aboriginal peoples were evicted from the territory in which they had lived for thousands of years.

Within Aboriginal communities, current policy emphasizes self-government. In the Northern Territory, land councils provide Aboriginal peoples with the means to organize their affairs independently of the state government. In other areas of Australia, community self-government has a more limited meaning, as the community land base is often small and its use restricted. In Queensland, for example, Aboriginal communities occupy land through restrictive, long-term government leases.

Nevertheless, legislation in the current period has a different character than it had in previous periods. The principal difference is that it recognizes that Aboriginal peoples have a right to organize themselves and to establish an independent identity within Australian society. This right is not well-established, and it remains controversial. It is not clear whether the Australian states are prepared to accept the presence of independent Aboriginal communities and organizations as part of a continuing framework that supports an independent Aboriginal society within Australia. The alternative view is that these measures are transitory, reflecting Australia's belated recognition of the original act of dispossession and of the need to provide compensation.

Social Policy and Defining 'Aborigine'

Fundamental to any separate set of social policies is a working definition of those people to whom it is meant to apply. This is true whether the policy is to disregard their existence, to provide them with protected status, to assimilate them, or to give them control over their communities. The practical process of making these distinctions can take no other form than an official act of racial definition.

During the initial contact period there was no difficulty in determining who was an 'Aborigine.' Aborigines were black, uncivilized, and pagan. This meant that they were not British subjects and, hence, were excluded from all citizenship rights. As a result of this definition, Aboriginal peoples were outside the law, outside the legal definition of a person, and were vulnerable to being attacked, robbed, and killed. The 1837 House of Commons Select Committee on Aborigines was not satisfied with this definition and argued for defining the Aborigine as a British subject with rights derived from the Crown's possession of the colony and from specific policy declarations. Governor MacQuarrie's proclamation of 1816, extending British law to Aborigines, is an example of such a declaration.[11] The right extended by MacQuarrie was, however, qualified by a provision for declaring Aborigines outlaws, thereby depriving them of the protection of the law. The practical enforcement of such laws depended on the visual recognition of a person as an Aborigine, sometimes assisted by a rudimentary definition referring to Aboriginal 'blood.' Their effect was to make all Aboriginal peoples subject to a form of double jeopardy, through which they could be dealt with either under the normal provisions of Australian state law or (at the discretion of a local police officer or official) as Aborigines and hence as outlaws.

Policy and administrative practice during the periods of protection and assimilation, respectively, required clear legal definitions of the persons to whom the authority of the protector(s) was to apply. The principal approaches to definition were: (1) defining descent, (2) administrative or judicial recognition, and (3) exemption from civil restrictions intended for Aborigines.

Defining Descent
Definitions based on the principle of descent, also referred to as 'blood,' began by recognizing the 'full-blooded' Aborigine, both of whose parents were known to be Aborigines. The second category consisted of the so-called half-caste people, who had one Aboriginal parent and one non-Aboriginal parent. These people were usually considered to be Aborigines, often with some qualifying clause referring to lifestyle. An example of such a clause may be found in the South Australia legislation of 1934, whose definition of Aborigine includes a half-caste person who is married to an Aborigine and a half-caste person who lives with and associates with Aborigines and their children.[12]

Recognizing who was or was not an Aborigine became more difficult where people of less than half Aboriginal descent were considered, and, as time passed, it became impossible to base administrative decisions on a knowledge of descent. As a result, defining who was or was not an Aborigine became, increasingly, a matter of administrative determination.

Administrative or Judicial Recognition
The second approach to defining who was and was not an Aborigine depended on a register and an administrative or judicial decision. Legislation in this form did not necessarily completely replace earlier definitions, and it sometimes had supplementary provisions for defining persons as Aborigines who could not be dependably so classified under earlier definitions.[13]

However, in the Northern Territory Welfare Ordinance, 1953, the replacement of definitions based on descent was completed, and the reference to 'Aborigine' was withdrawn in favour of a register of people who met the definition of a 'ward':

Section 14. A person may be declared a ward if by reason of: (a) his manner of living; (b) his inability, without assistance, adequately to

manage his own affairs; (c) his standard of social habit and behaviour; and (d) his personal associations, that person stands in need of such special care of assistance as is provided by [the] Ordinance.
Section 15. Persons under the control of 'Aboriginal' legislation of South Australia, Western Australia, or Queensland become wards upon entering the Northern Territory.

Through the Aborigines and Torres Straits Islanders Affairs Act, 1965, Queensland obtained similar discretionary power. This act established the category of 'assisted Aborigine,' meaning any person 'having a strain of Aboriginal blood' who is declared by the director to be an 'assisted Aborigine.'[14] A person who was subject to such a declaration could appeal, but the appeal process took as long as a year to complete and, meanwhile, the director exercised the powers of the act over the person's property, residence, and children.[15] At the federal level, a similar approach was adopted by the Social Services Act, 1959: 'An Aboriginal native of Australia who follows a way of life that is, in the opinion of the Director-General, nomadic or primitive is not entitled to a pension, allowance, endowment, or benefit under this Act.'[16]

These administrative definitions provided sweeping powers to officials to classify people as Aborigines and, thereby, to place them outside the benefits and protection of Australian law.

Recognition by Exemption

The use of exemption applied a reverse logic to the process of defining who was and was not an Aborigine in that it provided a process through which a person who was clearly of Aboriginal descent could be defined as an Australian citizen. These were the Aboriginal people who did not behave like stereotypical Aborigines and who were 'successfully' assimilated. These people were to be rewarded for their European behaviour by being excluded from the legal class of Aborigines to whom the special provisions of the law applied. An example is provided by the Commonwealth Social Services Consolidation Act, 1947, which reads:

Section 111. An Aboriginal native of Australia shall not be qualified to receive an unemployment benefit or a sickness benefit unless the Director General is satisfied that, by reason of the character and of the standard of intelligence and social development of that native, it is desirable that this section should not be applied.

Exemption provisions in state law were numerous and invariably discretionary. The Northern Territory Aboriginal Ordinance, 1936, contains the provision that: 'The Chief Protector may declare a person to be deemed not a half-caste for purposes of Aboriginals Ordinance 1918-33, and may revoke such declaration.'[17] The South Australia Aboriginal Affairs Act, 1962, contains an administrative provision to the effect that '[A Register of Aborigines is to be compiled and maintained by the board, which] shall from time to time remove therefrom the names of those persons who, in its opinion, are capable of accepting the full responsibilities of citizenship.'[18]

Removal from the legal classification of 'Aborigine,' 'Assisted Aborigine,' 'Native,' 'Ward,' or other similar designations was not permanent. The administrative authority could revoke such declarations where the Aboriginal person failed to maintain what was considered to be the proper standard of behaviour; nor was such a status necessarily transferable to children, who, in some jurisdictions, reverted to the classification of being legally Aborigines at age twenty-one.[19]

Exemption and revocation of Aboriginal status were central to the application of the principle that the primary purpose of social policy was to bring Aborigines to a level of development which would enable them to become full members of the white community. Not surprisingly, this process was never able to shed its inherent racism. In the end, the existence of a process of qualification and revocation meant that a person with Aboriginal 'blood' was subject to a different law and, unlike an immigrant, could never become a full Australian citizen.

To this tangle of regulatory provisions must be added the additional confusion which derived from state jurisdiction. Each state maintained its own legislative code, with the result that the person who was an Aborigine in one jurisdiction was not necessarily an Aborigine in another. When the state protection statutes were repealed in the 1960s and 1970s, this legal confusion as to who was or was not an Aborigine disappeared. In the current period, use of an official legal definition has been rendered less necessary, as state services and regulatory provisions are supposed to be universal. Nevertheless, at a working level, distinctions are still necessary, as, in some communities, there are separate agencies which work with Aboriginal peoples, and sometimes administrative policy requires that they be given special consideration. In practice, the application of these distinctions tends to be guided by appearance. Social workers, nurses, and/or police officers make their own judgements as to who are Aboriginals, and they refer such persons to what they consider to be the appropriate agencies.

During the same period there was a change in terminology, with Aborigine being replaced by Aboriginal. Ted Evans, in 'The Mechanics of Choice,' describes this change: 'There was a period in the sixties when there was argument and some uncertainty about "Aborigine" as against "Aboriginal"; one school favoured "Aborigine" as a noun and "Aboriginal" as the adjective. Today we seem to have settled for "Aboriginal" for all purposes.' There are also some current examples of policy based on the principle of self-management. Aboriginal peoples approve of the use of definitions of 'Aboriginal' in, for example, statutes dealing with: rights of access to, and residence on, reserves and heritage sites; rights of participation in community government; rights to hunt or fish, particularly for food; rights to benefit from administrative activities, grants, and representation provisions not available to other Australians as rights of citizenship; and rights to special consideration and benefits with respect to social legislation. For these purposes, definitions of Aboriginal have been inclusive, combining the elements of descent and custom. An example is provided by the Western Australia Aboriginal Affairs Planning Act, 1972, which contains the following definition:

> 'Aboriginal' means pertaining to the original inhabitants of Australia and to their descendants.
> 'Persons of Aboriginal descent' means any person living in Western Australia wholly or partly descended from the original inhabitants of Australia who claims to be an Aboriginal and who is accepted as such in the community in which he lives.[20]

There has also been some introduction of definitions which recognize tribal identity. The South Australia Pitjantjatjara Act, 1981, contains the following definition: 'Pitjantjatjara [is] defined as a person who is: (a) a member of the Pitjantjatjara, Yungkutatjara, or Ngaanatjara people and (b) a traditional owner of the lands, or part of them.'[21]

These definitions also illustrate a major change between current policy and earlier policies. The designation 'Aboriginal' still refers to a distinct identity, but government control of how it is defined and of the administrative task of applying it has, in some cases, been transferred to Aboriginal people themselves. In addition, the recognition of tribal names shows a growing sensitivity to the original identities of the Aboriginal peoples of Australia.

Number and Distribution of Aboriginal Peoples[22]

In the early years of contact, establishing the size of the Aboriginal population was of no particular importance, as, officially, it did not exist. Even when the Commonwealth of Australia was founded in 1900, the Constitution Act contained the clause: 'In reckoning the numbers of people of the Commonwealth, or of a State or other part of the Commonwealth, Aboriginal natives shall not be counted.'[23] In practice, census records of the Aboriginal population were established, but the instructions pertaining to them resulted in varying decisions to include or exclude full-blooded as opposed to half-caste Aboriginals and reduced the commitment to ensure that a complete census was obtained.

Initial contact with the Aboriginal population extended over a period of 150 years, and, during that time, a large proportion of them were killed. Estimates of the size of the pre-colonial (1788) population vary from 150,000 to 1,000,000, with 314,500 being the estimate offered by the Australian demographer L.R. Smith, who has studied the subject exhaustively.[24] Table 2.1 provides the available data as recorded in the official records of Australia.

The 1966 census, the last to use a definition of Aboriginal which was based on proportion of descent, recorded: 80,207 persons of half, or more, Aboriginal blood; 5,403 persons of half, or more, Torres Strait Island origins;[25] and 16,425 persons who were classified as Aboriginals with less than one-half Aboriginal blood.

Following the 1967 constitutional amendment, the census was no longer based on attempts to distinguish proportions of descent but, rather, on persons who classified themselves as of Aboriginal descent. The 1971 census records 115,593 such persons. At the same time, it has been estimated that 300,000 people had at least one ancestor who was Aboriginal.[26]

The number of Aboriginal children and the proportion of children in the Aboriginal population is of particular interest, as it provides the base data for establishing how many children were taken from their parents. Unfortunately, the enumeration figures with respect to children are extremely unreliable, and, for some years, are not available at all. The figures given are based on Smith's estimates.[27] The figures which were available showed that the proportion of Aboriginal

Table 2.1
Australian and Aboriginal population and proportion of children, 1881-1986

Year	Australian population	% children (0-14)	Aboriginal population	% children (0-14)	% Aboriginal
1881	2,250,194	38.96	89,659	24	3.98
1891	3,177,823	36.95	(48,397)		1.55
1901	3,733,801	35.14	93,333		2.49
1911	4,455,005	31.66	80,133		1.79
1921	5,435,734	31.73	71,836		1.32
1933	6,629,839	27.47	80,721	22	1.21
1947	7,579,358	25.05	75,965		1.00
1954	8,966,530	28.52	75,040		0.84
1961	10,508,186	30.24	84,470		0.80
1971	12,755,638	28.80	115,953	48	0.94
1981	14,576,330	24.76	159,807	44	1.10
1986	15,602,156	19.28	227,645	41	1.47

Sources: Base figures for the Australian population are from the Census of Australia. Figures for the Aboriginal population are from the Census of Australia for 1971 and 1981, and for earlier years from L.R. Smith, *The Aboriginal Population of Australia* (Canberra: Australian National University Press 1980). Data on children are not available for all years.

children was very low when compared with the proportion of children in the general population. This contributed to the view that the Aboriginal population was either dying out or being absorbed. Table 2.1 also shows that the Aboriginal population fell during the early years of contact. This fall was followed by a period of stabilization and then by strong growth.

The distribution of the Aboriginal population between the Australian states has influenced the importance of Aboriginal policy in each state. Table 2.2 provides estimates of the size of the Aboriginal population by state and as a proportion of the general state population.

The size of the Aboriginal populations as a proportion of state populations creates three principal categories: (1) in New South Wales, Victoria, South Australia, and Tasmania the Aboriginal population has been less than 1 per cent since 1901; (2) in Western Australia and Queensland the proportion of the population who are Aboriginal has declined to around 3 per cent; and (3) in the Northern Territory Aboriginal people were a majority for the first half of the twentieth century and still constitute one-third of the population.

The estimates for the individual states shows that in each of them there was a fall in the Aboriginal population on contact with Europeans, both in absolute numbers and as a proportion of the state population. This decline eventually ceased and was followed by a period in which the population was stable in absolute numbers, although decline as a proportion of the total Australian population continued. Finally, there is a period of Aboriginal population growth both in absolute and in proportionate terms, some of which can be attributed to the assertion of Aboriginal identity by persons who, in earlier periods, would not have been included in the Aboriginal population.

The most recent change in the distribution of the Aboriginal population has been its movement into urban and metropolitan Australian communities. Table 2.3 shows the urbanization of the Aboriginal population which has taken place since the 1960s.

The mainstream Australian population is one of the most urbanized in the world, with 56 per cent metropolitan, 26 per cent other urban, and 18 per cent rural in 1961; and with 62 per cent metropolitan, 22 per cent other urban, and 16 per cent rural in 1981. The Aboriginal population distribution contrasts sharply with this pattern. For most of the period since contact the Aboriginal population has been rural. This has meant that only a small proportion of the non-Aboriginal

Table 2.2

Aboriginal population as a proportion of state populations in Australia, by census year

Year	1901	1911	1921	1933	1947	1954	1961	1971	1986
New South Wales									
No.	6,895	7,329	7,551	9,688	10,874	12,000	13,598	23,873	39,011
%	0.5	0.4	0.3	0.3	0.4	0.3	0.3	0.5	1.09
Victoria									
No.	719	252	402	587	772	836	2,300	6,371	12,611
%	0.05	0.02	0.02	0.03	0.04	0.03	0.07	0.15	0.31
Queensland									
No.	20,000	20,000	17,000	16,957	20,560	21,835	47,448	31,922	61,268
%	4.0	3.3	2.2	1.8	1.8	1.6	3.3	1.7	2.37
South Australia									
No.	3,000	4,817	4,744	3,579	5,076	5,000	6,000	7,299	14,921
%	0.8	1.2	0.9	0.6	0.8	0.6	0.6	0.6	1.06
Western Australia									
No.	30,000	27,000	27,671	29,021	26,234	21,457	19,416	22,181	37,789
%	16.3	9.6	8.3	6.6	5.2	3.3	2.6	2.2	2.69
Tasmania									
No.	0	0	0	0	0	0	0	671	6,716
%	0	0	0	0	0	0	0	0.2	1.54
Northern Terr.									
No.	20,000	20,000	20,550	19,424	15,000	15,403	21,677	23,381	34,739
%	80.6	86.9	84.1	80.0	57.9	47.6	44.4	27.0	22.4

Year	1901	1911	1921	1933	1947	1954	1961	1971	1986
Aust. Cap. Terr.									
No.	0	0	0	0	0	0	0	250	1,220
%	0	0	0	0	0	0	0	0.1	0.4
Australia									
No.	80,610	79,938	77,918	79,256	78,897	76,531	110,439	115,948	227,645
%	2.1	1.8	1.4	1.2	1.0	1.8	1.0	1.0	1.4

Sources: Base figures for Australian population by state are from the Census of Australia. Aboriginal population for 1901-61 is from Sharon Stone, *Aborigines in White Australia: A Documentary History of the Attitudes Affecting Official Policy and the Australian Aborigine, 1897-1973* (Victoria: Heineman Education 1974). Aboriginal population for 1973 and 1986 is from the Census of Australia.

Table 2.3

Aboriginal population by urbanization, Australia, 1961-81

State	1961	1971	1981
New South Wales			
% Metro	10	27	32
% Urban	30	39	45
% Rural	60	33	23
Victoria			
% Metro	20	55	47
% Urban	30	30	40
% Rural	50	15	13
Queensland			
% Metro	>5	9	15
% Urban	20	32	41
% Rural	75	59	44
South Australia			
% Metro	10	25	33
% Urban	15	21	31
% Rural	75	44	36
Western Australia			
% Metro	>5	10	21
% Urban	10	30	36
% Rural	85	60	43
Northern Territories			
% Metro	0	0	0
% Urban	10	17	32
% Rural	90	82	68
Australia			
% Metro	>5	15	20
% Urban	20	29	39
% Rural	75	56	41

Sources: for 1961 and 1971: L.R. Smith, *The Aboriginal Population of Australia* (Canberra: Australian National University Press 1980), 247; for 1981: Census of Australia

population has actually come into contact with Aboriginals. Even in rural areas, contact was limited to the fringes of those small towns where the Aboriginal population was settled. While in the most recent policy period the trend towards a more urbanized Aboriginal population is strong, it remains the case that Aboriginal peoples are primarily a rural or 'fringe' dwelling population with whom most Australians have no contact at all. In addition, the contact which occurs in urban areas is with Aboriginal people who have left their rural roots and who are experiencing all of the problems attendant upon making the transition from rural to urban living.

The Administration of Aboriginal Affairs

During the colonial period, the administration of Aboriginal affairs was imperial and military. The direct military aspects of administration included those measures necessary for the security of the colony. In Van Diemans Land (Tasmania), the military was responsible for a campaign which resulted in either the death or expulsion of all Aboriginal peoples.

The imperial government was not necessarily hostile to Aboriginal peoples and, in some situations, believed that it should protect them from the convicts and immigrants who comprised the colonial settlement. It was during this period that there were also important attempts to introduce policies of 'instruction.'[28] This occurred in two principal forms: (1) educational institutions and settlements for Aboriginal peoples; and (2) missionary endeavours. The education of Aboriginal peoples was seen as difficult but not impossible, particularly if one took an intergenerational view and concentrated on Aboriginal children. In 1818 the Reverend Robert Cartwright wrote to Governor MacQuarrie:

> There can be no doubt of the success of a general Establishment of Schools for the young ... I think it will now be admitted by every candid person that the materials we have to work with, though extremely rude, are nevertheless good. Buried as is the intellect of these savages in Augean filth, we may yet find gems of the first magnitude and brilliance ... The small number of black children that have benefitted by the Native Institution may very properly be considered to be the first fruits of the harvest, and a pledge of your future success.[29]

During this initial period, Aboriginal children were left by their parents at a government 'Institution' for instruction, but there was no way of making them stay there. Instead, the approach was to encourage settlements of Aboriginal peoples through the provision of rations and industrial goods, principally tools, while separating them as much as possible from the settlers. Cartwright continues: 'Keep these black Natives entirely separate from our people until the Institution is become sufficiently strong, and the work of civilization so far advanced as to be proof against the evil practices and depraved examples of our countrymen.'[30]

The overall objective of social policy was to ensure that Aboriginal peoples would, in time, become an asset to the colonial economy; that is, that they would become 'better' people. Better not only than their ancestors, but also better than the settlers – many of whom were still viewed by the imperial government as members of a dangerous criminal class.[31] These ideas made a significant impression in London and were incorporated into the views of the 1837 House of Commons Select Committee on Aborigines.

Nevertheless, with the establishment of colonial legislatures, responsibility for Aboriginal administration was transferred to the settlers. This confirmed that Aboriginal administration had become an internal police matter for the Australian states rather than a colonial matter managed by the British Crown. Although the legislation enacted by the Australian states was called 'protection' legislation, it provided little protection for Aboriginal peoples. Indeed, as the settlers were in charge of both legislation and administration, while the Aboriginals were without full civil rights, 'protection' was interpreted as applying to the orderly process of settlement rather than to the rights of Aboriginals. Protection also came to mean the exercise of a paternalistic form of discretion in such matters as Aboriginal family life, residence, education, and alcohol use.

Each of the Australian states developed administrative departments with these or similar objectives. The powers of these departments included: (1) appointing a protector; (2) managing Aboriginal reserves; (3) supplying assistance to church missions; and (4) exercising special authority over Aboriginals on pastoral stations.

Appointing a Protector

The protector was a paid state official who had the power to appoint local protectors, each of whom was responsible for the Aboriginal people in a specific area. The protector was usually an official of the Department of Aboriginal Affairs or a local police officer but could be any citizen whom the government chose to appoint. Each protector was responsible for the administration of the state's protection act. All Aboriginal people within the area were subject to the protector's authority, which was extensive and discretionary. In most states the protector was able to: designate where an Aboriginal could, or could not, live; control by permit all employment of Aboriginals; approve marriages; act as the legal guardian of all Aboriginal children (including holding the power to separate them from their parents and consent to their adoption); make local regulations governing the conduct of Aboriginal people; manage reserves and Aboriginal lands; and control all assets of Aboriginal people.[32] This legislation was in keeping with the principles of the 1837 House of Commons Select Committee on Aborigines, which treated Aboriginal people as children. The committee assumed that the protector would be both charitable towards, and protective of, Aboriginal peoples. The protector was both administrator and magistrate and was often able to make decisions that could not be appealed; he could also enforce sanctions, including corporal punishment and detention.

The protector was not accountable to Aboriginals but did have to face the specific local interests of non-Aboriginal residents, employers, and missions – all of whom had access to the state legislature. The authority of the protector extended to all Aboriginal people whether or not they lived on a reserve. For those who did live on a reserve the protector had the additional powers of both lawmaker and magistrate.

Managing Aboriginal Reserves
Each state set aside some Crown lands for Aboriginal use. These were not treaty reserves in the Canadian tradition; they were state ordered land-use designations. As such, they could be revoked or changed without consultation with Aboriginal peoples. Such reserves provided a place to which Aboriginals could be sent as well as a place for their reformatories and schools. The protectors' powers over Aboriginal peoples in reserve areas increased to the point where they resembled those of a jail warden. Indeed, the residents of Aboriginal reserves were referred to in official documents as inmates.

Assisting Church Missions
The Australian states encouraged church missions to provide a refuge for Aboriginal peoples. The 1837 House of Commons Select Committee on Aborigines saw Christian missions as particularly suited to the task of 'civilizing' Aboriginals. They were also less expensive than were government settlements. In addition to receiving support from their home churches, missions raised funds through farming and commercial enterprises in an attempt to become economically self-sufficient communities. Government aid to missions

consisted principally of the use of the land and subsidies for education.³³ Protection legislation was also used to give missionaries authority to discipline Aboriginal peoples, while the police acted as a containment agency ensuring that Aboriginals stayed in, or went to, designated areas. The Australian historian C.D. Rowley, who documented the systematic destruction of Aboriginal society during the process of settlement, notes that:

> Under the Queensland legislation of 1897 and subsequent amendments, missionaries in charge were able to exercise quite strict control over Aborigines. Any difference from a prison farm was not marked ... The mission, then, was to become a multi-purpose institution through which the government could deal with some of its pressing problems by isolating them together. This enabled the removal of the part-Aboriginal child from the town fringe to a mission in Cape York – a power by no means unused – and such a decision would often be made on the basis of assumed Aboriginal descent.³⁴

Exercising Special Authority over Aboriginals on Pastoral Stations

The use of much of the interior of Australia for cattle grazing required a labour force that was familiar with the land and prepared to live at little cost. Local Aboriginal peoples offered such a labour pool. Special labour legislation exempted employers from having to pay minimum wages or having to make statutory insurance contributions, while, at the same time, it recognized employment contracts 'approved' by the protector of Aboriginals. This administration had a master-servant form and was unlike any other labour legislation in Australia.³⁵

Aboriginal affairs were administered through these institutions until the state protection acts were repealed in the period between 1967 and 1980. As the protection acts were repealed, the states integrated authority for services to Aboriginal peoples with general services. In most cases, no particular provisions were made for Aboriginal peoples, with the result that the services available to them were often completely inappropriate. For example, consider the extension of labour legislation to the Aboriginal peoples who were living on pastoral stations in the interior of Australia. The pastoral stations were not able to pay the wages required under general legislation and, thus, reduced their use of Aboriginal labour. As a result, Aboriginal peoples were evicted in large numbers from the lands on which they had lived since before white settlement. Problems of this type have since been recognized, and, in the 1980s, it was accepted that modifications of policy were needed in order to provide for better recognition of the needs of Aboriginal peoples.

Commonwealth Institutions
The constitutional changes made in 1967 gave the Commonwealth government (i.e., the Australian federal government) power to legislate for Aboriginal peoples throughout Australia. The Commonwealth government has used this power to establish new institutions for the advancement of the interests of Aboriginal peoples. A ommonwealth Department of Aboriginal Affairs was created and has become a major source of funding for Aboriginal organizations. In 1980, the Aboriginal Development Commission was formed, and its mandate was as follows:

> *Purpose*: ... to further the economic and social development of people of the Aboriginal race of Australia and people who are descendants of the indigenous inhabitants of the Torres Strait Islanders, and, in particular (as a recognition of past dispossession and dispersal of such people), to establish a Capital Account with the objective of promoting their development, self-management and self-sufficiency.[36]

The commission was wholly comprised of Aboriginal people and had an Aboriginal director. It pursued three principal types of activity:
(1) housing grants and loans, both for ownership and for rent by Aboriginal peoples ($A63m loaned in 1987-8)
(2) economic development through direct loans to small businesses owned by Aboriginal peoples and through long-term infrastructure and enterprise development schemes managed and staffed predominantly by Aboriginals (a total of $A26m was loaned in 1987-8)
(3) acquisition of sites and areas of particular significance to Aboriginal peoples ($A3.3m expended in 1987-8).

In 1990, the commission was merged with the Commonwealth Department of Aboriginal Affairs to form the Aboriginal and Torres Strait Islander Commission (ATSIC). ATSIC's members are chosen through local elections and regional councils; the individual commissioners are chosen by regional councils and are the official representatives of Aboriginal peoples.

In the Northern Territory, the Commonwealth government established three land councils to provide Aboriginal peoples with the power to manage their own lands. This was done through the Northern Territory Aboriginal Land Act, 1980,[37] which provides for: Aboriginal land trusts to hold Aboriginal land; Aboriginal control of access to Aboriginal land; investigation of Aboriginal claims to land; control by traditional Aboriginal owners of mining and development activities on Aboriginal lands; and payment of royalty equivalents to Aboriginal benefit trust accounts. These powers are subject to conditions on the expenditure of mining revenues and continue a form of supervision and trusteeship over the land and Aboriginal affairs. Nevertheless, the Aboriginal land councils of the Northern Territory provide more real power to Aboriginal peoples than has existed since white contact.

The present situation contains many uncertainties. On the one hand, the state authorities remain committed to policies of integration with limited modifications to recognize the interests of Aboriginal peoples; on the other hand, the Commonwealth government has encouraged the development of separate institutions for Aboriginal peoples. The polices of the Commonwealth government are regarded as controversial and unrealistic by many Australians.

The former minister of Aboriginal affairs and governor general of Australia, Sir Paul Hasluck, writes:

> Are they [Aboriginals] to be a minority living an artificial and pampered life, not supported by their own participation in what all other Australians are doing but by the bounty of those who earn the national income? Or are they to be living museum pieces? Or a sort of fringe community whose quaint customs are stared at by tourists? Will the separate development that is being pursued today have the result after two or three generations that persons of aboriginal descent find out they are shut out from participation from most of what is happening in the continent and are behind glass in a vast museum, or are in a sort of open range zoo? Or is it intended that their separate development will be carried to a point where they will become virtually a nation within a nation. That seems to me to be a dangerous absurdity – dangerous to Australia as a national entity in the world, dangerous for the future relationships of people with different ethnic origins in this continent and dangerous to the expanding hopes of Aboriginal people themselves. It is an idea that makes separate development not simply a transitional method but the permanent solution.[38]

In differing degrees this view was widely shared by the government administrators I met in Australia in 1990. They held the view that separate Aboriginal agencies are a blind alley which will result in further tragedy and disillusionment for Aboriginal peoples. In his 1988 commentary on Aboriginal affairs in Australia, the social policy analyst David Pollard writes:

> What white governmental policy makers, together with those who influence the policies of both major political parties, have been attempting to do in Aboriginal Affairs policy since 1972 is to settle the debt for the damage done to Aboriginal Society by the original occupation of Australia and by the subsequent government welfare policy.
>
> The debt of course is a construct: a way of explaining how whites in positions of authority ... justify the right of Aboriginal communities to these special measures. The 'settlement' of the debt will likewise be a settlement in white eyes – that is when they are satisfied that Aboriginal Affairs, as a separate stream of welfare benefits, has had its day and should be reabsorbed into the general welfare system.[39]

These views constitute a rejection of Aboriginal society – a rejection which has been part of Australian Aboriginal policy in both the eighteenth century (i.e., extermination) and in the nineteenth century (i.e., simply waiting for them to die out). Those who believe that genuine respect is due Aboriginal peoples despair at how those of European descent continue to assume that they have the right to subordinate all interests to their own. It is for this reason that Colin Tatz, in *Race Politics in Australia*, writes:

> Race relations in Australia can only get worse. My pessimism arises not only from the daily exercise of overt racism but also from the insolubility of four very basic – yet barely conceded – problems. First there is the psychological inability of whites to stop talking *about* blacks and to start talking *with* them ... Secondly, there is the growing trend among bureaucrats and liberal humanitarians to analyse the 'black' problem in terms of deficiencies of the victims ... The third problem lies in the reality that a mainstream society can never empathise with an oppressed minority. Finally, it is highly unlikely that white Australia can swallow the proposition that black progress is, in part, contingent on their rejection of white society ...

Integration, their ultimate goal, requires a period of separation first; the development of group cohesion, an awareness of the need for political and economic strength, a feeling of power arising out of knowing who they are; followed then by free participation in society at large, on their own terms.[40]

Thus, the Aboriginal Australian has been seen, since white contact, as a marginal person who needs to be managed to ensure that the settlement process is carried out in an orderly manner. Although there have been changes in the Aboriginal's legal status and in the institutions through which he or she is managed, there has been little change in white social attitudes. The Aboriginal Australian remains an outsider in Australian society, irrelevant to the interests and everyday life of most Australians.

3
Australia: Aboriginal Peoples and Child Welfare Policy

The policies of protection and assimilation which were followed in Australia until the 1970s subjected Aboriginal peoples to a police-state administration – an administration which could place them outside the normal protection of the law. Once subject to the power of state Aboriginal statutes and state administration, they were treated as parolees or institutional inmates without control of their assets, homes, labour, rights of association, or children. Children were a particular focus of attention, as it was through the absorption of the next generation of Aboriginal peoples that assimilation was expected to take place. When the state protection statutes were repealed, responsibility for the policy of assimilation was assumed by general-purpose social agencies, including the children's services of each state. Assimilation was then referred to as integration. In the 1980s, these policies were eased somewhat through the development of measures specific to Aboriginal peoples. This chapter examines major features of the history of Australian family and child welfare policy towards Aboriginal peoples.

Child Welfare Jurisdiction in Australia

In Australia, responsibility for family and child welfare comes under state jurisdiction (as did Aboriginal affairs until 1967, when it became a jurisdiction shared between Commonwealth and state governments). As a consequence, there can be substantial differences among the policies of various states. However, these policies tend to become similar to one another as, over time, those introduced in one state are either also adopted by other states or, eventually, abandoned altogether.

To attempt to discuss family and child welfare measures in all states would require a level of detail not possible within the context of this discussion. Instead, this book examines policy and administrative practices in effect in New South Wales, Queensland, and the Northern Territory. In New South Wales, there is a substantial number of Aboriginal peoples (although that number constitutes a small minority of the total state population), and there are well-developed welfare services. In Queensland, Aboriginal peoples constitute a higher proportion of the total population than they do in New South Wales, and services for them have focused on assimilation longer than has been the case in other states. In the Northern Territory, Aboriginal peoples were relatively unaffected by social policy until the postwar period, and they constitute a major segment of the population.[1] These three states are marked on Map 1 (p. 15), which also shows the principal locations mentioned in this chapter.

New South Wales

The legal scholar, Richard Chisolm, divides the Aboriginal child welfare history of New South Wales into four policy periods: (1) the period of early contact, 1788-1883; (2) the period of the Aborigines Protection Board, 1883-1940; (3) the period of the Aborigines Welfare Board, 1940-69; and (4) the period of the Child Welfare Department, 1969- .

Early Contact, 1788-1883

During this period there were several attempts to intervene in the lives of Aboriginal families and children, but they were not enforced by law. Missions and early government institutions provided incentives, in the form of food supplies, blankets, and other European goods, for Aboriginal families to leave their children in school. However, Chisolm indicates that the judgement of the early administrators and missionaries was that 'these early efforts at "civilising" the children appear to have largely been failures.'[2] The reason for failure was attributed to the stubbornness and inferiority of the Aboriginal peoples, who did not seem to appreciate the advantages being offered them. This perception contributed to the decision to establish more thorough and formal control over the lives of Aboriginals through the establishment of the Aborigines Protection Board.

Aborigines Protection Board, 1883-1940

The purposes for which the Aborigines Protection Board was formed included a deliberate systematic effort to train, educate, and employ

Aboriginal children. In the early phases of the board's work, this process centred on concentrating Aboriginal peoples on reserves and providing their children with training to make them suitable for farm labour (boys) and domestic service (girls). These training objectives remained central to the board throughout its life, but early attempts to induce them to send their children to school and to place their youth in employment encountered strong resistance from Aboriginal families.

In 1911, the board acquired additional powers, including the power to separate children from their parents. Separation took three major forms:

(1) On Aboriginal reserves, children were separated from their parents through being made to live in dormitories. Daily contact with parents was not allowed.
(2) Outside reserves, Aboriginal children were removed from their parents and placed in dormitories on reserves or in designated residential institutions. Visiting was not encouraged.
(3) Where possible, Aboriginal children were placed with European families to assist with farm labour or domestic service.

According to Rowley, these policies were intended 'to break the sequence of indigenous socialization so as to capture the adherence of the young, and to cast scorn on the sacred life and the ceremonies which remained as the only hold on the continuity with the past.'[3] The system was comprehensive and efficient; childhood for Aboriginal children became an institutional experience. In 1921, the board stated in its annual report that 'it would be difficult to find any child over school age out of employment, or not an inmate of the Board's homes.'[4] According to Chisolm, the effect of this intervention was to create inmates and apprentices. Policy would be a success when the boy or girl became a dutiful servant, and it would be a failure when he/she did not.

Coral Edwards, an Aboriginal woman who spent most of her childhood in one of the board homes, recounts the sad story of Jane King, who was taken to the Cootamundra Home in 1923. Jane spent her life either doing housework or being in mental hospitals, dressed whenever possible in the 'high heels, hat, handbag, [and] beautiful dress' that she had been taught to wear, perpetually ready to take a broom and sweep and clean. As Edwards concludes, 'If the Aborigines Protection Board still existed today, its members might be very pleased with Jane. She had learnt her lessons well.'[5]

Inside the institutions the management of Aboriginal children was harsh. In 1933 the manager at Kinchella, the boys' home, was warned that 'he must not be drunk on duty. He must no longer use a stock whip on the boys, nor tie them up. He must not use dietary punishments. He must keep a punishment register, and he was no longer allowed to send the boys out as labour on local farms.' Six years later, there was another inquiry at Kinchella into what the board called 'sexual deviance.'[6]

In 1937, the chief protectors from all the Australian states attended a conference in Canberra. The record of the conference shows that the protectors believed that 'the destiny of natives of aboriginal origin, but not of full blood, lies in their ultimate absorption by the people of the Commonwealth,' while

> the general policy in respect of full blood should be (a) to educate to white standard the children of detribalised natives living near centres of white population and subsequently place them in employment (b) to keep the semi-civilised under a benevolent supervision ... and (c) to preserve as far as possible the uncivilised native in his normal tribal state.[7]

The policy of 'ultimate absorption' for children of mixed descent was given explicit meaning by A.O. Neville, commissioner of Native affairs in Western Australia, in the conference proceedings:

> To achieve this end, however, we must have charge of the children at the age of six years; it is useless to wait until they are twelve or thirteen years of age. In Western Australia we have power under the act to take any child from its mother at any stage of its life, no matter whether the mother is legally married or not ...
>
> It is well known that coloured races all over the world detest institutionalism. They have a tremendous affection for their children ...
>
> Our experience is that they come to regard the institution as their home ... These homes are simply clearing stations for the future members of the race ...
>
> You cannot change a native after he has reached the age of puberty, but before that it is possible to mould him. When the quarter caste home, in which there are now nearly 100 children, was started we had some trouble with the mothers [but after some visits they] were ... usually content to leave them there, and some eventually forgot all about them.[8]

The effect of the conference was an increased commitment to the policy of assimilation in states like New South Wales, where it was then a hundred years since Aboriginal peoples had been in full contact with Europeans. In 1940, this renewed commitment to the policy of assimilation was signalled by the replacement of the Aborigines Protection Board with the Aborigines Welfare Board.

Aborigines Welfare Board, 1940-69

The Aborigines Welfare Board took over the institutions of the Aborigines Protection Board. The new board's first annual report provides the data on which Table 3.1 is based and indicates the inclusiveness of the Aboriginal child assimilation system.

Table 3.1

New South Wales Aboriginal children and the welfare board, 1940

Situation	Characteristics	No. of children	
Board's homes	Fully institutionalized, removed from families	107	(2.3%)
Apprenticeship	Fully removed from families, living with Europeans as servants	50	(1.1%)
Stations	Highly institutionalized, sleeping in dormitories, controlled contact with families	1,771	(37%)
Reserves, camps	Living with families, subject to administrative controls by police	885	(18.7%)
Nomadic	Free of European influence	176	(3.7%)
Other	Unknown, but some children in institutional care by missions and other agencies	1,745	(37%)
Total		4,734	(100%)

Source: Peter Read, *The Stolen Generations*, Occasional Paper No. 1 (Sydney: Ministry of Aboriginal Affairs 1982)

These figures indicate a minimum rate of 400/1,000 Aboriginal children living away from their parents in New South Wales in 1940. This year also marked the beginning of the period in which Aboriginals were subject to the dual jurisdiction of the welfare board and of child welfare legislation. This dual legislative authority makes it more difficult to establish the full extent of removal for subsequent years.

Placement practices also changed with the introduction of foster home 'boarding-out' relationships, initially for children unsuited to institutional life, but, later, as the preferred option. Some placements were made with Aboriginal families, presumably those which were 'successfully' assimilated. However, the main objective became placement in the European community. In 1955, the board was able to report: 'Efforts were made late in 1955 to secure foster homes for these children amongst white people. Furthermore, this was regarded as being a positive step in implementing the Board's policy of assimilation.'[9] In the following year's report, this initiative was described as 'an unqualified success.' As in other parts of Australia, there was a specific focus on Aboriginal peoples of 'lighter caste,' the objective being to merge them with the white population.

Peter Read estimates the total number of children removed from their parents between 1940 and 1969 to be at least 5,625 – approximately 4,000 of whom were removed under the authority of the Aborigines Protection Board, while 1,600 were removed under child welfare legislation.[10] These were instances of complete removal, not including the segregation and institutionalization of children on reserves through the dormitory system. Contact with parents was not encouraged in the board's homes. Peter Read describes the effect of these measures:

> Little by little the view was put across that blacks on the reserve were dirty, untrustworthy, bad. There were generally no black staff to whom children could relate. Partly because it was presented with no opposition the propaganda had its successes. Some children left the homes ashamed of the colour of their skin. Girls have stated that they used to cross the road in order to avoid an Aboriginal man, not just because they were taught to, but because in the end, they themselves had come to believe that he was a threat – dirty, brutal, black.[11]

While many of the staff were kindly and well-meaning, the homes were not easy to staff, and former staff members recall many periods when their numbers were inadequate.[12]

The existence of parallel child welfare systems in New South Wales, one for white children and one for Aboriginal children, continued until the late 1960s. In 1967, at the time of the constitutional amendment which made Aboriginal peoples full citizens, New South Wales held legislative hearings on Aboriginal welfare. In the 'Statement of the Department of Child Welfare and Social Welfare,' the director of the department argued for a single child welfare system.[13] This advice was accepted, and a decision was made to discontinue the work of the Aboriginal Welfare Board. In 1969, the Child Welfare Department took sole responsibility for the welfare of all children in New South Wales.

Child Welfare Department, 1969-

This period of administration began by continuing the policy of assimilation. However, because families and children were no longer identified as Aboriginal, they no longer showed up on official statistics. The policy change which took place in New South Wales in 1969 should not be minimized; simply being Aboriginal was no longer a cause for having one's children removed. The homes at Cootamundra and Kinchella were closed. Removal of children was dependent upon identifying neglect, abuse, or delinquency, and a court decided how departmental authority should be exercised.

The number of children removed from their homes diminished, but when, in the 1980s, research workers examined the records of the Child Welfare Department, they found that Aboriginal children were still overrepresented. Table 3.2 shows the number of Aboriginal children in care in 1966, 1969, 1976, and 1980.

The number of children in care, both Aboriginal and non-Aboriginal, continued to fall in the 1980s; but the proportion of Aboriginal children in care or in correctional institutions has remained much higher than has the proportion of non-Aboriginal children in the same situation. This high representation of Aboriginal children in care, along with the fact that most care resources were non-Aboriginal, was an important argument for the adoption of the Aboriginal Child Placement Principle. (This and associated policy and administrative changes are discussed in the final section of this chapter.) Thus, in New South Wales, Aboriginal child welfare policy has reflected public attitudes towards Aboriginal peoples.

Queensland

The overall policy framework for Aboriginal administration in Queensland is similar to that discussed for New South Wales, except that the latter continued the formal policy of assimilation into the 1980s and was much slower to integrate Aboriginal and general social

Table 3.2

New South Wales Aboriginal children in departmental care, 1966, 1969, 1976, and 1980

Placement	1966[a]	1969[a]	1976[b]	1980
Children's homes				
Abor. children	69	144		69
Total children	831	896		779
% Aboriginal	8%	16%		16%
Foster care				
Abor. children	145	313	630	430
Total children	4,074	4,796	4,580	2,431
% Aboriginal	4%	7%	14%	17%
Corrective institutions				
Abor. children	58	116	118	105
Total children	1,158	1,282	1,014	577
% Aboriginal	5%	9%	12%	18%
Abor. children in care/1,000	48	67	55	41
Non-Aboriginal children in care/1,000	4	4	4	3

Note: Underrepresentation of aboriginal descent is probable.
[a] Figures for 1966 and 1969 do not include children under the care of the Aborigines Welfare Board. In 1969, 308 children were transferred, increasing the proportion of Aboriginal children in care to 13 per cent.
[b] Children's homes and foster care are combined for this year.
Source: Chris Milne and Aileen Mongta, *Aboriginal Children in Substitute Care* (Sydney: Aboriginal Children's Research Project 1982)

services. There are four policy periods in Queensland: (1) the period in which there was a chief protector of Aboriginals administration, 1897-1939; (2) the period of the Aboriginal Preservation and Protection Act, 1939-65; (3) the period of the Aborigines and Torres Strait Islanders Affairs Act, 1965-84; and (4) the period of the Queensland Department of Family and Child Services, 1970- .

Chief Protector of Aboriginals Administration, 1897-1939

The Aboriginals Protection and Restriction on the Sale of Opium Act, 1897, was primarily designed as a measure to remove Aboriginal peoples from areas where they were in conflict with settlers. The early history of the settlement of Queensland was harsh. The Aboriginal population was well-established and resisted the loss of its land. In response, the Queensland government employed Aboriginal trackers to search out and kill or capture other Aboriginals. Elsewhere, poisoned flour was distributed to terrorize the Aboriginal population, killing children indiscriminately along with the adult population. This history of genocide is well known to historians but is still not reflected in the public record. The *Department of Community Service Newsletter* of November 1984 refers to Kilcoy, near Cherbourg, as 'significant for the calibre of the free settlers it attracted and their contribution to the development of the state of Queensland.' There is not a word about the fact that Kilcoy was one of the centres from which poisoned flour was distributed to the local Aboriginal population. Nor can one find in Mount Isa a monument at the place where, for decades, the slopes were littered 'with the bleached bones of warriors, gins and piccaninnies.'[14] The history contained in the 1987 annual report of the Ministry of Community Affairs sees fit to mention only the following:

> Queensland was a frontier of European expansion. Graziers, farmers and merchants were pushing out from the more settled areas of Moreton Bay and taking possession of the land as they went. The discovery of gold in various parts of Queensland caused a rapid influx of Europeans and resulted in conflict with the Aborigines.[15]

The Aboriginal reserves which were established as refuge areas for the remnants of the population were organized as controlled communities, and they resembled total institutions. Within the settlements, the authority of the chief protector extended to every aspect of the Aboriginal person's life. Each year, the annual reports of the chief protector contained a schedule of the local protectors and the 'Number of Natives Controlled by Each Protector.'[16]

The most studied Aboriginal reserve is the community of Cherbourg, which was established in 1905. For many years, Cherbourg (known as Barambah in early records) was considered to be a model of Aboriginal community administration. The early history of the settlement records many 'removals to station': 1905 = 64; 1912 = 46; 1913 = 72; 1915 = 144; 1916 = 158; and so on.[17] These were Aboriginal men, women, and children who were taken by the police and forcibly settled at Cherbourg. There was no attempt to preserve Aboriginal families or clan units. As a result, the anthropologist Tennant Kelly was able to identify members of no less than twenty-eight clans at Cherbourg in 1937.[18] In a follow-up study in 1976,

Klaus-Peter Koepping confirmed that twenty-six clans continued to live at Cherbourg. Of these, only one was originally from the area.

The early annual reports of the protector provide a detailed schedule of the people who were taken to the Queensland Aboriginal communities as well as notes on their behaviour. The character of this administration can be seen from the following short extract from the 1909 annual report:

Children and Women
The following list of young women and children rescued from a life of destitution, immorality and neglect, and placed in healthier and more comfortable circumstances will show that the Department has not been inactive in its operations for the welfare of this section of the community. There are now eighty-eight of these unfortunate children at school at Barambah.

Many of the young women have married steady hard-working boys, and gone to service with them as married couples on stations or as police trackers. With a magnanimity that was as amusing as commendable, where the woman had children by an earlier marriage or otherwise, the boy has apparently taken them as well as the mother to his heart and home.

Nellie, a half-caste, was sent to Brisbane and placed in service.

Ida, an aboriginal woman serving a sentence in Stewart's Creek Gaol, was certified insane and sent to the Goodna Lunatic Asylum.

Daisy, Albert, Norman, and Kathleen, neglected children, were taken from unhealthy surroundings at Nebo, and sent to school at Barambah.

Langlo Louise, who left her aboriginal husband at Mount Morris and lived in immorality with a white man, was removed to Barambah.

Bella McLean, a half-caste domestic servant in Brisbane, was sent to Barambah for immoral behaviour, and for absconding in service.

This list continued for several pages, showing, year by year, how a moralistic and intrusive process was applied to the management of Aboriginal peoples. The early reports are illustrated with photos of naked or partially clad Aboriginals. These photos have headings such as 'Types of Men – Mornington Island,' 'Full-blooded Aboriginal Child, 3 years old – Barambah,' 'Group of Women with Piccaninnies – Mornington Island.'

It was during this period that the 'dormitory' system of child management was established. Each settlement had a dormitory to which children could be assigned to live. These children might have parents who lived in the community, but often they were children from other communities who were removed from their homes as an act of discipline and sent away to prevent their parents from contacting them. The dormitories were also used to house children removed from Aboriginal parents living in the wider community. These placements give no indication of a clear policy – most, it appears, were carried out in the general pursuit of what was considered to be 'discipline.'

Aboriginal Preservation and Protection Act, 1939-65
The 1937 Conference of Protectors referred to earlier led to a clarification of the policy of assimilation. The Queensland government believed that assimilation should be achieved through a period of 'identity reorientation, [following which] the Aboriginal population would be effortlessly absorbed into the larger European population, leaving scarcely a trace behind it.'[19] The provisions of the Aboriginal Preservation and Protection Act indicated that a period of increased, and more rigorous, discipline was a necessary step towards assimilation. The 1982 Department of Aboriginal Affairs annual report summarizes the history of Queensland Aboriginal legislation and refers to the 1939 act in the following manner: 'This Act [the 1896 Act] was replaced in 1939 by the Aboriginals Preservation and Protection Act. Its main aspects were totalitarian control, restricted freedom of movement [pass required], imprisonment without trial, and corporal punishment without trial.'[20] Regarding authority for child welfare, the 1939 Act read:

Guardianship of Minors
18.(1) The Director shall be the legal guardian of every aboriginal child in the State while such child is under the age of 21 years, notwithstanding that any parent or relative of such child is living, and may exercise all or any of the powers of a guardian where in his opinion the parents or relatives are not exercising their own powers in the interests of the child.

(2) The Director may in this capacity consent or refuse to consent to the marriage of any aboriginal who is under the age of 21 years.

(3) Notwithstanding anything contained in the Adoption of Children Act, 1935, the Director may, subject to such conditions as

may be prescribed, execute agreements between or on behalf of aboriginals in the State of Queensland for the legal custody of aboriginal children by aboriginals or other persons who in his opinion are suitable persons to be given legal custody of such children.

These powers were extensively used. When children were removed from their parents, the Australian Child Endowment was paid to the institution caring for them. Endowment records provide an indication of the extent of Aboriginal child institutionalization in Queensland. In the 1949 annual report, it was recorded that 854 Aboriginal families were receiving the federal child endowment payment, and that 'a close check is being made on every individual account ... to ensure that the expenditure by parents is in keeping with the purpose for which the payment is made.' However, there are 1,702 children 'wholly maintained in Mission and Government Settlement institutions [where] the endowment is paid to the institution's funds.' Ten years later, in the 1958 report, the pattern continues, with the child endowment being collected for 1,598 children in institutions. These figures suggest that the ratio of Aboriginal children removed from their parents in Queensland was of the order of 300 to 400 per 1,000.

Aborigines and Torres Strait Islanders Affairs Act, 1965-84
The 1961 Native Welfare Conference was convened by the Commonwealth government in Darwin, and it led to a reassertion of the policy of assimilation. In a statement from the conference, the policy of assimilation was stated in the following terms:

> The policy of assimilation means in the view of all Australian governments that all aborigines and part-aborigines are expected eventually to attain the same manner of living as other Australians and to live as members of a single Australian community, enjoying the same responsibilities, observing the same customs and influenced by the same beliefs, hopes and loyalties as other Australians.[21]

'Eventually,' referred to the fact that in the states and territory,

> the position [of an Aboriginal] is somewhat like that of a minor who is basically a citizen but who, because he is under the age of 21 years, may not be able to do everything that other inhabitants of Australia

may be able to do, and may be protected and assisted in ways in which the adult is not protected and assisted.

This 1961 conference was influential in Queensland's decision to replace the Aboriginals Preservation and Protection Act, 1939, by the Aborigines and Torres Strait Islanders Affairs Act, 1965. The Queensland historian Lyndall Ryan, in his account of the career of Queensland premier, Bjorke-Petersen, writes:

> The legislation at first appeared to have all the ingredients of assimilation legislation ... But the rest of the Act followed earlier legislation whereby Aboriginal lives were controlled and defined by the department. Aborigines and Islanders were defined as any person charged with having 'a strain of Aboriginal blood' and were categorised as 'assisted' or 'exempt.' The 'assisted' Aborigines and Islanders lived on reserves at the Director's pleasure ... On the reserves ... Aboriginal children were usually separated from their parents from the age of four and placed in dormitories until adolescence ... The only life style that was acceptable to the Director was one of unquestioning obedience and gratitude, coupled with a hard-working desire to become 'just like white people.'[22]

The 1965 act was amended several times during the 1970s, partly because of pressure asserted by the Commonwealth government to modify racist legislation. In 1975, the government introduced the Racial Discrimination Act and the Aboriginal and Torres Strait Islanders Act, giving the latter the power to override many of the discriminatory provisions of the Queensland acts. These powers were not used, but they invoked much opposition from the then-director of Aboriginal welfare, P.J. Killoran:

> The philosophy of difference that has been embarked upon by the Commonwealth is the first step in the process of separate development ... It is, however, to pursue and deepen difference as a source of reconciliation that the Commonwealth has expanded its activities throughout this country, and in its train has initiated and extended prejudice and tension.[23]

Nevertheless, the threat implicit in this Commonwealth legislation, together with criticism from the churches and from academics and professionals, in the end led to legislative and administrative change. The Aboriginal social policy scholar Matthew Foley, writing in 1981, records that 'the overall effect of the legislative activities of the 1970's has been to dismantle many of the legal structures of protectionism affecting reserve life.'[24] Coincident with these changes was the extension to reserves of the Department of Family and Child Service child welfare program.

Queensland Department of Family and Child Services, 1970-
The date at which the Queensland Department of Family and Child Services took full responsibility for Aboriginal child welfare is not clear, as it appears that the transition was gradual (the Aboriginal affairs department and its successors maintained dual authority with the new department until 1984). As in New South Wales, initially, Aboriginal children and families did not appear in the records of the family and child services department, as, on the grounds that they would be discriminatory, no records of aboriginal status were kept. However, the Commonwealth government gathered such data for 1978, and it 'revealed that 35.5% of children in institutional care in Queensland were of Aboriginal and Islander descent. There were no black child care officers employed by the Department of Family and Child Services. Very few black foster parents have been recruited.'[25]

These policies remained in effect until 1985, when there was a change in internal policy. Following consultation with Aboriginal child care agencies, the department committed itself to implementing the Aboriginal Child Placement Principle and sought to develop a close and positive working relationship with the Aboriginal and Islander community. This was to include:

(a) increased capacity for Aboriginal and Islander Community Agencies to respond to child and family welfare issues,
(b) changes in the way the Department responds to issues of Aboriginal and Islander child welfare, and,
(c) a strengthening of the process of communication and of the working partnership between the Department and the Aboriginal and Islander community.[26]

Data collection was also revised so that official data were once again gathered on the Aboriginal origins of children in care. Table 3.3 shows the number and proportion of Aboriginal children who were subject to court orders in Queensland in 1987. Not all these children were living away from their parents, as, under Queensland child welfare legislation, children could be returned to their families while still under court order. As in New South Wales, Aboriginal children remain overrepresented among children subject to court orders.

As may be seen, Queensland Aboriginal child welfare policies have

Table 3.3

Aboriginal and Torres Strait Islander (ATSI) children under orders, Queensland, by type of order, 1987

Type of order	ATSI children	Total children	% ATSI children	% of total children
Care and control	187	557	33.6	4.1
Care and protection	463	2,114	21.9	10.2
Care and protection (voluntary)	179	806	22.2	3.9
Supervise (offence)	117	458	25.6	2.6
Protective supervision	34	335	10.1	0.7
Queen's pleasure	3	4	75.0	0.1
Children in care/1,000	39	7[a]		

[a] Aboriginal and Torres Strait Island children have been excluded from this calculation of the proportion of children in care.
Source: Department of Family Service, Queensland

followed a similar pattern to those in New South Wales but have often been more extreme, with explicitly racist attitudes being blatantly expressed in public policy.

Northern Territory

The operation of Aboriginal family and child welfare policy in the Northern Territory confirms the existence of the same major policy periods evidenced in New South Wales and Queensland; but there are important differences – differences which may be attributed to the area's remoteness. Apart from around Darwin and Alice Springs, Europeans have always been a small minority in the Northern Territory. Thus, until the Second World War, many Aboriginal peoples were able to retain a traditional life. The Aboriginal presence remains substantial today, and Aboriginal peoples are visible on the streets, in the media, and in the practical politics of the Northern Territory. In addition, as referred to in the previous chapter, the land councils of the Northern Territory exercise direct management of the large Aboriginal reserves (40 per cent of the Northern Territory), controlling entry and land use. Finally, the Northern Territory is not a state, and the Commonwealth government retains powers over both the territorial government and the land councils.

The main policy periods in the Northern Territory are: (1) the period from initial contact up to the Bleakley Report, 1928; (2) the period of Commonwealth protection policies, 1929-50; (3) the period of the Hasluck-Geise Welfare Administration, 1951-72; and (4) the period of community self-government, 1973- .

From Initial Contact to the Bleakley Report, 1928

The Northern Territory was established in 1911, when Northern Australia was separated from South Australia. The Commonwealth government then assumed jurisdiction of a territory that was considered to be remote and inhospitable to Europeans. Aboriginal affairs are frequently discussed in the early administrator's reports, and, in 1912, it is noted that:

> Professor W. Baldwin Spencer of Melbourne University was appointed Special Commissioner and Chief Protector of Aborigines. He did not arrive until 15th January this year. It can be assumed he will try to improve the conditions of the Aboriginal natives and to overcome the antagonism that certainly exists to the Act.[27]

Spencer was concerned at what he considered to be the exploitation of Aboriginal peoples in the Northern Territory by Asians and Europeans:

> The aboriginal man's code of morality is different from that of the white man and he sees no wrong in lending his lubra [wife]. If it be within the limits of his own tribe he is ruled by definite laws defining to whom he may – in fact sometimes must – lend her, and to whom he may not. Asiatics and Europeans stand outside the pale of these laws.[28]

By 1912, the development of a 'half-caste' population in the Northern Territory told of the ineffectiveness of the policy of protection. Spencer recommended policies which would encourage white women to settle in the Northern Territory as well as policies that would prohibit unions between Aboriginals and Asians or whites. These prohibitions were to be enforced by exercising control over Aboriginal movements and residence.

Spencer recognized that 'the question of half-castes, other than the children of legally married men and women, is a somewhat difficult one to deal with.' After some discussion of their number and the fact that 'the white population as a whole will never mix with half-castes,' he concluded that:

> No half-caste child should be allowed to remain in any native camp, but they should all be withdrawn and placed on stations. So far as practicable, this plan is now being adopted. In some cases when the child is very young, it must of necessity be accompanied by its mother, but in other cases, even though it may seem cruel to separate the mother and the child, it is better to do so, when the mother is living, as is usually the case, in a native camp.[29]

The native camps referred to were the Aboriginal settlements that were established by the government at Darwin and Alice Springs to segregate the Aboriginal from the non-aboriginal population. In Spencer's view, 'the best and kindest thing is to place them [half-caste people] on reserves with natives, train them in the same schools and encourage them to marry amongst themselves.'

In 1920, the administrator reported that it was 'difficult to make more than an intelligent guess at the number of Aboriginals in the Territory.' Twenty thousand was the best estimate which could be made, and the problem of applying any social policy to that number of people was considered to be beyond the power and resources of the administration. In comparison, the half-caste population was small and was concentrated around Darwin and Alice Springs. In 1921, the administrator indicated the policy for this more manageable population:

> There are 550 half-caste and quadroons in the Territory, 122 males, 147 females, 136 male and 145 female children. The birth of twenty half-caste and quadroon children were registered during the year and in only one instance was there sufficient evidence to allow the Court

making an order compelling the father of the child to contribute to his support.

Most of the half-caste women are prostitutes, but a few are married to white men and to Malays. Perhaps the establishment of an industrial school may be worthy of consideration, as there is little doubt these girls can be raised above the level of their black sisters and become useful servants.[30]

In accordance with the racist theory of the period, half-castes were considered to be superior to full-blooded Aboriginals. This being the case, half-caste people warranted a more concerted education than did full-blooded Aboriginals. Aboriginal habitation near Darwin and Alice Springs was controlled by confining Aboriginals to controlled-access camps. In 1928 Bleakley reported a social policy focused on 'rescuing half-caste children from the camps and sending them to a home for care and education.'[31]

Bleakley was the chief protector of Aboriginals in Queensland. In 1928, he was invited to undertake a review of the Territory's Aboriginal administration and to produce a report to guide policy. He approved the approach being taken to the management of the Aboriginal and half-caste population and made many suggestions aimed at making it more efficient.

Commonwealth Protection Policies, 1929-50

The Commonwealth government policy with respect to the Aboriginal peoples in the Northern Territory was consolidated on the basis of Bleakley's report and was issued in 1933 as a formal statement of objectives. These were:

(a) to preserve the aboriginal races;
(b) to ensure that the nomadic tribes have adequate land to enable them to pursue undisturbed their natural mode of living and to provide ample supplies of native foods;
(c) to protect the aboriginal employee and to ensure that he derives adequate remuneration and benefits from his employment;
(d) to protect the aboriginal women from moral abuses on the part of Europeans and other races;
(e) to collect half-castes and train them in institutions to enable them eventually to take their places in the ordinary life of the community.[32]

In towns, the practical task of removing half-caste children fell on the police, and in rural districts it fell on patrol officers. The work was systematically carried out until 1950. At least some of the patrol officers detested their task. Ted Evans, a patrol officer who was later to be a senior administrator in the Territory, wrote:

> My patrol district included the Wave Hill/Victoria River Downs regions ... In 1950 I was given instructions to remove a total of seven children, mainly from Wave Hill and neighbouring stations. Despite my efforts to assuage the fears of both mothers and children, the final attempt at separation was accompanied by such heart-rending scenes that I officially refused to continue to obey such future instructions.[33]

The children removed from their Aboriginal mothers were placed in institutions referred to as half-caste homes. Before the Second World War, they were accommodated in a home within the Aboriginal Khalin compound on the outskirts of Darwin. During the war, these children were evacuated to Alice Springs. After the war, a new home, known as the Retta Dixon Home, was established under church auspices in Darwin. Similar facilities were operated in Alice Springs and various other places in the Northern Territory. The number of children in these homes at any one time was around 400, and this represented all the known half-caste children in the Territory.

Full-blood Aboriginal children were affected to the extent that they saw or heard of children being taken away, but they were not, themselves, at risk. The purpose of this policy was to protect Aboriginal life, and it led to the establishment of extensive Crown land reserves where Aboriginals could live in comparative safety.

Hasluck-Geise Welfare Administration, 1951-72

Paul Hasluck (who was later knighted and became governor general of Australia) was appointed as minister for the Northern Territory in 1951. He was committed to the policy of assimilation that had been developed at the Commonwealth conference in 1937, but which had not been implemented with regard to full-blood Aboriginal people in the Northern Territory. Furthermore, the assimilation policy for the half-Aboriginal population was full of contradictions. In order to distinguish the half-caste people who were not subject to the same restrictions as were Aboriginals, they were required to wear a permit, known as a 'dog tag,' around their necks!

Hasluck was not impressed by either these policies nor by the calibre of staff available to him in Darwin, and he went about recruiting capable young men with 'intelligence, energy, an interest in people, and capacity to learn from experience. Some enthusiasm for unpopular causes (or sense of mission ...) would help.'[34] The man selected to be director of welfare was Harry Geise. Together, Hasluck and Geise produced a welfare administration for the Northern Territory that was unsurpassed in the thoroughness with which it applied the policy of assimilation.

This administration believed it important to replace explicitly racist terminology with welfare terminology. References to 'full-blood Aborigines' and 'half-castes' were replaced by references to 'wards of the state.' The target for change was not race but lifestyle. Implementing the policy required classifying all the people in the Territory, and it led to the first administrative enumeration of Aboriginal peoples, with most of them being classified as wards.

For twenty years, from 1952 to 1972, the Northern Territory Welfare Branch annual reports document continuing progress in extending an effective welfare administration to the wards. Table 3.4 shows the extent of assimilation.

In addition to these measures, there were high-school programs that provided opportunities for the most capable young Aboriginal people to attend schools outside the Territory as well as an ambitious feeding program that provided Aboriginal peoples and their children with European-style meals. Between 1952 and 1972, the Northern Territory Welfare Ordinance was revised several times to replace legislation based on race with legislation based on professional judgement.

To the welfare administrators of the day, the achievements of this administration speak for themselves. There were many more educated Aboriginals than there had been before; Aboriginals were better fed and healthier than they had been since white contact; there was a strong, positive emphasis on giving Aboriginal children the best possible chance to take their place as equals in Australian society; and, in addition, those features of Aboriginal life not in conflict with assimilation (e.g., art and music) were valued.

Nevertheless, assimilation remained the main objective of this administration. The effect of the feeding, pre-school, and school programs was to remove people from their traditional way of life and to break down the traditional Aboriginal community.[35] Under these child welfare and juvenile correctional programs, children were removed

Table 3.4

Northern Territory welfare administration, 1952-72

Service	1952-3	1957-8	1962-3	1967-8	1972-3
Aboriginal population	13,490	16,297	18,671	20,431	22,798
Aboriginal children[a]	4,655	7,414	9,013	9,810	10,468
Children in school	529	1,940	2,919	4,761	6,442
Children in pre-school	0	0	180	548	1,101
Children in care	0	0	154	266	347
Children in receiving homes	0	0	135	665	515
Part-Abor. children in homes	425	337	293	178	201
Abor. children in care/1,000	all known part-Abor. children	n/a	64	113	101

[a] Estimate of number of Aboriginal children in each year developed from available data on the proportion of children in the Aboriginal population on missions and government settlements.

Source: Northern Territory Administration annual reports

from their parents more often than they had been under earlier administrations. In accordance with the best welfare thinking of the day, Aboriginal children were increasingly placed in foster homes in non-Aboriginal communities. However, children placed in these homes felt more isolated than they had in the old Retta Dixon Home, where they at least had the support of their peers.[36] Finally, the 1971 annual report contained a reminder that the Northern Territory's preoccupation with the children of part-Aboriginal descent had not been lost:

A foster care program in the Northern Territory has several unique factors which make such a program difficult to implement. These include:

(a) Racial Factors of children fostered by the Branch at present 24% are of full-Aboriginal descent, 73% part-Aboriginal and 3% European. This breakdown is not representative of the Territory racial composition and it is extremely difficult to match the child's race to that of foster parents. Most part-Aboriginal children have been fostered by white people, and full-blood Aborigines by full-blood Aborigines.[37]

Community Self-Government, 1973-
Australia's election of the Whitlam labour government in 1972 ended the comprehensive application of the policy of assimilation. Aboriginal welfare was divided among different territorial and Commonwealth departments. The feeding programs were disbanded, as regular social security was extended to Aboriginal peoples. Cyclone Tracy (1973) also took its toll, destroying the Retta Dixon Home in Darwin. The Whitlam government's Aboriginal policy emphasized community self-government and community development. Its objective was to negotiate terms for the transfer of administrative control to the Aboriginal land councils, which were formed as a type of parallel government for Aboriginal peoples residing on reserves in the Northern Territory. New Aboriginal organizations were funded by the Commonwealth government, and it appears that policy shifted from a concern with issues of child welfare to a concern with community issues, particularly substance abuse and family violence. However, statistical data on services are not available. The Commonwealth Department of Aboriginal Affairs, which, in 1973, inherited many of the welfare department's responsibilities, provided no data on children or families during its four-year life. The Northern Territory Department of Community Development, which succeeded the Commonwealth Department of Aboriginal Affairs in 1977, provided no statistical data until it published its 1986-7 annual report.

In the 1986-7 annual report, the number of children in care is 200, and, although Aboriginal origin is not reported, I was told that less than half of these children were Aboriginal. In 1976, the Commonwealth Department of Community Development was criticized in court for 'child stealing' and was unable to obtain court support for the adoption of an Aboriginal child by an American couple.[38] As a result, territorial administration appears to have concentrated its child protection and guardianship services on the non-Aboriginal population. Field staff interviewed in Alice Springs seemed to be uncertain as to the mandate of child welfare service vis-à-vis the

Aboriginal community. The main emphasis appears to have shifted to the correctional system (in 1987-8, 464 children were subject to correctional orders – 304 of them were referred to as Aboriginal).

Commonwealth Aboriginal Child Welfare Policy

In 1967, the Commonwealth government obtained shared jurisdiction (with the states) over Aboriginal affairs. The Commonwealth government has used its legislative authority to enact enabling legislation, creating the Aboriginal Development Council, the Department of Aboriginal Affairs, and, in March 1990, the Aboriginal and Torres Strait Islanders Council. These bodies provide support for a number of Aboriginal services. Important contributions to Aboriginal child welfare have been made by: (1) the Aboriginal Legal Service; (2) Aboriginal child care funding; (3) the Australian Law Reform Commission study of Aboriginal customary law; and (4) the Royal Commission into Aboriginal Deaths in Custody.

Aboriginal Legal Service

The Aboriginal Legal Service was established to ensure that Aboriginal peoples were properly represented in court, including with respect to family and child welfare matters. In addition to providing this important service, the Aboriginal Legal Service has been a major contributor to policy development. Good examples of this are to be found in the development of the Aboriginal Child Placement Principle.

Aboriginal Child Care Funding

The Commonwealth Department of Community Services provides funding to the Aboriginal and Islander child care agencies, which have been developed in all major urban areas in Australia. The agencies provide an independent Aboriginal presence in both service and policymaking. This funding has also been extended to the Link-Up program. The impact of both these services is discussed in the concluding section of this chapter.

Australian Law Reform Commission Study of Aboriginal Customary Law

With Commonwealth funding, the Australian Law Reform Commission completed a major study of Aboriginal customary law in 1982 and, in so doing, provided a much improved understanding of how, in both legislation and common law, more sensitivity could be shown to the Aboriginal family. The commission recognized that Aboriginal peoples see themselves as living under 'two laws,' and it accepted their argument for court recognition of Aboriginal customary law.[39]

Royal Commission on Aboriginal Deaths in Custody

The mandate of the Royal Commission on Aboriginal Deaths in Custody (1990-) was to determine why there was a much higher proportion of Aboriginal Australians than non-Aboriginal Australians in custody. One reason for this state of affairs was attributed to the disruption of Aboriginal family life caused by family and child welfare programs.

Current Policy and Practice Changes

During the 1980s, there have been two major types of change in Aboriginal child welfare in Australia: (1) that brought about by Commonwealth-sponsored Aboriginal child welfare organizations; and (2) that brought about by the modification of mainstream state child welfare services.

Commonwealth-Sponsored Aboriginal Child Welfare Organizations

An important change in the 1980s was the development of Commonwealth-sponsored Aboriginal child welfare resources and agencies. These agencies work independently as well as in combination with established state agencies to provide Aboriginal peoples with services as well as support from other Aboriginals. The two principal family and child welfare services which are available to Aboriginal peoples throughout Australia are Link-Up and the Aboriginal and Islander child care agencies.

Link-Up is an organization that was begun in New South Wales by the oral historian Peter Read and by the Aboriginal leader Coral Edwards. It now has offices in every state and works with Koori and Murri adults (the names by which most New South Wales and Queensland Aboriginals, respectively, refer to themselves) to locate the members of disrupted families and to help them find their way home. Link-Up provides counselling and personal support and emphasizes that the task of tracing family contacts is only the first step in reunion – reconnecting with one's family takes time and can bring great joy as well as great pain.[40] Link-Up is supported by the Commonwealth government and has good working relationships with many social service agencies. However, official government records on Aboriginal adoption remained closed in 1990 in New South Wales, Queensland, Western Australia, and the Northern Territory. Nevertheless, Link-Up has been very effective in building informal networks to overcome this problem.

The Aboriginal and Islander child care agencies (AICCAs) are both service and advocacy organizations for Aboriginal child welfare. Independent Aboriginal child care agencies are supported by the Commonwealth government in more than twenty locations throughout Australia. There is also a national umbrella organization, the Secretariat of the National Aboriginal and Islander Child Care (SNAICC). These agencies provide child welfare support services such as day care, parent education, youth work, and community development. They also cooperate closely with state statutory, protection, and correction agencies. This cooperation includes providing advice, finding resources, and tracing family connections. It is primarily through AICCAs that the Aboriginal Child Placement Principle is implemented. In addition to Commonwealth support, AICCAs are supported by contracts and fee-for-service relationships with state agencies. Most of this funding is 'soft,' requiring a continuing process of application, reapplication, and evaluation. This makes it difficult for the agencies to stabilize their services and their staff. The extent of cooperation with state agencies varies from time to time and from state to state. Where there is a comprehensive relationship between the state and AICCA, the latter is notified of every Aboriginal child with whom a statutory agency is working, participates in all planning and case management, and controls placements; where the relationship between the state and AICCA is less comprehensive, the former decides which Aboriginal children to refer to the latter. AICCAs are urban agencies, located in major towns and cities; service to rural Aboriginal communities and peoples is restricted to visits.

As advocacy organizations, the aims of AICCAs and SNAICC are:

- To establish culturally relevant National Legislation relating to Aboriginal and Islander child development.
- To eliminate abusive child welfare practices that result in unwarranted Aboriginal and Islander parent-child separations.
- End discrimination that prevents Aboriginal and Islander families from qualifying as foster care or adoptive parents.
- To demand from State and Federal Child Welfare Departments and

other welfare agencies immediate access to records and other relevant information which will facilitate the return of Aboriginal and Islander persons to family, extended family and Aboriginal and Islander Communities.
- That the care custody and control of Aboriginal and Islander children be the sole prerogative of the Aboriginal and Islander communities.[41]

Modification of Mainstream State Child Welfare Services
The principal change in mainstream policy and practice has been the introduction of the Aboriginal Child Placement Principle. The placement principle was developed by members of the Aboriginal Legal Service, who argued that the best interest of the Aboriginal child were not being served by placement processes which ignored Aboriginal identity.[42] In the *Aboriginal Law Bulletin*, Richard Chisolm indicated that

> [it] involves two components. First, there is a guideline for the placement of children: they should be placed (in descending order of preference) with members of their own immediate or extended family; or with members of their community or with other Aboriginal people. Only if none of these placements can be made should they be placed in the care of non-aboriginal people. Second, there should be aboriginal participation in the decision-making process. Opinions differ about what this second component should involve. Aboriginal claims to self-determination or sovereignty suggest that Aboriginal people should have authority to determine placement while more conservative opinion would merely seek to ensure that Aboriginal views are taken into account when the decision is made.[43]

The placement principle made Aboriginal status an important administrative consideration in all placements. In addition, this principle has been introduced into legislation in Victoria, New South Wales, and the Northern Territory. Although none of the statutes place an absolute obligation on the child welfare agency to place an Aboriginal child only with Aboriginal people, the New South Wales legislation indicates that any other approach must be regarded as a last resort:

> An Aboriginal child shall not be placed in the custody or care of another person under this part unless – (a) the child is placed in the

care of a member of the child's extended family ...; (b) if it is not practicable for the child to be placed in accord with paragraph (a) ... the child is to be placed in the care of a member of the Aboriginal community to which the child belongs; (c) if it is not practicable for the child to be placed in accord with paragraph (a) or (b) ... the child is [to be] placed in the care of some other Aboriginal family ...; or, (d) if it is not practicable for the child to be placed in accordance with paragraph (a), (b), or (c) ... the child is to be placed in the care of a suitable person ... *after consultation with* – (i) members of the child's extended family ...; and (ii) such Aboriginal welfare organizations as are appropriate in relation to the child.[44]

Applying the placement principle requires a working definition of 'Aboriginal child.' In practice, many agencies appear not to have this, and they make decisions on the basis of the degree of colour, parental preference, and placement availability. Advocates of this principle argue for its application to all children of Aboriginal descent:

Aboriginal people frequently argue that *all* children with Aboriginal blood should be regarded as Aboriginal. There are two arguments often used to support this. Firstly, they point out that since contact, white people have used a variety of definitions of 'Aboriginal' to suit their purposes, and for whites to determine the question of Aboriginal identity is a particularly damaging and vicious form of oppression ... The second argument is that the social identification of a person with Aboriginal blood is Aboriginal.[45]

The Aboriginal Child Placement Principle has also brought about an end to the adoption of Aboriginal children by non-Aboriginal parents. In addition to these policy and practice changes, there have been some administrative changes in the staffing of state child welfare agencies; some states have adopted affirmative recruitment policies aimed at increasing the number of Aboriginals employed as staff members.

In each state, specific changes in policy towards Aboriginal families and children have followed general changes in attitude. Aboriginal adults were left on the margins of Australian society while attempts were made to absorb their children into non-Aboriginal society. These attempts included major parent-child separations – separations which have extended over several generations and which have resulted in the severe disruption of families.

Through the development of the placement principle, and through the support of Aboriginal family and child welfare organizations, Australia appears to have made a start in reversing the policies of assimilation and integration which have been dominant since the cessation of the early acts of genocide. However, these policies have been very damaging to Aboriginal peoples. Every Aboriginal person in Australia has his or her personal stories and scars. As a result, Europeans are feared and, sometimes, hated. Yet it is important to point out that they are hated not as individuals but as a group – a racist group. As Peter Read writes:

> Ignorance is no defence. The whites were so convinced of the rightness of their own way of life that they excluded all others. So deep was the idea of the worthlessness of Aboriginal society in New South Wales that hardly anybody, from the highest levels of administration to the lowest, got past the old irrelevancies that they respected or were friendly with certain Aborigines. What was required was an appreciation of Aboriginal life ways in their own right, not as lived by particular individuals. Most of the officials did not arrive at the starting point, that is, the recognition of the existence of New South Wales Aboriginal culture, let alone take the second step, which was to acknowledge its validity.
>
> The blacks whose families remained intact have known all along what the Board was trying to do and why. For generations Aborigines have suffered. Perhaps in time whites will suffer in the knowledge of what they have done. But they can not expect forgiveness.[46]

After two hundred years of assimilation and family and child welfare turmoil, it would require several generations of peace and separate development for Aboriginal peoples to rebuild the clan and family ties that were so deliberately assaulted. It is not clear that this will ever happen.

State agencies continue to work with Aboriginal children and families within the structure of a single child welfare law – a law which was framed by and for mainstream Australian society. The accommodations which are made through the placement principle and through the recognition of AICCAs do not change the fundamental imposition of European law on Aboriginal life.

In addition, as mentioned in Chapter 2, the general assumption of Australian writers and officials is that, eventually, Aboriginals will be assimilated into white society. In other words, it is generally believed that, although there may be a case for compensation for past wrongs, and although there may be a case for transitional arrangements, in the end there will be one integrated society living under one set of public institutions and laws.

4
Canada: The General Structure of Canadian Indian Policy

European policy towards First Nations peoples in North America was influenced initially by the competition between France, England, and Spain. In contrast to Australia, where Aboriginal peoples were not needed, First Nations peoples were important allies in the process of colonial competition, and relations with them were too important to be left to the local interests of early colonists. This established a pattern of centralized attention to First Nations affairs which was inherited by the Canadian government in 1867 (the date of Confederation). The history of Canadian Indian policy can be divided into six principal periods, each of which has left some mark on the general structure of such policy, on the definition of 'Indian,' and on the institutions of government through which Indian social policy was conducted.

History of Indian Policy
The six periods of Canadian Indian policy used in this discussion are: (1) the period of early contact, 1534-1763; (2) the period of the Royal Proclamation, 1763-1830; (3) the transitional period from Royal Proclamation to Canadian social policy, 1830-67; (4) the period of assimilation, 1867-1950; (5) the period of integration, 1951- ; and (6) the period of the assertion of self-government, 1970- . The last two periods coexist, although there is a gradual, uneven, and incomplete movement towards self-government. The treatment of the historical periods is abbreviated and introductory, with attention directed selectively to those aspects of social policy which have had a continuing impact on First Nations peoples.

Early Contact, 1534-1763
On 20 July 1534, Jacques Cartier, concluding his first visit to what

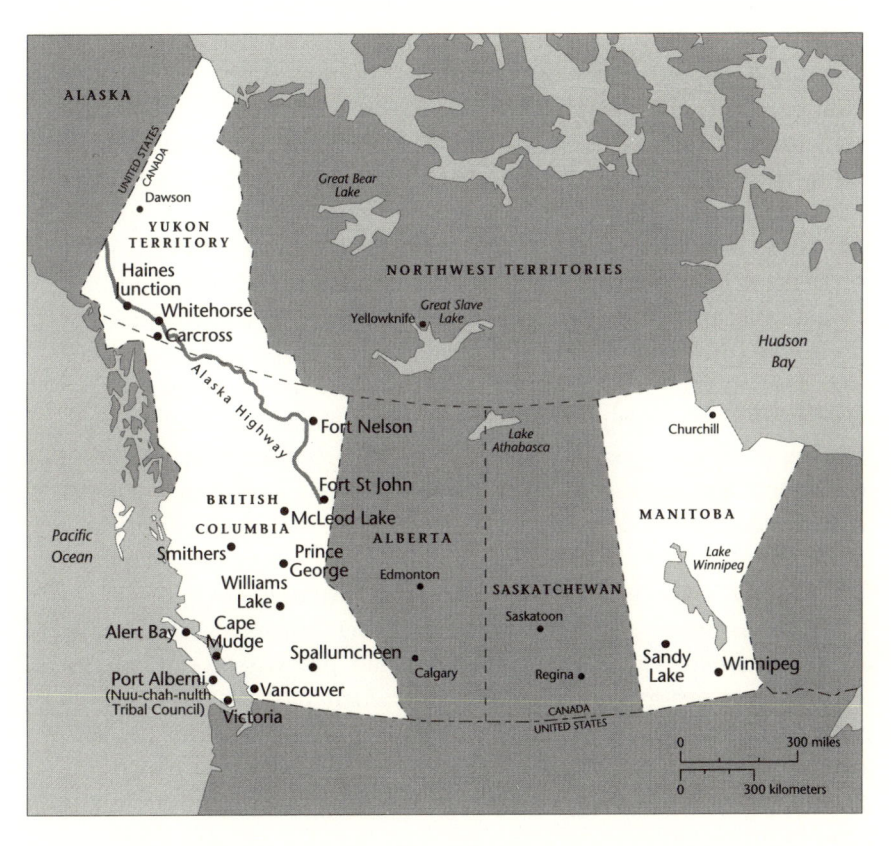

Map 2 Western Canadian research sites and relevant place names

would become Canada, erected a cross at St Jonquiere, Québec, and then departed for France, taking with him several First Nations people, following a mass baptism.[1] For the next 200 years, the Algonquin and Huron people had to deal with increasing French trade, church missions, settlement, and militarization. French military activity was directed primarily at Britain and Spain, with whom France competed for control of the 'New World.'

At first, First Nations peoples probably regarded the French presence as a novelty, not comprehending its long-term implications for their health, the control of their lands, and the destruction of their ways of life. However, the French Jesuits missionaries had no doubt about their obligation to implant the 'Faith' and to save First Nations souls.

The 1537 papal bull of Pope Paul III recognized that 'the Indians are truly men and are not only capable of understanding the Catholic faith but desire exceedingly to receive it.'[2] By 1634, general theological conclusions had been reached about 'Indians,' thus providing the basis for a systematic mission policy. It had been concluded that Indian religion (it was assumed there was only one) was vague and useless but, as a result of this, was not likely to be a serious impediment to conversion to Christianity. The Indian mind was considered to be a tabula rasa, just waiting to receive the teachings of Christianity. The process of conversion included a period of persuasion and instruction, followed, often on a mass basis, by baptism. The newly baptised would then be brought within the discipline of the church in order to stabilize them in their newly acquired faith. This required that education continue, that all use of their earlier religions cease, that sources of temptation offered by French traders (eg. alcohol, promiscuity, etc.) be removed, and that breaches of these prohibitions be disciplined by the church through penance and other penalties.

The Jesuits were relatively successful in their objectives, particularly in places where First Nations peoples had permanent settlements. Because conversion was more difficult when First Nations peoples were nomadic, the Jesuits perceived an advantage in encouraging agricultural settlements. Although there were incidents in which the Jesuit presence was rejected by First Nations communities, in the main, Christianity was accepted.

The early Jesuit missionaries, along with their successors, aimed at establishing, with First Nations peoples, a more perfect world than the one they had known in Europe. The efforts of these missionaries influenced all subsequent social policy. Of particular importance was the belief that First Nations peoples should be converted to Christianity.

Royal Proclamation, 1763-1830
The Royal Proclamation of 1763 was a result of British military policy and recognized the importance of First Nations allies in the victory over the French in the war of 1755-1830. The Royal Proclamation provided a foundation for British law in North America that has never been repealed and which is recognized in both American and Canadian law. In Canada, this was most recently confirmed when it was cited in Section 25 of the Canadian Constitution Act, 1982.

Prior to the Royal Proclamation, each of the British North American colonies had conducted its own relationship with First Nations peoples; this led to a lack of consistency and unity. In 1755, during the early stages of the war with France, the British government established an Indian Department and appointed a superintendent of Indian Affairs. The department was responsible 'for political relations with Indian people, protection from traders, boundary negotiations, and the enlistment of Indian people during times of war.'[3] The superintendents appointed by the British were not always successful in providing a unified administration, and they did not always prevent the colonists from appropriating First Nations lands (with or without payment). However, Britain was successful in the general conduct of its war with France both in Europe and in North America, and, at the Treaty of Paris, France ceded its North American territories, except the islands of St Pierre and Miquelon, to Britain.

First Nations peoples, led by Pontiac, were not prepared to recognize either British rule or the French surrender of what they considered to be their territory. Their concern was exacerbated by the reputation of the British for not controlling their colonists and not providing hospitality in their forts, as did the French traders. These conditions led to what is known as Pontiac's Rebellion, in which several British forts were captured. The Royal Proclamation of 1763 was drafted on the basis of advice from the colony concerning measures necessary to 'conciliate ... the Indian Nations, by every act of strict Justice ... by affording them Protection from any Encroachments on the lands they have reserved to themselves, for their hunting grounds.'[4]

The Royal Proclamation was addressed not only to the First Nations but also to the newly acquired colony of Québec. The proclamation gave Québec its first constitution under British rule, defined its boundaries, and recognized that land outside the colonial boundaries was 'reserved' as 'hunting grounds' for First Nations peoples:

> And whereas it is just and reasonable, and essential to our interest, and the Security of our Colonies, that the several Nations or Tribes of Indians with whom we are connected, and who live under our Protection, should not be molested or disturbed in the Possession of such Parts of Our Dominions and Territories as, not having been ceded or purchased by Us, are reserved to them, or any of them as their Hunting Grounds.
>
> And We do hereby strictly forbid ... all our loving Subjects from making any Purchases or Settlements whatever, or taking Possession of any of the Lands above reserved, without our especial leave and License for that Purpose first obtained.

Administration of the proclamation was another matter. Resources were inadequate to support an administration which conflicted with the expansionist interests of the settlers. In 1774, the British government annexed the entire area of former French administration to the colony of Québec in order to provide a base for a civil administration. This action contributed to the general dissatisfaction with British rule in the Thirteen Colonies and to the American Revolution. Following that revolution, new boundaries were drawn, and, in 1791, Upper and Lower Canada were established. However, the Royal Proclamation of 1763 remained the legal base for the conduct of British Indian policy. The idea that Indian policy should be unified and conducted through a superintendent derived from this period.

Transition from the Royal Proclamation of 1763 to Canadian Social Policy, 1830-67

This transition was seen as a sensitive period in relations between First Nations peoples and the British Crown. In Britain, the 1837 House of Commons Select Committee on Aborigines was developing a new set of policies based on a worldwide view of Britain's imperial and civilizing role. The committee recognized that this role would result in changing the treatment of the Crown's First Nations allies in North America, but it did not wish to embarrass the British government by advising an immediate change in policy. As a result, the committee declined to make recommendations with respect to North America:

On the subject of relations between the British colonies in North America and the Aborigines on that continent, your committee abstains from offering any specific suggestions because they understand that Her Majesty's government have for some time been engaged in correspondence respecting it with the Lieutenant Governor of Canada ... Your committee are unwilling to embarrass the Government by suggestions, which, being proffered during the pendency of discussions of the subject, might proceed on imperfect grounds and point to erroneous conclusions.[5]

Colonial correspondence from 1837 concerning the Indian Department in Upper and Lower Canada shows that the time in which First Nations peoples had been viewed as necessary military allies was past. The Royal Proclamation of 1763 is cited, but the colonial policies which had been based on it, particularly the giving of 'presents' in place of 'substantial Advantages of Territory,' are to be replaced by an administration aimed at 'inducing the Indians to change their present ways for more civilized Habits of Life, namely their Settlement: ... compact Settlements should be formed ... giving them Agricultural Implements, but no other Description of Presents.'[6] Of particular importance in this change of policy was the schooling of First Nations children, which followed in the footsteps of the Jesuits. The Canadian governor, Lord Gosford, forwarded a report to London which indicated the policies to be followed:

> Before the Conquest of this Country the Indians were under the Especial care and Direction of the Jesuit missionaries ... who became themselves their Instructors in so much of the Knowledge of Arts and Life as they thought it advisable to impart to them.
>
> Believing it however to be incumbent on the State to prepare the younger Generation of Indians for another and more useful Mode of Life, the Committee [Committee of the Executive Council, Québec City, 1836] would earnestly press upon His Majesty's Government the necessity of establishing Schools among them in which the Rudiments of Education shall be taught ...
>
> But though in natural Capacity, in Docility, and the Faculty of Observation, the Indians do not yield to any Race of Men ... a considerable Time must probably elapse before Ancient Habits and Prepossessions can be so far broken through that they become sensi-

ble to the Benefits of such Training for their Children. It may therefore be necessary to make it a condition of their continuing to receive Presents either for themselves or to their families, that they should send their Children to such Schools: and it may be hoped that the Clergy will lend their Aid in recommending and enforcing the Measure, as a necessary Part of any Plan for assimilating the Indians as much and as soon as possible to the rest of the Inhabitants of the Province.[7]

'Presents' were thus to be made conditional on behaviour rather than on recognition of treaties and the transfer of territory and land rights from First Nations peoples to colonists.

The assumption that the colonial administration had the right to govern First Nations peoples was based on the fact that, as London was going to eventually give it this responsibility anyway, it would be best if this could be done without subjecting it to 'the Burden of supporting a Race of indigent People whom the Policy of the Government has kept apart from the rest of the Society, has trained to an Aversion to Labour, and has in measure incapacitated from becoming useful Members of the Community.'[8] This assumption was compatible with the thinking of the 1837 House of Commons Select Committee on Aborigines, which had been encouraged by field reports from North American missionaries entered before it as testimony that First Nations peoples were in urgent need of Christianity and civilization:

> In the foregoing survey we have seen the desolating effects of unprincipled Europeans with Nations in a ruder state. There remains a more gratifying subject – the effect of fair dealing and of Christian instruction upon heathens.
>
> True civilization and Christianity are inseparable: the former has never been found, but as a fruit of the latter.
>
> As soon as they were converted, they perceived the evils attendant upon their former ignorant wandering state; they began to work, which they never did before; they perceived the advantage of cultivating the soil; they totally gave up drinking; they became industrious, sober and useful.[9]

These optimistic (not to say presumptuous and self-serving) reports were based, in part, on missionary experience with a new and practical form of organization which appeared to serve the need for education, settlement, protection of converts, proselytizing, and self-sufficiency. The church historian Foster Grant recognizes this new organization in his study of the role of the church in Indian policy: 'These developments inaugurated a new era in Indian missions, marked by the centrality of residential schools to which young people would be removed from parental influence in the hope that they would become effective emissaries of Christian civilization among their people.'[10] This endorsement of the residential school as a central instrument of social policy was formally recognized in Canada by the Bagot Commission in 1842.[11]

Additional measures undertaken prior to Confederation included the passage of legislation in the 1850s which, for the first time, established a legal definition of 'Indian,' and which vested all First Nations lands and property in the hands of a commissioner of Indian lands. Lands so vested could not be sold without Crown consent, and First Nations peoples resident on them, along with their spouses, were exempted from taxation.

Assimilation, 1867-1950
By the time of Confederation, all the basic features of Canadian Indian policy were in place, but they were scattered in a series of statutes and lacked a consolidated administrative structure. At Confederation, control of First Nations matters was assumed by the federal government, which, under Section 91(24) of the Constitution Act, 1867, was given jurisdiction for 'all Matters' coming under the subject 'Indians, and Lands reserved for Indians.'[12] One of the earliest Canadian enactments was the 1868 establishment of the predecessor to the Department of Indian Affairs, through An Act Providing for the Organization of the Department of the Secretary of State for Canada and for the Management of the Indian and Ordinance Lands.

Statutory consolidation occurred in the Indian Act, 1876.[13] This single act made provision for: the definition of 'Indian'; the recognition, protection, management, and sale of reserves; the payment of moneys to the support and benefit of Indians, including, specifically, 'contribution to schools frequented by such Indians'; the election of councils and chiefs; Indian privileges, particularly the exemption from taxation and from debt obligations of all types; provision for receiving the 'evidence of non-Christian Indians' in criminal prosecutions; special measures for the control of intoxicants; and provisions for 'enfranchisement.' The act was to be administered through agents of the superintendent of Indian affairs. These officials corresponded in all but name to the protectors advocated by the 1837 House of Commons Select Committee on Aborigines.

A provision for 'enfranchisement' was central to the statute – an enfranchised Indian ceased, in law, to be an Indian. Enfranchisement was only available to adult males, but, on being granted, it extended to their spouses and minor children. Two routes to enfranchisement were provided. One route was through demonstrating knowledge of how to farm in a European manner (upon demonstrating this skill over a three-year probation period, the man could take possession, in fee simple, of a parcel of land and become enfranchised). The other route was simpler – the man had to qualify to be a minister, lawyer, teacher, or doctor.

The Indian Act, 1876, was conceived as a complete code for the management of Indian affairs. It included a process for the sale of First Nations land and for providing First Nations peoples with full citizenship when they so qualified. Clearly, assimilation was its objective. Significantly, in law, there was no process whereby a former Indian or a descendant of an Indian could become, again, an Indian. The Indian Act, 1876, was drafted with the eastern Canadian First Nations peoples in mind. However, the application of the act to all First Nations peoples in British North America followed from its effective administration in British Columbia, the Prairies, and the North.

Resistance from First Nations peoples was met with amendments to the Indian Act – amendments which made its provisions even more effective. John Tobias details this extensive process of tightening the provisions of the act in the period up to the 1940s.[14] When First Nations bands elected their traditional leaders, the act was amended (in 1884) to give the government the power to depose those considered to be immoral, incompetent, or intemperate and to prevent their re-election. When traditional First Nations customs, in the view of missionaries or Indian agents, interfered with progress towards assimilation, legislation was introduced to ban them (e.g., in 1884 the potlatch [BC] and the Sun Dance [Prairies] were banned). In 1920, provisions requiring First Nations peoples to seek permits to appear in traditional dress and to perform traditional dances were written into the Indian Act; when the First Nations peoples of Manitoba and the Northwest Territories persisted in continuing to hunt and fish, the act was amended so that the game laws applied to them as well as to non-aboriginals (1890); when schools on the reserves were not well attended and First Nations parents failed to send their children to residential schools, provisions permitting the governor-general-in-council to issue regulations and to commit children to such institutions were written into the act (1894); when these provisions failed to obtain consistent attendance, the act was strengthened by classifying as delinquent all children who did not attend and by making their parents subject to criminal penalties (1920); and when First Nations peoples failed to apply for enfranchisement, provisions making it compulsory were written into the act (1922).

This process of tightening the administration of the Indian Act ended with the Second World War. In 1946, a joint committee of both the Senate and the House of Commons was established to review the provisions of the act and of Canada's administration of Indian affairs. The committee, reporting in 1948, proposed new guidelines for future Indian policy. These included:
- a political voice for women in band affairs
- more self-government and financial assistance for bands
- equal treatment for Indians with respect to intoxicants
- the provision of bands with the power to incorporate as municipalities
- instructions to Indian Affairs officials to assist Indian peoples in learning about self-government
- easing of enfranchisement conditions and the early extension of the franchise to all Indian peoples
- cooperation with the provinces in extending service to Indian peoples
- education of Indian children with non-Indians in order to better prepare the former for assimilation.[15]

Integration, 1951-
The 1951 Indian Act emphasized practical measures for integrating services to First Nations peoples with services to all Canadians, but its primary objective remained assimilation. Measures that followed from the act included:
- the development of agreements with the provinces for the provision of services to Indian peoples, including their integration into the regular school system
- a major 1966 survey of the social, educational, and economic situation of Indian peoples, together with recommendations for

education, economic development, federal-provincial relations, political development, welfare, and local government[16]
- the beginning of a consultative process, aimed at a more fundamental revision of the Indian Act, with national Indian organizations.[17]

The final step in this policy of integration was introduced in 1969, when the federal government issued a White Paper and announced its intention to absolve itself from responsibility for Indian affairs through repealing the Indian Act. Services would be transferred to the provinces, reserves would become the fee-simple property of bands, and Indians would become Canadians, differing from other Canadians only in ethnic origin, not in law.[18]

First Nations peoples completely rejected the White Paper, and, as a result of their opposition, it was formally withdrawn in 1973. This had the effect of strengthening national First Nations organizations, particularly the National Indian Brotherhood. The secretary of state provided core funding to First Nations peoples to support their land claims research. This gave the National Indian Brotherhood a capacity for sustained effort that had not existed since white contact. However, despite the formal withdrawal of the White Paper, in its day-to-day operations the Department of Indian Affairs and Northern Development (DIAND) continued to focus on integration.

Self-Government, 1970-
Since 1970, First Nations organizations have sought recognition of the right of First Nations peoples to govern themselves. Two decades of debate have not yet produced a model for public policy that has been accepted by the federal/provincial governments, the Canadian public, or First Nations peoples. Nevertheless, the following events and changes signal the potential recognition of internal decolonization and the independent self-government of First Nations peoples:

(1) A sustained campaign by national First Nations leaders and organizations for recognition in discussions relating to the Canadian Constitution. This campaign was hard-fought, for, although the federal government supported the recognition of a First Nations presence in the discussions, there was substantial provincial opposition, particularly from the western provinces. When Pierre Elliott Trudeau's Liberal government realized that it could only reach consent with the provinces if it agreed not to recognize First Nations peoples, the result was inevitable – First Nations peoples were not recognized in either the 1981 federal-provincial agreement on a constitutional amending

formula or in the Charter of Rights and Freedoms. Determined lobbying permitted limited recognition of 'the existing aboriginal and treaty rights of the aboriginal peoples of Canada' in the Canadian Constitution Act, 1982,[19] with aboriginal defined as including the Indian, Inuit, and Métis people. The Charter of Rights and Freedoms was qualified so as not to abrogate or derogate from any aboriginal, treaty, or other right or freedom that pertained to the aboriginal peoples of Canada, including (a) any rights or freedoms that have been recognized by the Royal Proclamation of 7 October 1763 and (b) any rights or freedoms that 'now exist by way of land claims agreements or may be so acquired.'[20] Finally, a commitment was given to convene a constitutional conference 'respecting constitutional matters that directly affect the aboriginal peoples of Canada.' This constitutional process ended in deadlock because provincial governments could not agree as to what, exactly, self-government might mean.[21]

(2) The introduction of practical measures for recognizing self-government and for enabling First Nations communities to exercise it. This approach was commended by the House of Commons Special Committee on Indian Self-Government (the Penner Committee) in 1983.[22] The committee was made up of MPs and three non-voting representatives from First Nations organizations. Following extensive hearings, it produced a report that argued for an expansion of the concept of self-government so that 'Indian First Nations' would be recognized as a 'distinct order of government in Canada.' The committee recognized that, at a practical level, band administration had been greatly strengthened by, for example, the assumption of responsibility for welfare, education, and child welfare. Economic development has also been important, with many bands developing the capacity to conduct substantial economic enterprises on reserve lands.

(3) Progress has been made towards settling outstanding land claims with aboriginal peoples in Québec, the Northwest Territories, and the Yukon Territory. Together with existing treaties, a framework for recognizing the legitimacy of aboriginal land rights exists in all of Canada, with the exception of BC. The Canadian courts have played a major role in this process, particularly in BC, where provincial opposition to aboriginal land rights has been strongest. As a result, a body of case law has developed that provides legal recognition of the existence of aboriginal jurisdiction, particularly in those areas of Canada where aboriginal rights were superseded without following any due process of law.

(4) The influence of the Charter of Rights and Freedoms. The Charter of Rights and Freedoms has been used to challenge the definition of Indian contained in the Indian Act. This definition was found to be discriminatory, as men and women were treated differently. In addition, the charter has been used to set aside the process of disenfranchisement. As a result, the Indian Act has been amended to provide a route whereby a person of aboriginal descent can in some circumstances reassert his or her legal aboriginal status.

These moves towards greater recognition of First Nations peoples exist alongside government actions which suggest that the objective of assimilation remains deeply rooted in Canadian Indian policy. For example, the Indian Act, 1951, is still the formal basis for policy. Today, this statute is administered in a manner that permits local decision-making autonomy at the band level – but what can be permitted can also be withheld. The expansion of government funding has provided bands with resources for the exercise of a limited form of self-government, but, as such expansion entails the development of extensive accountability mechanisms, it has also simultaneously limited the *exercise* of self-government. In fact, the result can be viewed not as 'self-government' but as the effective administrative/bureaucratic management of First Nations peoples. The model for this form of self-government is basically municipal; that is, limited functions are exercised by a local jurisdiction which lacks full fiscal autonomy and which is supervised by a senior level of government. The Indian Affairs Branch of the DIAND remains the central federal body concerned with First Nations peoples.

The provinces also provide many services to First Nations peoples through a single service-delivery system. This is legitimated through the use of Section 87 of the Indian Act, 1951, which states that: 'All laws of general application from time to time in force in any province are applicable to and in respect of Indians in the province, except to the extent that such laws are inconsistent with this Act.' However, in many areas of social policy, including the fields of health regulation and family law, the Indian Act is silent. Thus, the effective legislative body is not the band or tribal government but the province. This continues the basic thrust of pre-1969 Indian policy vis-à-vis the integration of First Nations services with regular provincial services.

Finally, evidence exists that assimilation could very easily be reintroduced. In 1985, Eric Nielsen, deputy prime minister and Conservative MP for the Yukon, chaired a task force that conducted a review of all government programs. The section of the report dealing with First Nations programs was reminiscent of the 1969 statement:

> The solutions ... recommended were that DIAND should be dissolved, some programs shifted to other federal departments, and then all programs were to be transferred to the provinces for delivery to Native peoples ... Comprehensive land claims were not to be dealt with ... Funding for native political organizations to support their development in all areas but the constitutional talks was to be ended and the funds diverted to bands ... and ... a media management strategy [should be] designed to minimize the public relations damage that they anticipated would occur when the 'clients' became aware of the recommendations.[23]

When this report was leaked, the government disowned it. Nevertheless, it damaged the credibility of Brian Mulroney's Conservative government and provided evidence that support for the 1969 objectives of integration and assimilation were still present.

The Definition of 'Indian' in Canadian Social Policy

During the early period of contact and military alliance, no definition of 'Indian' was needed. The individual First Nations defined themselves, and, although they were collectively referred to as Indians, they were also individually recognized as separate peoples. First Nations peoples have more than fifty different languages and eleven major linguistic families.

The critical step towards the development of a single, unified social policy occurred when, in 1850, the following definition appeared in legislation pertaining to First Nations peoples:

> [Indians may be defined as] persons of Indian blood, reputed to belong to the particular Body or Tribe of Indians interested in such lands and their descendants ... persons intermarried with any such Indians and residing amongst them, and the descendants of all such persons ... persons residing among such Indians whose parents on either side were or are Indians of such Body or Tribe, or entitled to be considered as such: And ... persons adopted in infancy by any such Indians, and residing in the villages or upon the lands of such Tribe or Body of Indians and their Descendants.[24]

This definition was broad and open to interpretation, but its significance was, as J.R. Miller indicates, that 'the civil government, an agency beyond the control of Indians, a body in which Indians were not even eligible to have representation, arrogated to itself the authority to define who was, and who was not, an Indian.'[25]

An effective administration designed to assimilate First Nations peoples required a more precise definition to ensure that the requisite services were properly targeted. The Indian Act, 1876, provided a much more precise legal definition:

The term 'Indian' means
   First. Any male person of Indian blood reputed to belong to a particular band
   Second. Any child of any such person; and
   Third. Any woman who is or was lawfully married to any such person

Special provisions in the 1876 act deal with the 'illegitimate,' 'absentees,' and 'half-breeds,' all of whom may or may not be 'Indians,' based on an administrative decision made by the superintendent of Indian affairs or his agent. An Indian woman who married 'any other than an Indian or a non-Treaty Indian ... cease[d] to be an Indian.' The definition of 'Indian' was tied to the definition of 'band,' so that every Indian was, by law, a band member, entitled to a vote in the affairs of the band, entitled to live on a specific reserve, and entitled to enjoy the financial or other benefits that related to the band. The act also defined two other categories of 'Indian'; the 'non-Treaty' Indian was 'any person of Indian blood who [was] reputed to belong to an irregular band [not recognized through a Treaty] or who follow[ed] the Indian mode of life,' and the 'enfranchised Indian' was someone who, following the grant of letters patent, had ceased to be an Indian.

The implications of these definitions were enormous. They effectively transferred power from First Nations communities to civil officials who were bound to follow the rules of their own culture. Major cultural impositions occurred due to European assumptions that the head of a household had to be male; that women and children could and should be related to as though they were forms of property; and that 'illegitimacy' and 'half-breed' were both valid, meaningful concepts. In addition, partially concealed within the Indian Act, 1876, was an administrative mechanism which became of great significance in later statutes. This was the requirement that, for administrative purposes, every 'Indian' had to be a member of a 'band.' This requirement resulted in a list of band members eligible to vote in band elections who, together with their dependants, were also eligible for other benefits. At the time of the act, there were many First Nations peoples, particularly in the west, who, being 'non-Treaty' members of 'irregular' bands, were beyond its administrative apparatus. This changed with the extension of settlement and the concomitant replacement of a definition of 'Indian' based on 'blood' and 'mode of life' with one based on registration. Thus, in the Indian Act, 1951, the definition of 'Indian' was shortened to 'a person who pursuant to this Act is registered as an Indian or is entitled to be registered as an Indian.' Being an Indian had thus become an administrative matter determined by having one's name on a list maintained and managed by an Indian affairs department.

This list of who counted as a legal Indian was an important measurement tool for the then Department of Northern Affairs and National Development, which, first, had to ensure that it was complete and accurate and, second, that it reflected the rate of enfranchisement. The legal structure of the policy of assimilation provided First Nations peoples with the means to get off this list (through enfranchisement and/or marriage), but it did not provide them with the means to get back on it. Furthermore, these rules applied to all members of the immediate family of the male head of a household. Administrative complexity abounded and is illustrated by that fact that some persons were denied Indian status through the 'double mother' rule. When a non-Indian woman married an Indian man she became a legal Indian, as did her offspring. However, should one of the sons of the couple marry a person who was not legally an Indian, then their children would not legally be Indians (because it was thought that 25 per cent legal Indian heritage was inadequate to qualify one as an Indian).[26]

The administration of the definition of 'Indian' under the Indian Act was accompanied by a gradual recognition, in law, that there were many persons of aboriginal heritage to whom it did not apply. Initially, these people were identified through being defined as not legally Indian. The Métis were one such group. When the Manitoba Act, 1870, was passed, provision was made for the distribution of 'scrips,' or land grants, which gave some recognition to Métis agricultural land use prior to mass European immigration and settlement. As a consequence, the Indian Act, 1886, was amended to provide that 'no half-breed in Manitoba who has shared in the distribution of half-breed lands shall be counted as an Indian.' The Indian Act, 1952, excluded Inuit, while recognizing them as aboriginal people: 'This Act does not apply to the race of aborigines commonly referred to as Eskimos.'

References in other statutes to Indian, Native, and Aboriginal provide yet more grounds for confusion over to whom special legal provisions based on aboriginal descent apply.[27] These principally arise where it is recognized that persons other than those who satisfy the definition of Indian in the Indian Act – a definition which was integral to one-way assimilation – have historic rights to land usage. Being defined as Indian was never intended to convey permanent rights to anyone; it was intended to determine to whom assimilationist social policies should be applied. Thus, where aboriginal rights have received some recognition in law, different definitions of 'Indian' have had to be used. The Constitution Act, 1982, now provides the highest level of legal recognition for First Nations, Inuit, and Métis peoples, who are referred to collectively as 'the aboriginal peoples of Canada.'

During the period since 1969, growing recognition has been given to broad terms like 'Aboriginal' and 'Native' to indicate entitlement rights, and there has also been a major change in the Indian Act. Following passage of the Charter of Rights and Freedoms in 1982, the federal government introduced legislation to correct the Indian Act's discriminatory provisions concerning women. By the time of the charter's passage, Canada had already been judged as not complying with the United Nations Covenant on Civil and Political Rights. This was a result of an action brought by a woman who, having lost her Indian status through marriage, had been prohibited from living on a reserve.[28] The changes in the Indian Act following this challenge were substantial and included removing sex discrimination clauses, abolishing the concept of enfranchisement, restoring Indian status and band membership to those individuals and their children who had lost them through the operation of discriminatory clauses, and providing bands with the power to pass by-laws, thus giving them limited control over their members. However, persons who had relinquished their Indian status through enfranchisement could not simply resume it – they had to go through an application process.

And establishing the case for resumption of status could be difficult, particularly for persons who had been adopted and who could only assume their aboriginal descent.

Number and Distribution of Indian People

There are two principal sources of data on the number and distribution of Indian people: the records of DIAND and the Census of Canada. These serve different purposes and are not in agreement with each other. DIAND's records have the administrative purpose of recording those persons for whom it has, or has had, responsibility. As indicated in the previous discussion, there have been important changes in the administrative definition of 'Indian' – changes which have affected the number of people recognized by DIAND. By contrast, the Census of Canada has counted people by their ancestral and linguistic origin, with its principal orientation being a French/English/Other classification system. In *1971 Census of Canada: Profile Studies – Ethnic Origins of Canadians*, it is noted that 'Canada's Native peoples tend to be peripheral characters, their actions and life style recounted only in so far as they affected the European colonist.'[29] Census definitions of origin were subject to the requirement that a respondent define his or her descent by naming a single male ancestor. Even the wording of the questions on origin ('on first coming to this continent'), used as late as 1981, illustrated the census's lack of recognition of aboriginal peoples. The Métis also represented a particular challenge to these definitions, as is reflected in the following note to the 1981 census: 'Métis are descendants of people of mixed Indian and European ancestry who formed a distinct socio-cultural entity in the 19th century. The Métis have gone on to absorb the mixed offspring of Native people and groups from all over the world.'[30] The 1986 census introduced a question which did not presume immigrant origin, a single descendant, or paternal primacy: 'Do you consider yourself an aboriginal person or a native Indian of North America, that is, Inuit, North American Indian or Métis?'[31]

In this study no attempt has been made to reconcile data from these different sources. Current scholarly estimates of aboriginal ancestry indicate that Canada has 1,000,000 persons of aboriginal descent; 265,000 'treaty' Indians; 85,000 'non-treaty' Indians; 35,000 Inuit; 102,000 Métis; and 500,000 assimilated Indian people.[32] The figures for treaty and non-treaty Indians are derived from the DIAND register. As a result of this historic register, the changing geographic and historic distribution of these First Nations peoples is well documented (see Table 4.1). To illustrate the difference between what is shown on the register and what is shown by census declaration, Table 4.1 gives both figures for 1981. The 1986 figure is from the census.

Throughout the last 100 years, the recognized status Indian people of eastern Canada have represented less than 1 per cent of the population. In the western provinces of Manitoba, Saskatchewan, Alberta, and British Columbia (and also in Northern Ontario), the last 100 years includes an early period in which First Nations peoples were overwhelmed by the process of settlement and became small minorities in their own land. However, even when only status Indians were counted, they remained more significant minorities than was the case in eastern Canada. The addition of Métis people (as people of aboriginal descent) to the census enumerations of the 1980s had a particularly strong effect in Manitoba and Saskatchewan, where one in twelve people identified themselves as descended primarily from the original occupants of the land. In the Yukon and Northwest Territories, aboriginal peoples have always been relatively numerous. In the Yukon, the Klondike gold rush resulted in First Nations peoples becoming a minority, but, as the gold rush population left, the former again became a significant percentage of the Yukon population. In the Northwest Territories, the addition of Inuit people to the count of aboriginal people in the 1981 and 1986 censuses also had a substantial effect on the proportions of aboriginal to non-aboriginal people.

A general conclusion from these figures is that people of aboriginal descent were turned into minorities by the settlement process rather than by a decline in their actual number. Furthermore, the official 'count' of Indian peoples maintained by DIAND significantly underrepresented the importance of aboriginal descent. Personal pride in aboriginal descent and the aforementioned changes in how it is defined are increasing Canadian sensitivity to its importance to social policy.

The composition of the families of First Nations peoples differs from that of the families of mainstream Canadians. This difference is particularly apparent in the proportion of children in the First Nations population and the proportion of children in the mainstream population, respectively; in the early years of the century, the former was much lower than was latter. This was interpreted as being a clear sign that First Nations peoples were disappearing. In the period from 1930 until the present day, the proportions have reversed, with First Nations children now making up a much larger proportion of the total First Nations population than non-aboriginal children do of the general Canadian population (see Table 4.2).

The extent of rural as opposed to urban living is difficult to ascertain, as DIAND's records are primarily oriented to establishing whether First Nations peoples were living on- or off-reserve. Although most reserves are rural, 9 per cent are considered to be urban, and an additional 21 per cent are semi-urban.[33] The proportion of First Nations peoples living off-reserve rose from 15.9 per cent in 1966 to 27.4 per cent in 1976.

The growing number of First Nations peoples living in major urban centres is also shown in Table 4.3, which indicates that more and more status Indians are living in major urban centres. However, First Nations peoples remain, primarily, rural dwellers. In contrast, most Canadian social policy has been developed in order to respond to social problems resulting from industrialism, urbanization, and immigration.

Administration of Indian Affairs

As in Australia, in Canada the separate legal status of aboriginal people was accompanied by the development of administrative mechanisms which differed from those which were used with regard to general social policy. These mechanisms have included treaties, Indian agencies, federal-provincial administrative agreements, federal and/or provincial administrative agreements with bands, and centrally funded national First Nations organizations.

The principle of treaty relationships between First Nations and European peoples was established as early as 1664, when the Two Row Wampum Treaty was concluded at Albany, New York. The principles of the treaty were recognized in 1983 by the Canadian House of Commons Committee on Indian Self-Government. It quoted Chief Michael Mitchell of the Akwesasne, who saw the treaty as

> symboliz[ing] two paths or two vessels travelling down the same river together. One, a birch bark canoe, will be for the Indian people, their laws, their customs and their ways. The other, a ship, will be for the white people and their laws, their customs and their ways. We shall each travel the river together, side by side, but in our own boat. Neither of us will try to steer the other's vessel.[34]

These early principles of mutual respect were widely used in 'Peace and Friendship' agreements that were made during the early part of

Table 4.1

Indian people by province, Canada, 1871-1986

Year	Nfld.	PEI	NS	NB	Que.	Ont.	Man.	Sask.-NWT	Alta.	BC	Yuk.	NWT	Total (000s)
1871		323 0.3%	1,666 0.4%	1,403 0.5%	6,988 0.6%	12,978 0.8%		56,000		23,000 63%			102 2.7%
1881		281 0.3%	2,125 0.5%	1,401 0.4%	7,515 0.5%	15,325 0.8%		56,239		25,661 51%			108 2.5%
1891		314 0.3%	2,076 0.5%	1,521 0.5%	13,361 1.0%	17,915 0.8%		51,249		34,202 35%			120 2.5%
1901		258 0.2%	1,629 0.4%	1,465 0.4%	10,142 0.6%	24,674 1.1%	16,277 6.3%	26,304 12.4%		28,949 16%	3,322 12%	14,921	127 2.4%
1911		248 0.3%	1,915 0.4%	1,541 0.4%	9,993 0.5%	23,044 0.9%	7,876 1.7%	11,718	11,630	20,134 5.1%	1,489 17%	15,904	105 1.5%
1921		235 0.2%	2,048 0.3%	1,331 0.3%	11,566 0.5%	26,436 0.9%	13,869 2.2%	12,914 1.7%	14,557 2.5%	22,377 4.2%	1,390 33%	3,873 47%	110 1.2%
1931		233 0.2%	2,191 0.4%	1,685 0.4%	12,312 0.4%	30,638 0.9%	15,417 2.2%	15,268 1.6%	15,258 2.1%	24,599 3.5%	1,543 36%	4,046 43%	122 1.2%
1941		258 0.3%	2,063 0.3%	1,939 0.4%	11,863 0.4%	30,366 0.8%	15,473 2.1%	13,384 1.4%	12,565 1.6%	24,875 3.0%	1,508 30%	4,052 33%	118 1.0%
1951		273 0.3%	2,641 0.4%	2,139 0.4%	15,970 0.4%	34,571 0.8%	17,549 2.2%	16,308 1.9%	13,805 1.5%	27,936 2.4%	1,443 16%	3,772 24%	136 1.0%

Year	Nfld.	PEI	NS	NB	Que.	Ont.	Man.	Sask.-NWT	Alta.	BC	Yuk.	NWT	Total (000s)
1961		341	3,561	3,183	20,453	42,688	23,658	23,280	19,827	36,229	1,869	4,598	179
		0.3%	0.5%	0.5%	0.4%	0.7%	2.6%	2.5%	1.5%	2.2%	13%	20%	1.1%
1971		432	4,524	4,280	26,985	54,072	34,422	35,072	28,343	46,955	2,661	6,277	244
		0.4%	0.6%	0.6%	0.4%	0.8%	3.5%	3.8%	1.7%	2.2%	14%	18%	1.1%
1981		430	6,035	4,240	39,275	71,285	39,940	37,615	36,320	54,600	2,866	6,720	318
		0.4%	0.8%	0.6%	0.6%	0.8%	3.9%	3.9%	1.6%	2.0%	12%	25%	1.3%
1981*		625	7,795	5,515	52,395	110,060	66,280	59,200	72,050	82,645	4,045	15,910	491
		0.5%	0.9%	0.8%	0.8%	1.3%	6.4%	6.1%	3.2%	3.0%	17%	45%	2.0%
1986	9,555	1,290	14,220	9,375	80,490	167,375	85,235	77,650	103,930	126,625	4,995	30,530	711
	1.6%	1.0%	1.6%	1.3%	1.2%	1.6%	8.1%	7.7%	4.4%	4.6%	21%	60%	2.8%

Source: Indians are as reported by the Department of Indian Affairs in annual reports from 1871 to 1981. These figures do not include the Inuit, Métis, or people of Indian descent who, through enfranchisement, had lost Indian status. The 1981* and 1986 figures are from the Census of Canada. Base figures for the Canadian population, from which the percentages are derived, are from the census.

Table 4.2
Children, aged 0-16, in the Canadian and status Indian populations

Year	Canadian population	Canadian children	% Canadian aged 0-16	Indian population	Indian children	% Indian aged 0-16
1901	5,371,315	1,839,223	34	127,941	21,473	22
1911	7,206,443	2,371,047	32	105,942	29,664	28
1921	8,788,483	3,019,560	34	110,596	32,982	29
1931	10,376,786	3,281,776	31	122,920	37,284	30
1951	14,009,429	4,520,357	30	136,407	58,610	43
1961	18,238,247	6,398,678	35	179,126	83,885	47
1971	21,568,310	6,380,900	29	244,023	116,578	47
1981	24,343,180	5,481,100	22	318,090	119,398	38

Source: Census of Canada for Canadian population and Department of Indian Affairs for status Indians

Table 4.3

Indian and Inuit in urban centres, Canada, 1951-81

City	1951	1961	1971	1981
Calgary	62	335	2,265	4,740
Edmonton	616	995	4,260	8,240
Hamilton	493	841	1,470	4,925
London	133	340	1,015	2,300
Montreal	296	507	3,215	12,525
Pr. Albert	211	225	1,045	2,485
Pr. Rupert		880	1,780	2,760
Regina	160	539	2,860	6,095
Saskatoon	48	207	1,070	3,050
Toronto	805	1,196	2,990	15,940
Vancouver	239	530	3,000	9,955
Winnipeg	210	1,082	4,940	13,165

Source: Information Canada, *Perspectives Canada* (Ottawa: Queen's Printer 1984), 244

the eighteenth century in what are now the Maritime provinces.³⁵ However, these principles had already been set aside when, following the Royal Proclamation of 1763, the 'treaty' became the primary instrument of settlement. Treaties were then used in Ontario and throughout the Prairies in a systematic process which, in British law, 'cleared' the land for settlement. In his review of treaties, Frideres writes: 'With a few subtle differences, all the Western treaties provided for reserve lands; monetary payments, and occasionally ribbons and flags at the treaty signing; suits of clothing every three years to chiefs and headmen; yearly ammunition and twine payments; and some allowance for schooling.'³⁶ The purpose of the treaties for the Canadian administration was expressed by Indian Commissioner J. Provencher in 1873:

> There are two modes wherein the Government may treat the Indian nations who inhabit this territory. Treaties may be made with them simply with a view to the extinction of their rights, by agreeing to pay them a sum, and afterwards abandon them to themselves. On the other side, they may be instructed, civilised and led to a mode of life more in conformity with the new position of this country and accordingly made good industrious and useful citizens.³⁷

First Nations peoples entered such unequal agreements because they were under great pressure at the time: the death toll from smallpox and other epidemic disease was very high; the buffalo had been hunted to extinction; and the Indian people in the United States had been defeated in battle and massacred. On the Prairies, the railroad surveyors were at work laying out the right-of-way for the railroad. Change was inevitable. In 1880, the government's representative, Alexander Morris, attempted to reassure the Cree with the following words:

> You know my words are true; you see for yourself and know that your numbers are lessening every year ... We want you to have homes of your own where your children can be taught to raise food for themselves from the good mother earth. You may not all be ready for that, but some, I have no doubt are, and in a short time others will follow.³⁸

The time was one in which terms dictated by a dominant authority could not but be accepted.

Treaties were not used to manage the settlement process in most of BC, in the Yukon, or in the Northwest Territories. In the case of BC, reserves were created by Crown land surveyors based on what was known of First Nations land use. Such reserves were neither negotiated nor covered by any treaty. Furthermore, the government had the right to change their boundaries at any time based on new knowledge, settlement needs, or any other factor it considered relevant. The provisions of the Royal Proclamation of 1763 were deemed not to apply to a territory that was then unknown. In the case of the Yukon and Northwest Territories, the areas remained so remote that it was unnecessary to deal with the issues of land use and possession until the middle of the twentieth century.

Although treaties were widely used during the settlement process, the administration which was established under the Indian Act, 1879, and its successors provided the means to control all lands and First Nations peoples, whether or not they were covered by treaty. Principal features of this administration included: (1) the superintendent of Indian affairs and his agents; (2) the Indian band; (3) the church mission; and (4) the residential school.

The Superintendent of Indian Affairs and His Agents

The administration of the Indian Act was placed in the hands of a superintendent, who, through that act, was given wide discretionary powers with which to govern the affairs of First Nations peoples. The superintendent's administration was brought to First Nations peoples by agents, each of whom was responsible for designated reserves, bands, and individual status Indians.

The powers provided by the Indian Act were extensive, and they were progressively increased as the agents encountered issues with which, in their opinion, First Nations peoples needed their direction. By the time of the Indian Act, 1927, the agent's powers included control of First Nations property, schooling, labour on public works, hunting, right of assembly, ceremonies (many of which were prohibited), and residence. In other words, there were relatively few areas of everyday life in which a First Nations person was able to exercise the ordinary powers of an adult citizen. The logic which dictated that the Indian was not a citizen until enfranchised entailed the corollary that it was the Indian agent, not the Indian him or herself, who should exercise a citizen's powers on the Indian's behalf.

The Indian Band
The internal self-government of the reserve community was placed in the hands of the band. The band was not a traditional First Nations form of government, nor were band territories and reserves necessarily situated in traditional jurisdictions. The band was a creation of the Indian Act, 1876, and it entailed a prescribed mode of election along with limited powers. Both the process of election and the exercise of band powers was subject to the overriding discretion of the Indian agent, who could set aside decisions which, in the view of Indian affairs, were unacceptable. Thus, when bands elected traditional chiefs whom the department considered corrupt, these elections were set aside and new ones were ordered. Nevertheless, band administration did provide for a limited degree of local autonomy, organization, and control, and First Nations peoples did not entirely reject it. A common pattern was for the First Nations community to have two internal governments – a traditional government, consisting of hereditary chiefs and elders, and an elected band government pursuant to the Indian Act.

The Mission
The church mission was a third important component of Indian affairs administration. Whereas the authority of Indian affairs focused on physical control and the authority of the band focused on providing a limited form of local government, the mission's authority was focused on 'morality.' It was through the mission that it was hoped that First Nations people would become Christian, civilized, and educated – fit to be enfranchised. Each of the denominations was encouraged to take responsibility for specific bands and reserves. This offered administrative economy and avoided unseemly local competition between denominations. Once a First Nations person became a Roman Catholic, an Anglican, or a free church member, Indian affairs was scrupulous in ensuring that these distinctions were recorded and respected. Thus, churches became part of the administration of Indian affairs. However, priests and ministers viewed themselves as guardians of their flocks, of 'our' Indians, and would take the side of First Nations peoples when they saw what they considered to be abuses of power on the part of Indian agents.

The Residential School
The fourth major administrative component of Indian affairs was the

residential school. The description and discussion of the residential school is reserved to the next chapter, where family and child welfare measures are discussed in more detail.

First Nations Organizations

Independent of the aforementioned formally mandated administrative mechanisms (the superintendent of Indian affairs, the band, the church, and the residential school), First Nations peoples maintained their own organizations in order to provide an independent expression of their interests. The origins of these organizations can be traced to the need to resist the administration imposed on them through the Indian Act. Frideres notes that

> it was not until 1870 that the first Indian political organization in Canada was formed – the Grand General Indian Council of Ontario and Quebec ... Their major concern was with the government's implementation of Indian policy.[39]

A competing organization, the League of Indians of Canada was established in Ontario in 1918 and, during the 1920s, it also had considerable success in the Prairies. Meanwhile,

> in British Columbia the Nishga Indians formed the Nishga Land Committee in the latter part of the 19th century. This organization was the genesis of their concern with land claims ... By 1915 a supporting organization, the Allied Tribes of British Columbia, was created to lobby for land claims.[40]

The present discussion does not permit a full presentation of the history of administrative relationships between the Canadian government and independent First Nations organizations, but the early and continuing activity of the latter offers important evidence of aboriginal resistance to the Indian Act.

As indicated earlier, the Indian Act remains substantially as it was in 1951; but, since 1969, the administration of Indian affairs has changed enormously. At the field level, Indian agents have been withdrawn and their powers over the day-to-day affairs of First Nations peoples are not exercised. The band councils have grown in both authority and administrative capacity and now exercise control over band affairs. The missions have been replaced by churches (often with

First Nations ministers) and have become advocates of renewal and autonomy. The residential schools are closed, and all that remains of them are their decaying shells. Many First Nations bands now operate band schools, where their children receive their primary education.

Nevertheless, DIAND continues, and, although it has an increasing number of First Nations employees (25 per cent during the 1980s),[41] these people remain concentrated at its lower levels. And the executive and senior management levels are still committed to the objective of managing the 'Indians.' Despite lack of support from either First Nations peoples or provincial governments, the pre-1967 assimilationist policy of integrating First Nations services with mainstream services continues. This is best seen in the continuing use of federal-provincial mechanisms to extend provincial services to First Nations peoples. First Nations children now attend provincial schools; but every First Nations child is carefully counted so that the province can be reimbursed by the federal government. As a result, First Nations peoples are still not provincial citizens in practical, everyday matters of social policy – their services are determined not by elections and provincial taxes but by negotiations and agreements between federal and provincial governments.

First Nations peoples have not, in the main, sought provincial services; instead, they have sought direct federal support for the services which they provide directly to their members. Federal funding has also been provided to First Nations groups in an attempt to resolve outstanding land claims. In the Arctic and the Yukon, master agreements have been reached. In British Columbia, there is still no framework for an agreement with any of the First Nations. Progress towards such an agreement is immersed in federal-provincial bickering over the proportion of settlement costs which each should pay. In many other parts of Canada, there are disputes arising over the general disregard of historic treaty obligations.

There has also been a major increase in the power and influence of national First Nations organizations. As indicated earlier, the National Indian Brotherhood, established in 1968 as an organization for status Indians, became the leading organization in opposing the 1969 White Paper. When the White Paper was withdrawn in 1973, the Brotherhood was sufficiently established to succeed and endure as a national organization (eventually having a headquarters in Ottawa with a staff of as many as fifty). In 1980, the Brotherhood was replaced by the Assembly of First Nations (AFN), reflecting the fact that the national organization needed to represent specific First Nations rather than First Nations individuals.

The current period of administrative activity tends to be characterized by uncertainty, conflicting objectives, and political manoeuvring between DIAND, First Nations, and provincial governments. Occasionally, as in the child welfare field, there are opportunities for these three parties to agree on some limited common goals.

5
Canada: First Nations Family and Child Welfare Policy

From the passage of the Indian Act, 1876, until the 1960s, child welfare for First Nations peoples was dominated by a massive attempt to use educational methods to change both their cultures and their characters. This attempt at large-scale social engineering was fundamental to the policy of assimilation. The church-operated residential school was the central institution used in this strategy. When the policy of assimilation was replaced by the policy of integration, child welfare strategy was again used in an attempt to ensure that the next generation of First Nations children did not emulate that of its parents. Children separated from parents whom welfare authorities considered negligent or abusive were either raised in foster care or were adopted. As part of the current move towards self-government, many First Nations communities are taking control of their own child welfare programs in order to ensure that the next generation is raised within the context of its own culture. This chapter examines the principal phases of the history of First Nations child welfare, with a particular focus on the reasons behind the policies and on the extent of their impact on First Nations peoples.

Child Welfare Jurisdiction
In Canada, responsibility for family and child welfare, including education, comes under provincial jurisdiction, as it does in most federal states. However, as discussed in the previous chapter, responsibility for First Nations peoples and, specifically, for status Indians, is federal. As federal law and constitutional obligations take precedence over provincial ones, it is the federal government which has primary responsibility for establishing family and child welfare policy and programs for status Indians. This authority is not always fully exercised.

In the period from 1876 to the early 1960s, federal authority vis-à-vis family and child welfare policy for status Indians was directly exercised, but, since then, such authority has been delegated to the provinces. Nevertheless, the consistency with which DIAND has acted has resulted in similar developments in First Nations child and family services throughout the country. Those differences that do exist are the result of the differences among various First Nations cultures and histories as well as differences in the willingness of various provinces to cooperate with federal Indian policy. As a result of continuing federal control, Canadian policy towards First Nations peoples is more unified than is Australian policy towards Aboriginal peoples.

To attempt to fully discuss provincial and territorial variations with respect to family and child welfare policy would entail a separate discussion of each of the ten provinces and two territories. As this would occupy more space than is available, the provinces of British Columbia and Manitoba, along with the Yukon Territory,[1] have been chosen to illustrate some variations in policy and practice. These provinces and the locations mentioned in this chapter are marked on Map 2 (p. 71). Manitoba is a province in which 8 per cent of the population are status Indians, pursuant to the Indian Act, and at least another 8 per cent are Métis or non-status Indians. It is a prairie province, in which First Nations land was ceded to the Crown by treaty. In the early 1980s, Manitoba First Nations peoples developed a series of child welfare agreements with the province and with the federal government. These were the first of their type, and they offer one comprehensive model for providing First Nations peoples with authority for child welfare.

British Columbia has a smaller proportion of First Nations peoples than does Manitoba – 4.6 per cent – and very few Métis. In BC, First Nations land was annexed by an act of the British Parliament; with respect to resident First Nations peoples, this was done, for the most part, in the absence of both treaty and discussion.[2] Although child welfare agreements have been developed in the late 1980s, unlike those in Manitoba, their approaches are extremely varied, they are not comprehensive, and they are not universally supported by First Nations peoples.

The Yukon Territory is a remote area where status Indians form 21 per cent of the population and where, until the Second World War, most First Nations peoples were relatively untouched by the Canadian government. A child welfare agreement exists with one of the Yukon bands. In addition, the Yukon illustrates some of the difficulties which small, remote communities have in assuming authority for child welfare.

As indicated in Chapter 4, provincial authority is extended to First Nations peoples living on reserve land through the operation of Section 88 of the Indian Act, 1876.[3] This section has the effect of incorporating into the act all provincial law which is not contrary or alternative to federal law. Section 88 does not have the effect of transferring any fiscal obligation from the federal government to the provinces. As a result, the federal government remains responsible for the cost of all services to status Indians. As the provinces rarely fund First Nations services from their own revenues, control over family and child welfare programming for status Indians is determined by what services the federal government is prepared to fund.

In addition to status Indians living on-reserve, the Canadian Constitution recognizes that Inuit, Métis, and non-status Indian people of aboriginal descent also have rights that pre-date Confederation. In recent times, they, too, have increasingly sought distinct institutions which are sensitive to their respective cultures and heritage.[4]

However, this chapter deals principally with family and child welfare measures for status Indian people. Status Indians have been the subject of separate laws, separate programs, and separate institutions. As all status Indians are registered, there are also separate records on their rights, location, band membership, children, and services. The records were initially developed to keep track of band members and of the obligations of the Crown pursuant to treaties with First Nations peoples. When the role of the Crown towards First Nations peoples changed from one of protecting and preserving to one of managing and assimilating, the records were used to show the progress they were making towards becoming 'civilized.' In the latest period, the records reflect the federal government's obligation to reimburse the provinces for the services they provide to status Indians.

To reiterate, there are three principal stages of First Nations family and child welfare policy, each of which are characterized by differences in policy, law, and administration: (1) from 1867 to the 1960s, family and child welfare policy towards status First Nations peoples was, avowedly, an integral part of the general policy of assimilation; (2) in the 1960s, this policy was gradually replaced by a policy of integrating services for status Indians with services for non-aboriginal people; and (3) in the 1980s, policy changed again – this time, under the terms of tripartite (federal-provincial-band/tribal council) agreements, it favoured some degree of community and administrative self-government.[5] These three stages provide the framework for this chapter. Discussion of regional and provincial variations between British Columbia, Manitoba, and the Yukon principally deal with period (3), in which First Nation peoples have had a more active role in initiating changes. The general form of these stages is similar to the principal stages of Aboriginal child welfare policy and practice in Australia.

Policy and Practice in the Assimilation Period, 1867-1960

The foundation for family and child welfare policy towards First Nations peoples in this period was provided by early missionary endeavours. These had been endorsed by the Bagot Commission, which was established in 1842 to provide guidance for colonial Indian policy in the period leading up to Confederation. The commission concluded that day schools were inadequate to the task of assimilating First Nations children. The Canadian historian J.R. Miller summarizes the commission's argument, which recognized a problem with earlier First Nations schooling policies – policies in which the children had remained under

> the influence that parents exerted when the young scholars returned from class. It recommended the establishment of boarding schools with farms in which children could be taught agriculture or a trade, assimilated in the absence of a parent's influence, equipped to forego annual presents, and readied to take up individual plots of land under freehold tenure.[6]

This early conclusion was confirmed by the Davin Report of 1879.[7] Jean Barman, a residential school historian, indicates the report's effect:

> The Davin Report approved American practice with the proviso that schools be operated so far as possible by missionaries, who had already demonstrated their commitment to 'civilising' Canada's Indians. The Department of Indian Affairs accepted the proposal ... Preference was given to the creation of large industrial residential schools located away from reserves, and, a few years later, to boarding schools nearer reserves for younger children. There, attendance would be ensured, and all aspects of life, from dress to use of English language to behaviour, would be carefully regulated.[8]

Day schools continued to be used but were considered to be less satisfactory than residential schools because they entailed greater parental influence and serious problems with regard to maintaining attendance.

Initially, the First Nations peoples' response to educational opportunity for their children was positive, but this did not extend to the deliberate attempt to reshape the latter's lives.[9] Nor were the early results of attendance at residential schools as fruitful as expected. Duncan Campbell Scott, a leading Indian Affairs Branch official, noted in 1913 that the 'most promising pupils are found to have retrograded and to have become leaders in the pagan life of the reserves.'[10]

The response of the Indian Affairs Branch was to decide that the early policy, with its assumption of assimilation and civilization within one generation, was too optimistic. The Department of Indian Affairs' annual report for 1897 noted that

> only the certainty of some practical result can justify the large expense entailed upon the country by the maintenance of these schools ... To educate children above the possibilities of their station, and to create a distaste for what is certain to be their environment in life would be not only a waste of time but doing an injury instead of confirming a benefit on them.

In 1904, Minister of Indian Affairs Clifford Sifton was equally forthright when he declared in Parliament: 'I have no hesitation in saying – we may as well be frank – that the Indian cannot go out from school, making his own way and competing with the white man ... He has not the physical, mental or moral get-up to enable him to compete. He cannot do it.'[11]

These concerns were reflected in a new, more frugal, policy, which was introduced in 1910. Barman uses excerpts from Duncan Campbell Scott to document the changes to a policy intended

> to fit the Indian for civilised life in his own environment ... To this end the curriculum in residential schools has been simplified, and the practical instruction given is such as may be immediately of use to the pupil when he returns to the reserve after leaving the school ... Local Indian agents should carefully select the most favourable location for ex-pupils [with] most careful thought given to the future of

female pupils [who should be] protected in so far as possible from the temptations to which they are often exposed.[12]

The temptations were seen as coming from white men of 'the lowest type,' to whom the girls were exposed due to the fact that their experiences at residential schools had made them 'too smart for the Indian villages.' Chief Assu of the Cape Mudge band in British Columbia recalls how this attitude affected his own experience:

> We got our start on education through the church school on the reserve and in the [residential] schools run by the churches in Port Alberni, Chilliwack and Alert Bay. The trouble was that Indians were only allowed to go to grade nine, and then had to get out ... I wanted my boys to go to high school so I went to see the Indian agent, M.S. Todd, and told him so. He said to me. 'Nothing doing!' I asked him, 'Isn't it for everybody?' and he answered me, 'Not for you people.'[13]

First Nations education was provided by the church, which received an operating grant from the federal government. As far as the church was concerned, the approach to First Nations education expressed by the Indian agent, Sifton, and Scott was not unwelcome, for its objective was to establish its own form of 'Christian citizenship.'[14] Paganism had first to be defeated, but, beyond that, there was the opportunity to build a better world – a world insulated to some extent from mainstream Canadian society. The assimilation of First Nations people into a society in which white people were too often greedy, drunk, and immoral was not what the church wanted to see. The Roman Catholics also wanted to ensure that First Nations peoples were kept from the influence of the Protestant majority.

Collaboration between church and state was close. Government financing of education served to support an organized church authority that was much stronger and larger than would have been possible on missionary donations. In addition, church officials tended to extend their power by assuming roles as magistrates, school inspectors, and Indian Affairs Branch officials. Bishop George Thonloe of Algoma noted: 'The very fact of the civil power being behind would, in the main, suffice to make clerical supervision more efficient.'[15]

On the coast of British Columbia, the church and state attempted to destroy the marriage system and the potlatch, both of which were central to Northwest Coast First Nations cultures. Halliday, the Indian agent in Alert Bay, wrote: 'No boy who has been trained at the Industrial School can get a wife by wooing her and following the ideas he has learned at school but must go back to the potlatch to buy one. One lad in speaking on this point said to me that one might as well be a eunuch as keep out of the potlatch.'[16] The assault on the potlatch culminated in Alert Bay in 1922, with a series of trials of First Nations peoples who had been charged with potlatching. Those convicted were imprisoned, and the regalia, dancing gear, and coppers (a traditional symbol of wealth used in the feast) were all confiscated. Shortly afterwards, in 1924, a new, two-storey brick residential school was opened, and all the school-age children were confined to it and its fenced grounds.[17]

After the Second World War, the concept of a separate set of segregated social institutions for First Nations peoples was called into question. The special joint committee of the Senate and House of Commons (which reviewed the Indian Act between 1946 and 1948) was urged to abolish separate First Nations schools; the revised Indian Act, 1951, committed the federal government to the integration of First Nations peoples into mainstream Canadian society. The new act provided authority for the federal government to negotiate agreements with the provinces for services (including education) to First Nations peoples.

Nevertheless, the role of the residential school in the suppression of First Nations cultures and in the preparation of First Nations children for Christian civilization continued into the 1960s. As in Australia, the period of overt assimilation lasted from the 1860s to the 1960s and intensified when, in the 1920s and 1930s, it was realized that aboriginal peoples were not disappearing or merging with the general population in the manner which had been expected. Table 5.1 shows the extent of the residential school system that operated from the 1890s to the 1960s and indicates several important features of the overall pattern of First Nations education during this period:

- In any one year there was a substantial proportion of First Nations children between the ages of six and fifteen who were in neither residential nor day school systems. While a minority of these would have been attending regular provincial schools, many were not in school at all.
- The low attendance figures for day schools provided an important reason why the residential schools were considered to be superior institutions.

Table 5.1
Status Indian children in school, Canada, 1901-61

Year	Residential school enrolment	Residential school average attendance	Day school enrolment	Day school average attendance	Indian children aged 6-15	No./1,000 Indian children in res. school
1901	1,698	1,517	7,878	4,600	14,362	118
1906	3,697	3,309	6,391	2,983	14,794	255
1911	3,842	3,382	7,348	3,381	15,590	247
1916	4,661	4,029	8,138	4,051	16,547	282
1921	4,783	4,143	7,775	3,931	17,028	281
1926	6,327	5,658	8,455	4,940	20,969[a]	301
1931	7,831	6,917	8,584	5,314	22,347[a]	350
1936	8,906	8,061	9,127	5,788	23,689[a]	375
1941	8,774	8,243	8,651	6,110	26,854[a]	330
1946	9,149	8,264	9,656	6,779	28,639[a]	319
1951	9,357	8,779	15,514	13,526	31,052[a]	301
1956	10,501	9,378	17,947	16,254	38,565[a]	272
1961	8,391		20,896		50,292[a]	166

[a] Numbers of Indian children, aged 6-15, estimated from counts taken in non-census years.
Source: *Canada Year Book*

- At their peak, approximately one-third of all First Nations children between the ages of six and fifteen were in residential school – their impact was felt by at least one of every two First Nations children. In some communities this meant that all its children were removed, while in others a specific selection of children were removed.

Residential schools were not evenly distributed throughout Canada. Table 5.2 shows the provincial pattern of distribution and the percentage of First Nations children in residential schools in each province. It shows that the concentration of residential schools was greatest in the Prairie provinces and in British Columbia, while day schools remained more common in Ontario and in eastern Canada.

In the Northwest Territories and in the Yukon Territory, the civilizing mission of the churches received little support from the Indian Affairs Branch. The Yukon historian, Ken Coates, characterizes government policy up until the Second World War:

> The federal government's objective for the Yukon Indians departed in several significant respects from declared national objectives in the period before 1945. Several of the elements contained in the Indian Act, including encouraging self-sufficiency, protection of natives from white society and support for their Christianization, found their way into Yukon practice although seldom as a result of deliberate administrative decisions. There was, by contrast, no commitment to assimilation. The authorities, even though aware of their power to force change, remained convinced that the Yukon Indians should be left as Indians.[18]

In practice, this meant that many First Nations children in the territories did not attend school at all. The 259 children reported enrolled in the Northwest Territories in 1936 were drawn from a known school-age population of 847 – an enrolment rate of 30 per cent, not including those children who were not enumerated.

With the construction of the Alaska Highway during the Second World War, the Yukon and the Northwest Territories became much more accessible. This was also a period in which universal access to services was emphasized. As a result, Indian policy in the North began to enforce education and to encourage settlement. Thus, in Canada as in Australia, the policy of assimilation was not applied fully until after the Second World War.

Table 5.2

Residential and day school enrolment by province, Canada, 1936

Province	Residential school enrolment	Day school enrolment	Total school enrolment	% res. school of total enrolment
BC	2,163	1,633	3,796	57
Alberta	1,917	37	1,954	98
Sask.	1,735	521	2,256	77
Manitoba	1,009	1,416	2,425	42
Ontario	1,618	2,890	4,508	36
Quebec	55	1,590	1,645	3
NS	148	281	429	19[a]
NB	0	330	330	
PEI	0	20	20	
NWT	193	66	259	75
Yukon	68	123	192	35

[a] % of children in residential school in the Atlantic region of Indian Affairs is based on enrolment in all three provinces.
Source: Department of Indian Affairs, *Annual Report, 1936*

Operating a Residential School

The residential school was the central institution through which Canadian child welfare policy was conducted during the assimilation period. The internal operations of all such schools were similar. In his 1967 book, *The School at Mopass*, the University of Victoria scholar, Richard King, provided a detailed account of how the typical residential school was run.[19]

The school at Mopass was the Anglican-operated residential school at Carcross, Yukon; it was built in 1946 to hold 150 students between the ages of 5 and 15. It was the successor to a much smaller residential school, which had operated in the Yukon since the gold rush of the 1890s. In 1962-3, when King was a teacher in the school, there were 116 children, only 2 of whom were older than 12. This institution offered five years of schooling, and the children left when these were completed. The assignment of children to the school was the complete responsibility of the local Indian agent, who based his decision on family need and responsibility as well as on the need of children for primary education.

> Sometimes children are removed from their homes and placed in residential school because of the neglect on the part of their parents who are told that the children will be allowed to stay at home if the parents 'straighten up.' At other times reluctant parents have been forced to keep their children at home because the agency thought that the sense of responsibility for the children's welfare would have a stabilising effect upon a disintegrating family situation.[20]

Basil Johnston, who was a pupil in a residential school in northern Ontario in a village named Spanish, provides a personal account of the effect of these policies in *Indian School Days*:

> The mothers and grandmothers cried and wept, as mine did, in helplessness and heartache. There was nothing, absolutely nothing, that they could do, as women and as Indians, to reverse the decision of 'the Department.' Already they had suffered the anguish of separating from husbands; now they had to suffer the anguish of being dispossessed of their children; later, they would have to suffer the alienation from the children who were sent away to Spanish. It is no wonder then that when my mother, during a visit to the hospital at Owen Sound, saw the Cape Crocker agent who was convalescing there, she expressed the sentiment that she wouldn't give two hoots if he never got better.[21]

In all the residential schools, children had to be in attendance for ten months of the year. They usually had to travel long distances to the school, and, once there, return was next to impossible. At the Carcross school they came from all over the Yukon. The Indian agent collected them in September and returned them in late June. In theory, parents could pay for them to go home at Christmas or Easter, but few did. For some children, the school was their only home, as the Indian agent did not approve of their parents.

Within the schools, only English could be used, and even the First Nations names of students were suppressed. At the Carcross school, the names recorded were often duplicated when only one English name was available (Joe Joseph, Tommy Thomas, Jimmy James), and always, for ultimate identification and assurance of payment, the government registration number was used. Internally, the schools were rigidly segregated between areas where children could go and areas where they could not. Boys were segregated from girls, and weekly and daily timetables were tightly regulated. The supervisory staff, usually young priests-in-training, indicated the end of one activity and the start of another by using a whistle (outside) and a bell (inside).

The curriculum of the school at Carcross had been established by adopting the BC Programme of Studies for Elementary Schools, which contained not one word of First Nations content. Although variations were possible, it took an unusual teacher or principal to assemble alternative or additional teaching materials and then to persist through the lengthy process of obtaining approval for their use. As a result, the curriculum lacked any local content.

Visitors to the school were not encouraged. As Richard King notes:

> The staff knows that many children are welfare cases and has heard lurid tales of drunkenness, sexual promiscuity and family neglect about various parents. No records are available to show which families are in such categories and which have children in the school simply because the family home is remote. The staff therefore tends to assume that the visitor is in the dissolute category ... The visitor is seated on a bench in the open hallway outside the chapel, and the child or children to be visited are brought to stand before the visitor during the interaction ... The visitor hugs the child, repeats its name several times, then sits and talks intermittently until the cumulative discomfort becomes intolerable and the visit ends with another hug, a few pats, and admonitions to be good and to write letters.[22]

In King's view, the residential school served to reinforce barriers between First Nations peoples and their overseers, inducing in the former passive, institutionalized behaviour which concealed their true selves and which led to their romanticization of the world from which they had been removed. Basil Johnston confirms this impression in his account of how the boys he knew lived from month to month and year to year with the hope of early release from the schools.[23]

The residential school curriculum failed even in preparing children for the limited roles which it had set for them. Johnston writes that, in 1945, Father Oliver, one of the school principals at Spanish, undertook a study of the school records from 1825 to the present. 'He found no record of a graduate of the school who had established himself in a business related to his interests [while in the school] or training, be it shoemaking, tailoring, swineherding, shepherding, milling, blacksmithing, chicken raising, dairy farming, canning, barbering, carpentry, plumbing or janitoring.'[24] Barman also draws attention to the inequality between the education received by First Nations students and that received by non-aboriginal students.[25]

In the end, the residential schools did not prepare First Nations children for life in any type of community: not for the First Nations community from which their parents originally came; not for the urbanized white communities to which some tried to go; and not for the idealized Christian community which existed only in the minds of the missionaries. In a documentary program made by Yukon First Nations peoples for the Canadian Broadcasting Corporation's northern television network, it is suggested that the residential school best prepared children for life in other institutional communities – particularly jails and mental hospitals, into which a disproportionate number of former students seem to have disappeared.[26]

There is also the difficult subject of the deliberate abuse of First Nations children which took place within the residential school system. King drew attention to the stories of dishonesty, cruelty, sexual deviance, and promiscuity which circulated in the school at Carcross. Johnston heard similar stories of other schools during his period at Spanish. More recently, there has been a series of prosecutions based on adults' memories of abuse, principally sexual abuse, as children. The following account from the *Vancouver Sun* concerning the Williams Lake residential school in BC is representative:

> Sellars spent almost nine years at this Catholic run school, where he was not only sexually abused by a priest, but cut off from his family, constantly hungry, frequently strapped, and put down along with his friends as a 'dirty little Siwash,' a cruel nickname he still does not understand ... An Oblate priest and brother have been convicted of sexually abusing more than 15 young natives at St. Joseph's in the 60s, and a third, Prince George Bishop Hubert O'Connor, also an Oblate, stands charged with molesting five young females while he was a supervisor ... There was also old fashioned discipline which rarely let up. Girls were strapped if they were caught looking at boys across the segregated playground. Kids were punished by having their hair chopped off. Boys who wet their beds had to wear the urine-stained sheets over their heads.[27]

Finally, the death toll in the residential schools in the early years of the twentieth century was significant, principally due to tuberculosis, pneumonia, and other epidemic infectious disease to which the children were exposed in the dormitories. Barman cites a 1902 estimate from Scott, in which he suggests that 'fifty per cent of the children who passed through the schools did not live to benefit from the education they received therein.'[28]

Policy and Practice during the Child Welfare Period, 1960-

The residential school was much more than an educational institution. Initially, it was intended to prepare young First Nations peoples for Christian citizenship; but, by the 1960s, it had also become a general welfare resource for the care of children who, in the view of local Indian agents, were not being competently cared for by their parents. (This is no doubt, in part, a commentary on the effect of residential schools, for most parents had, themselves, attended these institutions.)

The separate nature of welfare institutions for status Indians attracted attention during the 1946-8 hearings of the Special Joint Committee of the Senate and House of Commons. In a joint presentation to the committee by the Canadian Welfare Council (CWC) and the Canadian Association of Social Workers (CASW), it was argued that First Nations peoples should enjoy the same services that were available to other Canadians. This included the family and child welfare services provided by the provinces. Patrick Johnston summarized the argument:[29] 'The brief said that as wards of the federal government, "Indian children who are neglected lack the protection afforded under social legislation available to white children in the community."[30] The practice of placing children in residential schools was also condemned.' The brief concluded that the best way to improve the situation was to extend the services of the provincial departments of health, welfare, and education to the residents of reserves. The argument presented in the submission was accepted by the committee, and it led to changes in the Indian Act. In 1951, the act was amended, and, under terms of agreement to be negotiated with the provinces, provision was made for the operation of the aforementioned provincial services on reserves.

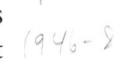

There were problems with the approach proposed by the CWC and CASW. In the 1940s, provincial family and child welfare services were provided principally through children's aid societies and were not available outside developed areas. However, in the postwar period, this problem was solved through the expansion of provincial child welfare services. Unfortunately, the services provided in the remote areas of provinces were modelled on the services that had been developed by the children's aid societies for use in urban areas. The objective of these child welfare services was to serve the best interests of the individual child through three principal activities: (1) offering counselling and support to families where children were not being well cared for; (2) offering a placement program, principally through foster homes, for neglected or abused children (for whom a children's aid society would obtain guardianship by application to a court); and (3) offering an adoption program to aid children needing permanent alternative parents.

Service in the remote areas of the provinces was provided by field social workers, but there were many limitations: the family service program called for professional counselling skills and strong support services; the placement program required foster homes and other more specialized resources; and the adoption service was primarily designed to serve unmarried mothers who voluntarily relinquished their infants so that they could be placed with a childless adopting couple. None of these services worked well outside urban areas, and First Nations communities also had to deal with the fact that they were not culturally connected to them. Nevertheless, as residential schools were closed and the students were integrated into provincial education systems, Indian affairs negotiated agreements with the provinces to devolve responsibility for children's general welfare onto provincial child welfare agencies.

These discussions did not result in a unitary pattern of services across Canada. The stance of each province towards extending services to First Nations families and children differed, and each sought its own financial arrangements with the federal government. All saw that serving First Nations peoples could prove to be expensive, and all sought terms which would be to their financial advantage. The result is referred to by Johnston as

> an incredible disparity in the quantity and quality of child welfare programs available to status Indians from one province to another. In some instances there are disparities within a province. This myriad of differing policy approaches results in unequal treatment of Indian children across Canada.[31]

In the federal government's Hawthorn Report (1966) on services to status Indians,[32] there was substantial discussion of First Nations child welfare and of the move to provide services through the provinces. The report expressed approval of a provincial role in First Nations child welfare, provided that the services it extended were those requested by First Nations peoples. Recommendation 56 states: 'All possible efforts should be made to induce Indians to demand and to accept provincial welfare services.' Recommendation 65 states: 'When Children's Aid Societies extend their services to Indian reserves, the appointment of Indians to the Boards of Directors should be sought, and consultations between the societies and the Band Councils should be encouraged.' These recommendations, with their concern for First Nations participation, were not followed when the transfer of authority took place between the federal government and the provinces.

At the working level, the transfer of responsibility led to provincial social workers receiving a series of allegations from Indian agents, rural school teachers, local police, priests, and other community authority figures concerning child neglect or abuse in First Nations communities. The response of the provincial child welfare authorities – often working from a great distance without local support services, and often finding it difficult to surmount the cultural barrier in order to communicate with First Nations peoples – was to remove the children from their parents and to place them in non-aboriginal foster homes. In the 1950s, the number of status Indian children per 1,000 in the care of provincial child welfare agencies had been so low that statistics were not kept; but by the mid-1960s, the number was already substantial, and it continued to increase until the mid-1970s. Table 5.3 shows the extent of this growth. The numbers in this table should be seen as minimum figures because informal placements, unbilled placements, and adoption placements are not included.

The impact of the adoption program on First Nations families and children was also substantial. This program operated, principally, without the voluntary consent usually required in the non-aboriginal community. Typically, children would be removed from their parents at birth, be declared children in care, and then the provincial child welfare agency would apply to the court to waive adoption consent. Placements were then made with non-aboriginal families. Table 5.4 shows the extent of this program.

In 1978-9, in BC, 26.3 per cent of all adoptions involved First Nations children, and in Manitoba that figure was 48.7 per cent. Children obtained from First Nations communities were not necessarily

Table 5.3

Status Indian children in care, Canada, 1966-7 to 1988-9

Year	Children in care	Children 16 and under	Children in care/1,000
1966-7	3,201	93,101	34.3
1970-1	5,156	95,048	54.2
1975-6	6,078	96,493	62.9
1980-1	5,716	94,916	60.2
1985-6	4,000	99,213	40.3
1988-9	3,989	102,529	38.9

Note: The total number of children in care is calculated from the total of days of care paid by Indian Affairs divided by 365, not including any preventative or alternative services.
Source: Department of Indian and Northern Affairs and Northern Development, *Basic Developmental Data* (Ottawa: Supply and Services 1989), Table 18

Table 5.4

Adoption of status Indian children, Canada, 1964-5 to 1985-6

Year	By Indians	By non-Natives	Total	Birth	Adoptions/ 1,000 births
1965-6	43	122	165	8,942	18.4
1970-1	36	205	241	8,756	27.5
1975-6	95	446	541	8,127	66.5
1980-1	127	441	686	8,459	81.1
1985-6	191	344	535	11,158	47.9

Source: Indian and Inuit Affairs, Resource Centre, Ottawa

placed in Canada; as late as 1980, a majority of Manitoba's First Nations adoptees were placed in the United States. The number of children permanently removed from First Nations families should be added to the number of children in care in order to understand the total impact of the child welfare system. In the late 1970s and early 1980s, one in seven status Indian children were not in the care of their parents at any one time, and as many as one in four status Indian children were spending at least some part of their childhood years away from their parents' homes.

There were also marked provincial and regional variations in the proportion of First Nations children in care. Patrick Johnston, working with partial data in the early 1980s, was able to show the main features of this pattern in Table 5.5.

It is also possible to compare the rate per 1,000 children in care between the status Indian and non-aboriginal population for those provinces with a significant First Nations population (see Table 5.6). These data had not been available prior to Johnston's research in the late 1970s. The data show that the provincial child welfare systems were removing First Nations children from their parents and communities at an alarming and unprecedented rate. In the North and in western Canada, the extent of the removal of children was such that status and non-status Indian peoples constituted 40 per cent or more of all children served, yet this fact was not acknowledged by attention to community, historical, or cultural differences.

Brad McKenzie and Peter Hudson of the University of Manitoba summarized the available explanations for this state of affairs in an article which drew heavily on Johnston's material.[33] The principal explanations discussed were:

(1) The psycho-social argument (i.e., that child neglect and abuse was the result of individual deviance). This was the dominant argument recognized in the child welfare system.
(2) The cultural change argument (i.e., that First Nations peoples were undergoing rapid social change, and that this was resulting in high rates of family dysfunction).
(3) The economic deprivation argument (i.e., that First Nations peoples were poor and deprived of adequate housing and social services, and that this resulted in increased use of the residual child welfare system).
(4) The historical argument (i.e., that First Nations peoples had been deprived of their lands and had been systematically institutionalized, thus losing the coping capacities of their own cultures and never obtaining alternatives).
(5) The racial argument (i.e., that First Nations peoples were being systematically rejected and stigmatized by the non-aboriginal majority).
(6) The colonial argument (i.e., that the child welfare system was part of a deliberate assault on First Nations societies, and that it was designed to change First Nations peoples). McKenzie and Hudson found this argument the most persuasive.

Table 5.5
Indian children in care (CIC) by province, Canada

Province	Year	Status CIC	Non-status CIC	Total Native CIC	Total all CIC	% Native of all CIC
BC	1978-9	1,692	1,208	2,900	7,369	39.2
Alberta	1978-9	1,498	1,085	2,583	6,844	37.7
Sask.	1978-9	1,390	500	1,890	2,909	65.0
Manitoba	1979-80	1,134	n/a	1,134[a]	3,788	29.9[a]
Ontario	1978-9	n/a	n/a	1,097	14,008	7.9
Québec	1978-9	590	12	602	28,870	2.1
NB	1978-9	n/a	n/a	80	2,270	3.5
NS	1978-9	n/a	n/a	81	1,959	4.1
PEI	1981	14	11	25	233	10.7
Nfld.	1978-9	n/a	n/a	108	1,221	8.8
NWT	1980	71	104	175	368	47.5
Yukon	1978-9	n/a	n/a	109	194	56.2

[a] Non-status includes Métis and persons of recognizable Indian descent as judged by departmental social workers for statistical purposes.
Source: Patrick Johnston, *Native Children and the Child Welfare System* (Toronto: James Lorimer 1983)

Table 5.6

Status Indian and Non-Indian children in care (CIC), Canada, 1978-9

Province	Status CIC	Status children	Status CIC/1,000	Other CIC	Other children (000s)	Other CIC/1,000
BC	1,692	21,241	79.6	4,469	545	8.2
Alberta	1,498	23,505	63.7	4,261	463	9.2
Sask.	1,390	20,830	66.7	1,519	230	6.6
Manitoba	1,134	19,518	58.1	2,654	245	10.8
Ontario	1,097	22,561	48.6	12,911	2,051	6.3
NWT	71	3,049	23.2	193	13.4	13.4
Yukon	109	996	109.4	85	5.4	12.0

Notes: The figures for status children in care for 1978-9 are from Johnston, *Native Children and the Child Welfare System*. Data for all 'status children' are from special tables available at the DIAND resource centre, Ottawa, for 1978-9. 'Other children in care' indicates non-Native children as calculated by deducting figures for both status and non-status children in care (from Johnston, *Native Children and the Child Welfare System*) from figures for all children in care on 31 March 1979 (from annual reports of the respective provincial departments of welfare). Data for all 'other children' are from the 1976 census, from which figures for status have been deducted. (In the case of Manitoba, where there was no estimate available for non-status and Métis children in care, they are indicated under 'other children in care.')

Sources: Patrick Johnston, *Native Children and the Child Welfare System* (Toronto: James Lorimer 1983); DIAND resource centre; provincial child welfare statistics; Census of Canada

By the 1970s, child welfare agencies had succeeded residential schools as the preferred care system for First Nations children. These agencies were most active in those regions of Canada where residential schools had been most prevalent; they were introduced to accomplish some of the same purposes as had the residential schools; and they were subject to some of the same types of internal child abuse problems as were the residential schools.

However, there are some important differences between the residential school period and the child welfare period. The child welfare system had not been designed to change the culture of First Nations people; it was designed for non-aboriginal people living in urban areas and was then extended to rural and First Nations communities in the name of equality of service. As has been mentioned, this extension of services overlooked significant differences between mainstream Canadian and First Nations cultures.

Children were removed from their parents without regard to differences of history, culture, or ethnicity because the assumption was that these factors were much less important than were physical health, diet, housing, absence of alcoholism in the home, and so on. It was assumed that children were pliable; once admitted to care or placed for adoption, the child welfare system regarded childhood as primarily a period of physical and emotional development in which prior heritage and culture were relatively unimportant. It was thought that the heritage and culture of the adopting parents or foster parents could be acquired by any child. Ethnic origin was not seen as a serious problem, for, although the children were unmistakably different from their non-adopted siblings, it was hoped that some basic education in the history and culture of First Nations peoples would provide them with sufficient understanding of their origins. Finally, it was believed that loving adoptive and foster parents would protect the children from any instances of racial prejudice to which they might be exposed.

In many ways, the child welfare system put First Nations children under more pressure to assimilate than did the residential school system. In the residential school First Nations children had the companionship of their peers, the annual return to their home communities and parents, the daily presence of many other First Nations peoples, and the knowledge that this was an experience that their parents had undergone. In addition, they knew that they were there because they were First Nations children. These familiar sources of support were not available in the child welfare system. The children were isolated from each other, usually losing contact even with their brothers and sisters. They were caught in the system not because they were First Nations children, but because their parents had been judged by social workers and a court to have treated them in an abusive or negligent manner. There was no promise of return to their home communities and people. Immense pressure was put on them to forget all those things which made them First Nations persons. No wonder that the records of First Nations children in foster homes and adoption homes contain repeated stories of the attempts of the children to scrub the brown colour off their skins. It was the colour which made them different, and, in some way which they could not understand, unacceptable.

The Indian Act, 1876, and the Indian affairs administration it produced, had the colonial and racist objective of ensuring that future generations of First Nations peoples would fit into a Christian civilization. In the mid-twentieth century child welfare system, most of the policymakers, social workers, foster parents, and adoptive parents would have rejected that objective. However, they simply made the assumption that the mainstream Canadian world was the only world worth having. Most wanted only the best for First Nations children. But, in the end, what they wanted did not matter very much – for their actions resulted in First Nations children feeling pressured to reject their own cultures in favour of another. And, with all this pressure, assimilation may have 'succeeded' had it not been for mainstream Canadians' racist attitude towards people who were visibly of First Nations descent. It was their visibility which prevented many First Nations peoples from being accepted in mainstream society and which, consequently, made it impossible for them to assimilate.

The change from the residential school period to the child welfare period in Canada corresponded to the change from Aboriginal welfare boards to state child welfare agencies in Australia. In both countries, the high proportions of aboriginal children in care were not anticipated, and it was twenty years before either government recognized the seriousness of the problems which had been created by their respective social welfare policies.

Changes in Current Policy and Practice, 1980-

The latest stage of family and child welfare policy vis-à-vis First Nations peoples came in response to the concerns identified in the 1970s. A distinctive feature of this stage of development is the initiative which First Nations peoples have taken in developing proposals of their own and in negotiating agreements with governments. As this occurs, First Nations peoples are developing service models which reflect the experiences of their communities, cultures, and histories. Although there is a general pattern to this change throughout Canada, there are also substantial variations between different First Nations peoples and different provinces. As a result, after some general observations on Canada as a whole, this section includes a detailed discussion of the specific changes that are occurring in Manitoba, BC, and the Yukon.

Concern that the child welfare system might be inappropriate for First Nation peoples had existed before the detailed work of Johnston in the late 1970s. The Hawthorn Report (1966) referred to the advantages of government agreements with First Nations bands and tribal councils. But this idea had not been systematically incorporated into policy. The earliest agreement which involved a band as a direct signatory was completed in 1973, and it was between the Blackfoot, the Alberta Ministry of Social Development, and DIAND.

In 1976, the tenth report of the Royal Commission on Family and Child Welfare Law (Justice Thomas Berger, chair), dealt extensively with First Nations families in British Columbia. Among its recommendations were procedures to ensure that bands were notified of all protection and adoption hearings affecting their children.[34] There were also proposals to provide First Nations families with adoption subsidies, so that First Nations children could be placed in their own communities. The band at Spalumcheen, BC, passed a 1980 by-law giving itself the authority to operate its own child welfare service.[35] The by-law could have been disallowed by the minister of Indian affairs, but, instead, it was allowed to stand, thus indicating the government's willingness to look at new ways of providing service to First Nations families.

In 1978, there was a year-long review of the delivery of social services to First Nations communities in Ontario. The review was undertaken on a tripartite basis, recognizing the interests of the federal government, the provincial government, and First Nations peoples. It included a field study of services in First Nations communities, using local First Nations interviewers.[36] The findings of the study included the following input from First Nations communities:

- It is unfair to place First Nations children in white homes.
- Fostering should be encouraged on reserves.

- Children's aid societies do not keep in touch – they just come in an emergency.
- A First Nations family service worker is needed on the reserve.
- The foster allowance should be increased to enable First Nations peoples to foster First Nations children.

In Manitoba, a tripartite committee prepared a report on First Nations child welfare in June 1980,[37] and this was speedily followed by a comprehensive proposal from the Four Nations Confederacy (encompassing all bands in the province). The proposal was directed to DIAND and dealt with three stages for the assumption of responsibility for child welfare: orientation, development, and operation. From these beginnings in the late 1970s and early 1980s there followed a rapid development of child welfare agreements between the government and various bands in the five years between 1982-3 and 1986-7. The scale of development can be seen in Tables 5.7, 5.8, and 5.9.

Each child welfare agreement that is included in these tables is an individual document which was negotiated between governments and bands or tribal councils. The services provided under the agreements varied; some covered only preventative and support services, leaving all statutory authority with the province, while others provided for the band or tribal council to exercise statutory authority pursuant to a province/band agreement. The signatories to agreements also varied. Where the agreement covered support funding, it was usually made between DIAND and the band or tribal council; where the agreement was for the exercise of statutory authority, there was sometimes a tripartite, band/province/department agreement and sometimes two separate agreements – a band/province agreement providing for the exercise of statutory authority and a band/department agreement providing for program funding.

The exercise of statutory authority by bands and tribal councils has usually required change in provincial legislation. Alberta, Manitoba, Ontario, and the Yukon have added major new sections to their child welfare legislation in order to provide a clear legal framework for band/province agreements, and similar changes are under consideration in the other provinces. Agreements have usually provided control over child welfare for First Nations families living on reserve lands, but there are a number of interesting provisions for services to families and children living off-reserve. These and other detailed variations which meet the needs of individual bands and provinces require further study at the provincial level.

Table 5.7
Agencies (bands) administering child welfare programs, Canada, 1981-91

Year	BC	Alberta	Man.	Ont.	Que.	Alt.[a]	Yukon
1981-2	1 (1)	1 (1)	2 (9)				
1982-3	1 (1)	1 (1)	5 (34)				
1983-4	1 (1)	2 (10)	6 (59)		1 (1)	3 (3)	
1984-5	1 (1)	2 (10)	6 (59)		3 (5)	6 (6)	
1985-6	1 (1)	2 (10)	6 (59)		5 (7)	9 (21)	
1986-7	2 (14)	3 (15)	6 (59)	1 (14)	5 (13)	11 (23)	1 (1)
1987-8	2 (14)	3 (15)	6 (59)	4 (56)	7 (15)	11 (23)	1 (1)
1990-1	2 (19)	3 (15)	7 (60)	7 (84)	7 (15)	11 (20)	1 (1)

[a] This refers to the Department of Indian Affairs, Atlantic region, including the provinces of New Brunswick, Nova Scotia, Newfoundland, and Prince Edward Island.

Source: DIAND, Ottawa, press release, 6 April 1988; data for 1990-1 from direct inquiry at department

Table 5.8

Staff employed by Indian child welfare agencies, Canada, 1981-8

Year	Agencies (bands)	Staff
1981-2	4 (11)	46
1982-3	7 (36)	105
1983-4	13 (74)	219
1984-5	18 (81)	275
1985-6	23 (98)	321
1986-7	29 (140)	415
1987-8	34 (184)	

Note: In addition, there were twenty tribal councils, representing 118 bands in British Columbia, Alberta, and Saskatchewan, which were in the process of negotiating agreements in 1988.
Source: DIAND, Ottawa, press release, 6 April 1988

Table 5.9

Federal expenditures on Indian child welfare, Canada, 1981-8

Year	Expenditure (millions)	% increase
1981-2	$34.7	
1982-3	37.6	8.2
1983-4	43.7	16.2
1984-5	50.8	16.2
1985-6	63.9	25.8
1986-7	70.6	10.5
1987-8	77.9	10.3

Source: DIAND, Ottawa, press release, 6 April 1988

The changes that have been made have been accompanied by both policy problems and administrative problems. Significant policy problems have arisen out of the attempt to divide jurisdiction for child welfare into two spheres, one for the First Nations communities and another for the non-aboriginal communities. It is often not clear what authority the First Nations sphere has, what persons it has under its jurisdiction, and what resources it has under its control in order to serve those persons. At the administrative level, obtaining First Nations staff to undertake child welfare work in First Nation communities for First Nation authorities has often not been possible.

In the period between 1987-8 and 1990-1, there have been few new agreements because DIAND introduced a moratorium in 1986, pending a policy review. This was released in 1989 in the discussion document *Indian Child and Family Services Management Regime: Discussion Paper*.[38] The paper was a response to the tripling of child welfare costs and what is referred to as 'unplanned and ad hoc growth.' As a result of this paper, new agreements could only be made when a minimum of a thousand children were included, child care services were excluded, and provincial legislation and standards were followed. The discussion paper also indicated that new agreements would only be possible 'as resources become available.' Although the document was referred to as a discussion paper, it has been treated as policy in the years following its release.

Child Welfare Agreements at the Provincial Level

Manitoba
Manitoba provides the best example of a comprehensive approach to First Nations child welfare through the use of tripartite agreements. The first comprehensive agreement for all child welfare services other than adoption was reached with the Dakota-Ojibway in July 1981. This was followed by additional agreements with other First Nations in 1982, 1983, and 1984, until all rural and reserve areas of the province were covered. In addition, in 1984 the Ma-Mawi-Wi-Chi-Itata Centre (We All Work Together to Help Each Other) was opened to provide non-statutory services to First Nations (both status and non-status) and Métis peoples in Winnipeg.

The child welfare agreements followed a 1980 joint report from the Manitoba Indian Brotherhood (MIB) and the federal and provincial governments. The guiding principles of these agreements were:

(1) Indians have special status as defined in treaties, and through provisions of the Indian Act;
(2) The family is the first resource for the nurturance and protection of children, but families do need support for their parenting role, and children, for a variety of reasons, may need substitute care;
(3) All children need care, nurturing, and protection;

(4) As a result of culture, geography, and past experience, Indian people have special needs;
(5) Preservation of Indian cultural identity is of importance in terms of both language and customs, within the framework of tribes, bands, extended families, and individuals; and,
(6) The provision of services must involve Indian people, recognize their priority needs and the current variety of service modes.[39]

A new child and family services act was passed in Manitoba in 1986 to provide a legal base for recognizing First Nations communities and for transferring to them authority to act as agents of the province (see Table 5.10).

Evaluations of the Manitoba child welfare agreements have been undertaken by staff of the School of Social Work at the University of Manitoba[40] and by the management consultants Coopers and Lybrand. Although each of the assessments recognizes that the First Nations-managed agencies have made substantial achievements, there are also some concerns. These include: the high proportion of children in care by court order; the under-use of homemaker and family day care services; the lack of accountability and responsibility for follow-up case services;[41] the difficulties due to multiple accountability

Table 5.10
Status Indian children in care, Manitoba, agreements, 1981-9

Year	Dakota/ Ojibway	AWASIS[a]	Anishinaabe	West region	South-east region
1981	68				
1982	85				
1983	108	116	37	35	30
1984	150	315	85	81	43
1985	174	286	134	106	81
1986	207	307	199	137	127
1987	212	373	n/a	105	160
1988	244	384	n/a	149	153
1989	258	382	n/a	179	n/a

[a] AWASIS is the First Nations agency responsible for child welfare services to communities in northern Manitoba.
Source: Manitoba, Department of Family and Child Services, 1981-9

to First Nations, to the Manitoba government, and to the funding conditions of the federal government; and the problem of attracting and retaining staff with accreditation in social work.[42] A central problem identified in both reports is the contradiction between 'respecting the reemergence of Indian self-government in so far as Indian family and child services is concerned, while at the same time [maintaining] ultimate [provincial] responsibility for the protection of Indian children and service standards.'[43]

In 1992, Justice Brian Giesbrecht concluded a report on an inquiry into the death of a thirteen-year-old boy (following a prolonged period of sexual and physical abuse on the Sandy Bay Ojibway reserve) with the following words: 'What is clear to me is that Lester Desjarlais had the right to expect more. His family let him down; his community let him down; his leaders let him down; then the agency that was mandated to protect him let him down, and the government chose not to notice.'[44] In this instance, the provincial agency had respected the jurisdiction of the Dakota Ojibway Child and Family Services Agency, which had been authorized to provide services to the Sandy Bay reserve. The agency staff had recognized that there was a serious problem of abuse, but, although the case worker had wanted to intervene, it had been decided to attempt to find a solution within the framework of the Sandy Bay community. Other examples could be given of the conflict between respect for First Nations jurisdiction and the welfare of individual children.

The problem of jurisdiction has also been difficult to resolve in urban areas, where there is a mix of status and non-status First Nations peoples, Métis, and non-aboriginal people. In Winnipeg (500,000 people), there are approximately 50,000 First Nations people. The First Nations social agency, Ma-Mawi-Wi-Chi-Itata (Ma-Mawi), was established in 1984 to serve this complex urban community. Ma-Mawi does not have any statutory authority; the responsibility for initiating court action and maintaining formal guardianship remains with provincial agencies. Ma-Mawi derives its authority from a philosophy of mutual support and empowerment based on a common recognition of oppression.[45]

Ma-Mawi's first annual report expressed this philosophy as follows:

> We understand the child welfare system as a system which has evolved, in the dominant culture, to deal with the problems of industrial society. Within the Native community, the child welfare system

is a system that deals with the symptoms of larger social problems – racism, poverty, underdevelopment, unemployment, etc. The theoretical base of Ma-Mawi-Wi-Chi-Itata Centre is grounded in the understanding of child welfare problems as the result of the colonial nature of relations between the aboriginal people and the Euro-Canadian majority ... We understand our practice, which flows from this theory, as a process of decolonization. We see this as a conscious process through which we regain control over our lives and resources.[46]

Ma-Mawi has an annual budget of over $2 million dollars and serves more than 500 families each year. The approach to services is comprehensive and is based on the support which First Nations peoples derive from extended family networks.[47] The philosophy of decolonization and empowerment is expressed in the administration and staffing of Ma-Mawi. All board members and staff of the agency are First Nations people. The Ma-Mawi computer is used to trace extended families. This ensures that connections to appropriate relatives are made wherever possible, and that, where this is not possible, service is provided by a person who fills the role that a relative would have filled.

The philosophy at Ma-Mawi recognizes that 'empowerment confers upon a collective the opportunity to decide what is of value within its indigenous traditions, and what is of value from external sources.'[48] Mainstream values and practices (e.g., the social work code of ethics) have a prominent place in the work of Ma-Mawi, but they are used alongside declarations of First Nations family teaching. Ma-Mawi aims to have good relationships with all Winnipeg and Manitoba agencies. One of its major strengths is its clear understanding of First Nations values. Ma-Mawi is not the only First Nations agency in Manitoba to articulate these values, but, as the largest such urban agency in Canada, it serves as a good example of First Nations understanding, policymaking, and practice.

British Columbia
In BC, the role of First Nations peoples in child welfare has developed in a piecemeal manner. In the 1980s, despite the lack of a comprehensive approach, First Nations peoples throughout the province were much more active in the child welfare field than they were in the 1970s. In the 1990s, the level of activity continues to increase.

University of Victoria professor Brian Wharf, in his review of child welfare developments in BC, refers to most of this activity as 'muddling through.'[49] The principal characteristic of 'muddling through' is local negotiation between provincial child welfare offices and First Nations bands. As First Nations peoples have become more aware of the effects of the child welfare system on their families and communities, they have asserted greater control over their relationship with the local offices of the Ministry of Social Services. The First Nations child welfare by-law passed in 1980 by the Spallumcheen band illustrates this forceful approach to policymaking. The by-law authorized the band to conduct its own child welfare program. Chief Wayne Christian was himself a former child in care, and he described his experiences with the child welfare system to Wharf:

> Much of Chief Christian's concern with child welfare practices were a result of his own experiences as a child in the care of Human Resources from age 12 until 18. He was removed from his mother's care along with his nine brothers and sisters and was profoundly influenced by the dissolution of his family. Chief Christian went through several foster homes, separated from his siblings by his choice, and finally settled in one for a number of years.
>
> Chief Christian states that his mother was almost destroyed by being without her children, and as a result turned to alcohol as a release. Chief Christian was able to make the change back to living on the reserve when he was 18 years old. One of his brothers was not as successful and committed suicide after being unable to cope with the transition from foster home to reserve life.[50]

To take control of child welfare, Chief Christian organized a protest on the front lawn of Grace McCarthy, the Social Credit minister of social services in Vancouver, refusing to move until the band's right to operate its child welfare program was recognized. In 1980, public sympathy was with the band, and the minister conceded.

Whereas in the 1960s and 1970s social workers were assisted by the police and a disinterested general public to 'invade' local First Nations communities, in the 1980s there was little mainstream community support for such actions (nor were social workers still confident that such direct intervention was appropriate). As a result, the day-to-day activities of social workers were dependent on First Nations cooperation with regard to providing information, keeping appointments, providing access to children, and using alternative child care resources. Achieving such cooperation required that respect be shown to local band chiefs and to community elders. Interviews were arranged through the band office, and advice was asked before action was taken. The initiative for reserve visits shifted from the social workers to the bands. In the course of time, these local arrangements were formalized as local protocol agreements.

In 1991, formal agreements with two tribal councils and two independent bands covered approximately 10 per cent of status Indian people living on-reserve in BC.[51] Most arrangements continued to be made at an informal and local level, and neither the agreements nor the local arrangements were recognized in the BC Family and Child Service Act. However, at the local level, the bands and tribal councils often controlled child welfare on the provincial reserves, and an increasing number of band social service staff were obtaining professional qualifications in social work and related disciplines. Thus, in BC, practice changed before policy.

Policy change was initiated in 1992, with the report of the Aboriginal Committee of the Family and Children's Services Legislation Review Panel. The report, *Liberating Our Children: Liberating Our Nations*, opened with the words:

> Your present laws empower your Superintendent of Family and Child Service and your family courts to remove our children from our Nations, and place them in the care and custody of others. The first step to righting the wrongs done to us is to limit the authority to interfere in the lives of our families, and to provide remedies other than the removal of our children from our Nations. This must be accompanied by the financial resources we require to heal the wounds inflicted upon us. Finally, as our Nations assert our own family laws to meet our contemporary needs, as we rebuild the authority usurped from our Nations, the laws of our Nations must have paramountcy over your laws as they apply to our people.[52]

The vision of an independent jurisdiction with its own laws is clear, but the process of putting it into place and the form that it will take are not yet defined. Following the publication of this report, a moratorium was placed on all adoption of First Nations infants and children; but the immediate result has included a growing number of infants and very young children in care whose mothers have abandoned them and whose families and communities are not known. At the working level, it seemed that the only available course was to extend protection to infants and children despite the clear intent to respect the request to recognize First Nations jurisdiction.

In BC, change in urban areas has been slow; there is no agency comparable to Ma-Mawi. The Indian friendship centres which can be found in most urban communities provide some support services to First Nations peoples living off-reserve, but they lack the professional sophistication of Ma-Mawi. Partly to compensate for the lack of autonomous urban First Nations social service organizations, the BC social services ministry has established a special unit for First Nations child welfare in Vancouver. The unit has been staffed, in so far as possible, by First Nations social workers.

Yukon Territory
The Yukon Territory has two of the main problems which characterize northern Canadian communities – it is remote and its population is small. The total population of the Yukon is 25,000 people, of whom 5,000 are of First Nations descent. These 5,000 people live in widely separated communities, and, in 1952, they were divided for administrative purposes by the Department of Northern Affairs and National Resources (the precursor of DIAND) into thirteen bands. The Champagne-Aishihik band, which is recognized as one of the strongest in the Yukon, has 500 members, 300 of whom live in Whitehorse (the provincial capital) and 200 of whom live in the band's principal community, Haines Junction (there are no reserves in the Yukon). Of these 500 people, 200 are children or youth.

In the 1970s, the proportion of First Nations children in care in the Yukon exceeded one in ten, and additional children were placed for adoption outside the territory. In the 1980s, this proportion has declined, and the Yukon government supports the principle of bands providing their own child welfare services. The Yukon Childrens Act was revised in 1984 to provide for the delegation of the power inherent in the office of the director of child welfare to any society serving as a band child welfare authority.

One such agreement, that with the Champagne-Aishihik, has been established. The band appointed a child welfare committee and employed a First Nations social worker to provide services to First

Nations families. There are substantial differences between the kind of practice appropriate to a community of 500 people, 200 of whom are children or youth (and all of whom know one another), and the kind of practice appropriate to mainstream child welfare systems.[53] For example, with respect to:

- *Protection complaints.* There was no such thing as an anonymous protection complaint. Instead, there was a daily monitoring of those families who were known to have problems providing to their children the kind of care which was in accord with community standards.
- *Intervention.* Intervention in the affairs of a family was a matter for the extended family. It was the extended family which had to take responsibility for its members, including children and youth. Foster homes could only be found when plans were made with family members and when a home for the child could be found with extended family members.
- *Court action.* The court was never used. The community either settled the matter internally or lived with the problem.
- *Permanent planning.* The mainstream Yukon child welfare system gave a great deal of attention to making the best decisions and plans for the future of children in care. Social workers then acted on these decisions. In contrast, the Champagne-Aishihik valued continuity of relationships and were prepared to live with chronic parenting problems over long periods. It was assumed that change would come as parents matured and as healing took place, and that, meanwhile, it was the responsibility of the grandparents to ensure that the child was cared for.

The problems of applying the aforementioned services were, principally, practical. There were few social workers who could provide the requisite culturally sensitive enabling role, and the cost of providing service on a daily and intensive basis was high. The economies of scale which could be achieved in a larger organization were not available. In addition, the Champagne-Aishihik agreement was not in accord with the policies for child welfare agreements contained in the 1989 DIAND discussion paper.

Assembly of First Nations (AFN)

The Assembly of First Nations is the national body which develops First Nations policy and which represents First Nations interests to the federal government. The AFN regards child welfare as a priority area for policy development and for the exercise of self-government. Its 1989 report on child care concluded:

> Our most basic recommendations are for immediate funding of community controlled native child-care as part of the enabling process. Such programs would provide First Nations' most precious resources with an early sense of security, stability, motivation and pride. In the long term complete jurisdiction over the lives of native children must be returned to those First Nations who are ready, and who will be a model for others.[54]

The AFN held a national child welfare conference in New Brunswick in 1988,[55] and it held a second conference in Winnipeg in 1991. The second conference focused on the development of a national strategy for First Nations child and family services. Among the issues discussed were:
- jurisdiction (i.e., the authority to govern children and families independently of the provincial and/or federal governments)
- interim mechanisms/models (i.e., the development of research, coordination, and funding mechanisms to provide the capacity to support First Nations and to pursue long-term objectives)
- services (i.e., the development and recognition of First Nations community traditions and approaches to child welfare at both national and regional levels)
- funding (i.e., looking at approaches to funding child welfare that avoid or reduce the problems of reinforcing provincial control).[56]

The tripartite child welfare agreements used to obtain First Nations management of child welfare were seen by First Nations organizations as steps towards the exercise of self-government. It was expected that this would lead to fewer children in care, more culturally appropriate services, and lower costs. So far, the record is, at best, mixed. Services are more culturally appropriate; but there are still many children in care, costs have grown rapidly, and the conflict between respecting First Nations jurisdiction and protecting the rights of individual First Nations children is unresolved.

Furthermore, it can be argued that the agreements are now becoming a means of governing First Nations organizations through the requirements laid out in the management regime. These reinforce the provisions of Section 88 of the Indian Act, whereby child welfare authority is subject to provincial policy and standards. In the end, this could easily lead back to the exercise of policies which integrate First Nations and non-First Nations services under provincial jurisdiction rather than forward to policies which contribute to the development of First Nations self-government. Although there has been a reduction in the proportion of First Nations children in care from 63/1,000 (1975-6) to 39/1000 (1988-9), the number in care remains five times higher than that in the non-First Nations community.

Conclusion

Family and child welfare measures have been an important part of Canada's general policy of assimilation from 1867 until the present day. The form of policy in each period has followed whatever the current understanding of the 'Indian problem' might be. In the last policy period, First Nations peoples have been recognized as entitled to exercise jurisdiction over child welfare measures so as to fulfil whatever they believe to be appropriate to their respective cultures and communities. However, fundamental policy problems with respect to individual as opposed to collective rights have not been settled, jurisdictions have not been clearly defined, and services remain dependant on funding from the mainstream Canadian community. Thus, although First Nations peoples have obtained more control over family and child welfare in Canada than have Aboriginal people in most parts of Australia, full control continues to be elusive.

Canadian public opinion remains divided as to whether or not First Nations self-government and, with it, full control of family and child welfare should become a reality. But each year shows some increase in public support for the aboriginal rights of First Nations people. Although progress has been slow, there are grounds for hope that the policy of assimilation, initiated by the British House of Commons, is at last being replaced by policies that reflect the continuing presence of First Nations peoples within Canadian society.

6
New Zealand: The General Structure of Maori Policy[1]

British imperial policy towards the South Pacific islands, including New Zealand, was developed in the early nineteenth century. The initial policy was one of non-interference and of respect for the sovereignty of the island people. This policy was set aside due to the growth of unplanned settlements of sailors, traders, escaped convicts, and missionaries. The British mission to govern to the ends of the world was also spurred on by the continuing process of competition with France and Germany as well as by the prospects for land sales should settlement be permitted. The policies towards the Maori people were based on the work of the 1837 House of Commons Select Committee on Aborigines.

History of Maori Policy

The history of Maori policy can be divided into five principal periods: (1) the period of initial contact, 1769-1840; (2) the period of the Treaty of Waitangi, 1840-6; (3) the assimilation period, 1847-1960; (4) the integration period, 1960- ; and (5) the period of Maori resurgence, 1975- .[2] These periods can be defined by specific events, but, in each of them, some features of later periods are foreshadowed and some features of earlier periods persist. In the present period, there is much controversy as to whether to pursue a policy based on the principles of integration or on the principles contained in the Treaty of Waitangi.

Initial Contact, 1769-1840

Although the Dutch explorer Tasman reached New Zealand in 1642, the period of initial contact leading to the establishment of a European government began in a concerted manner with the exploratory

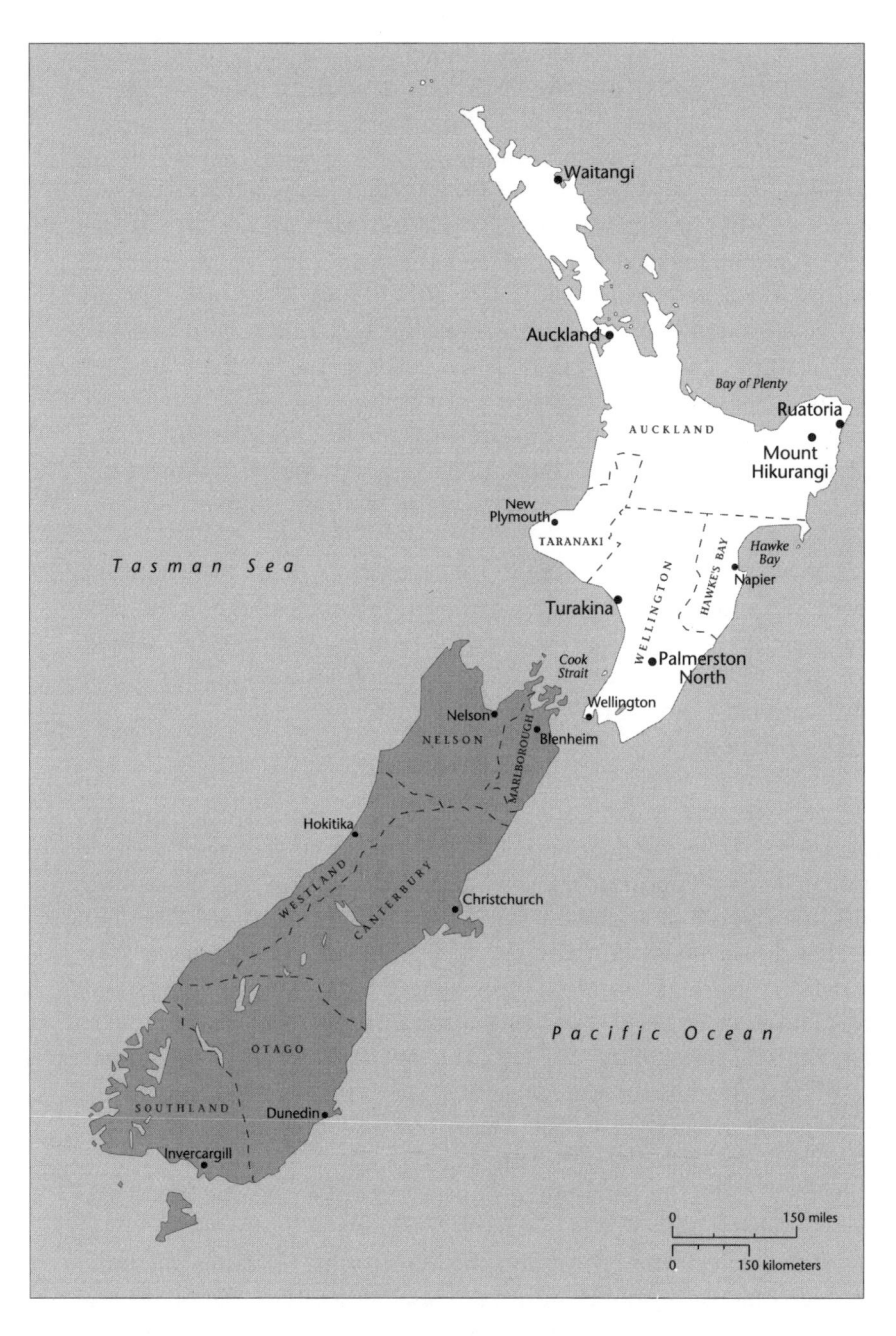

Map 3 New Zealand research sites and relevant place names

work of Captain Cook (1769) and ended with the completion of the Treaty of Waitangi (1840). The Maori people whom Cook encountered were firmly established in Aotorea (the North Island),[3] while on the South Island there were few communities. It appears that the Maori people had come to New Zealand from Polynesia around 800 AD, and that a sizeable population existed by 1200 AD.[4] They were divided into approximately twenty tribes on the North Island and three or four tribes on the South Island. Each tribe possessed its own territory and government and was a self-sustaining social unit, cultivating its land, fishing, and providing its own clothing and shelter. Although the tribes shared both a language and a culture, the social and historical differences among them were of great importance. Warfare among tribes was a highly developed art, providing not only such direct fruits of conquest as slaves and territory but also the opportunity to demonstrate skill and courage.

Following Cook's charting of the coastline, there had been no decision to proceed with any form of British settlement in New Zealand, as the territory was both remote and already settled. However, in the years after Cook's visit, there occurred an unplanned and scattered European (principally British) occupation, which had several components.

Those first settlements were based on local trade opportunities, sealing, and whaling. Ships plying the trade came from Sydney, Hobart, the United States, and Britain. In addition, there was also scattered contact with French traders. The missionaries were not far behind, with the Church of England padre appointed to the prison settlement in New South Wales bringing the first group of missionaries to New Zealand in 1814.[5] There were three main denominations represented: the Church of England, operating through the powerful and influential Church Missionary Society; the Wesleyans; and the Roman Catholics. The missionaries saw their role as not only bringing the message of the Gospel to the Maori but also as bringing them the knowledge and benefits of British society.

By the 1830s, the cumulative impact of contact on the Maori was already substantial. On the one hand, there was a profitable exchange of goods between the British and the Maori, with the latter obtaining European blankets, tools, and methods of agriculture; the Maori language was placed in written form by the missionaries; and the European presence made the Maori tribes more aware of their common heritage. On the other hand, the introduction of diseases had already resulted in epidemics and the loss of perhaps a quarter of the Maori population; the introduction of the musket had made warfare more deadly; the introduction of liquor had brought with it all its attendant problems; and disputes over land were frequent, as European acquisitions of land exclusively for profit conflicted with Maori traditions of community ownership. To the missionaries and to some Maori it was apparent that New Zealand needed a government which could bring law and order to the settlers.

The need for such a government was less apparent to the settlers and was opposed by the New Zealand Association, which had been formed in Britain with the intent of colonizing New Zealand by purchasing land from the Maori and selling it to prospective settlers. Some Maori leaders also questioned the need for a colonial government to be introduced into New Zealand. In addition, the Colonial Office in London was reluctant to expand the British Empire to a land that was viewed as remote and of questionable value. Nevertheless, the British government was persuaded that it had a moral responsibility to extend British rule to the settlements that were being established in New Zealand. In 1839, when Captain Hobson was sent to New Zealand to extend British sovereignty, his instructions expressed Britain's ambivalence. Lord Normanby, the colonial secretary, wrote to Captain Hobson:

> We have not been insensible to the importance of New Zealand to the interests of Great Britain in Australia, nor unaware of the great natural resources by which that country is distinguished ... On the other hand the Ministers of the Crown have been restricted by higher motives from engaging in such an enterprise [the colonization of New Zealand]. They have deferred to the advice of the Committee of the House of Commons in the year 1836 to enquire into the state of the aborigines residing in the vicinity of our colonial territories, and have concurred with the committee that the increase in natural wealth and power, promised by the acquisition of New Zealand, would be a most inadequate compensation for the injury which would be inflicted on this kingdom ... and with the calamity to a numerous and inoffensive people whose title to the soil and to sovereignty of New Zealand is indisputable and has been solemnly recognized by the British government. We retain these opinions in unim-

paired force, and though circumstances entirely beyond our control have at length compelled us to alter our course, I do not scruple to avow we depart from it with extreme reluctance.

The Queen ... disclaims for herself and her subjects every pretension to seize on the Islands of New Zealand unless the free consent of the natives, expressed according to their established usages, shall first be obtained.[6]

In launching this new colony, the Colonial Office was acting, at least in part, out of a desire to protect the Maori from the problems which European settlement had visited upon other aboriginal peoples.

The Treaty of Waitangi was the result of Hobson's attempt to convert these lofty objectives into a form that would be acceptable to the Maori chiefs and that would also clear the way for an orderly British settlement. The treaty was signed in 1840 by Hobson, representing the British Crown, and, eventually, by some 550 Maori chiefs, representing most Maori (but not all – indeed, the chiefs of a number of important tribes [e.g., the Waikato-Maniapoto, the Taupo, and the Rotorua] did not sign). In convincing the chiefs to sign, the missionaries were invaluable as advocates, intermediaries, and translators. They believed that some form of settlement was inevitable, and, through the Treaty of Waitangi, they sought to minimize its effect on the Maori.

The text of the Treaty of Waitangi is the subject of dispute because of language variations between the English text, which Hobson prepared, and the Maori text, which the English missionary William Williams prepared for the chiefs' signatures.[7] The treaty has a prologue and three articles. The prologue states the purpose of the treaty as being: the securing of the chieftainship of the chiefs and tribes of New Zealand; the governorship of the queen; and the stemming of the evils that would come upon the Maori people and the British from the lawlessness concomitant with the process of settlement. Article 1 provides for the chiefs to give to the queen the government of their lands; Article 2 obliges the queen to protect the Maori in the exercise of their government over their lands, villages, and treasures, and it establishes that the queen, through her local agents, has a right of purchase with respect to any lands they may wish to sell; and Article 3 gives to all the people of New Zealand the rights and duties of British subjects.

The Treaty of Waitangi is a unique document. Unlike the Canadian treaties, it was signed at a time when Maori people held most of the land and were many times more numerous than were the settlers. It recognized the prior existence of Maori title, and it did not restrict the exercise of aboriginal government to reserves. In addition, in exchange for the surrender of sovereignty the treaty recognized the Maori right to govern their own people, and it gave all Maori the status of British subjects. Thus, the Maori were recognized as full citizens a hundred years before such rights were extended to the Aboriginal peoples of Australia or to the First Nations peoples of Canada.

Government under the Treaty of Waitangi, 1840-6

Government under the Treaty of Waitangi lasted for only six years. A protectorate department was established in 1840, and its first and only head was George Clarke, a senior missionary of the Church Missionary Society. Clarke attempted to fulfil the obligations of the treaty. These included recommending a separate Maori justice system, recognizing Maori customs and law, and pursuing a conservative approach to the purchase of Maori land. The purchase of Maori land proved problematic. There were many more Maori interested in selling, and settlers interested in buying, land than the department had the funds or administrative capacity to process. In addition, there was a conflict of interest between the duty to protect the Maori and the obligation to purchase their land. In 1844, Hobson's successor as governor, Captain Fitzroy, acting on Clarke's advice, relinquished the Crown's monopoly on purchase in favour of a regulatory and dispute-settling role.

Land disputes were numerous, as members of the two cultures misunderstood who had the right to sell land and what was meant by the right of ownership. An attempt by the government to intervene in 1845 resulted in the Maori sacking of the British town of Kokrareka. The Colonial Office was aghast, dismissed Captain Fitzroy, and appointed Captain George Grey as governor. George Butterworth, the official departmental historian, writes:

> Grey believed that the best solution to native problems was to amalgamate the indigenous population into British society as quickly as possible. He was adamantly opposed to any recognition of Maori custom. He deliberately restructured the administration of Maori affairs so as to demote George Clarke and force his resignation. Clarke resigned in March 1846 and after he had left the Protectorate Department was disbanded.[8]

The period in which the Crown had attempted to establish an administration to fulfil its obligations under Article 2 of the Treaty of Waitangi was over. The missionaries were horrified. William Williams of the Church Missionary Society wrote that the Maori would now have 'to be told that the Treaty was a form of words without meaning ... They will naturally think that the missionaries have deceived them for some sinister purpose ... I do not see in this difficulty any alternative but that of returning to England ... Our influence with the natives will be ruined.'[9]

Assimilation, 1847-1960

George Grey's policy of 'amalgamation' or 'assimilation' (as it came to be called) was based on Article 3 of the Treaty of Waitangi, which had made all Maori British subjects. This policy disregarded the assurances given to the chiefs in Article 2 vis-à-vis their right to govern the Maori people. Grey introduced this change of policy in order to accelerate the process of settlement. By the 1850s, he was confident that his policy of amalgamation was working, and, in 1852, he believed that the time had come when government constitutional authority could be transferred from Westminster to New Zealand. This was done in a way that ensured that authority was transferred to the settlers rather than to the Maori. For, although the Maori were British subjects, they were effectively disenfranchised because they could only qualify to vote if they held individual titles to property – and very few of them did. A provision in the Constitution which could have been used to declare a number of aboriginal districts which would exist under Maori rule was never implemented. The Maori responded with a renewed sense of nationalism, as they tried to create a united front to meet the settler government and to re-establish their lost autonomy. The result was the establishment of a Maori king, Potatau the First. Two governments then existed in New Zealand, and the situation became increasingly tense in the latter 1850s. Open warfare began in 1860. The 'Maori Wars' or, as the Maori referred to them, the 'Pakeha Wars' lasted sporadically for seven years, and, in the end, the Maori 'rebels' (for they were now considered to be rebellious British subjects) were defeated. As a punishment, 3,000,000 acres of good farming land, suitable for settlement, were confiscated.

During the period of the Pakeha Wars and their immediate aftermath, the colonial government introduced measures to respond to

Maori grievances and to provide them with more effective rule. These measures proved to be enduring features of the New Zealand policy of assimilation. They were:
- The establishment of the Native Department in 1861. The department's mandate was to establish an effective government presence throughout Maori areas and to undercut the political appeal of the Maori chiefs.
- The Maori Land Act, 1862. This act gave the governor the power to establish the Maori Land Court. This court was established in 1865 and was empowered 'to enquire and decide who are the Maori people entitled under Maori custom to the Maori lands, to apportion their interest, and issue certificates of Title to them for such lands.'[10]
- The Native School Act, 1867. This act provided for the establishment of schools in each community. Earlier schools had been managed by missionaries and instruction had been provided in Maori, but, from 1871 on, instruction was permitted in English only.
- The Maori Representation Act, 1867. This act reserved four seats in the legislature for Maori representatives and established a separate Maori electoral role.

Maori reactions to these arrangements varied from rejection, to compromise, to acceptance. Rejection is seen in the establishment of a Maori supratribal Kotahitanga or 'parliament' at Orakei in 1879. The Kotahitanga persisted for twenty years, passed laws (which were not recognized by the New Zealand government), and sent delegations to London to seek implementation of the Treaty of Waitangi.

Acceptance and compromise was seen in the development of the new form of Maori leadership embodied by the Young Maori Party. The Young Maori Party was formed in 1897 by missionary-educated Maori who believed that the old ways had passed and who wanted to see the fulfilment of the promised equality of treatment of Maori citizens. The Maori electoral seats were seen as providing a practical means of achieving these objectives. Three outstanding leaders, Apirana Ngata, Maui Pomare, and Peter Buck were elected to the New Zealand legislature. *The Oxford History of New Zealand* notes that

> with the exception of Ngata, this group was characterised by its wholesale adoption of Pakeha culture and its readiness to scrap the surviving elements of its own. To them Maori society was degraded, demoralised, irreligious, beset with antiquated, depressing, and

pernicious customs. Their task ... was to reconstruct this society to make the race clean, industrious, sober and virtuous.[11]

As a group, they had accepted the view of Maori society held by their missionary mentors. 'There is no alternative but to become a pakeha' said Pomare in 1906 in the New Zealand House of Representatives.[12] This acceptance of the Pakeha view of Maori society gave the Young Maori Party credibility with the New Zealand government. Successive party leaders used this credibility to improve Maori social conditions. Apirana Ngata was particularly effective, both as an advisor to ministers and, from 1928 to 1934, as native minister. Because of his own prestige, he was able, in later years, to gain the support of both the New Zealand government and the Maori people with regard to the practical questions of Maori land use and community management. Apirana Ngata believed that Maori society had a future based on 'Maoritanga,' meaning

> an emphasis on the continuing individuality of the Maori people, the maintenance of such features of Maori culture as present day circumstances will permit, the inculcation of pride in Maori history and traditions, the retention in so far as possible of old time ceremonial [and] the continuous attempt to interpret the Maori point of view to the *pakeha* in power.[13]

An alternative to adopting Pakeha institutions was demonstrated by a succession of unorthodox transformations of missionary teachings into distinctively Maori religious organizations. The church historian, Allan Davidson, writes:

> The Maori movements led by Te Kooti, Rua, and the Tariao [morning star] faith established by Tawhiao, offered to their people a blend of traditional Maori values and rituals together with biblically based precepts and imagery within a religious framework which provided a sense of hope and meaning. These leaders and their movements were clear alternatives to the Pakeha dominated missionary churches.[14]

The establishment of the Ratana Church in the 1920s was particularly important because of the political influence it came to exercise. The Ratana Church was based in rural Maori communities and was led by Tahpotiki Wiremu Ratana. The church was Christian but unorthodox, based on a vision in which the Holy Ghost appointed Ratana as *Mangai*, the 'mouthpiece of God.' The Ratana Church rejected assimilation. In 1928, it formed the Ratana Political Party, and, by 1935, it had captured the four Maori seats from the representatives of the Young Maori Party. The party then entered into an alliance with the New Zealand Labour Party. The alliance was a fruitful one, leading to higher expenditures on Maori housing, schools, pensions, and land development. New Zealand had very few explicit policies which treated Maori people differently from settlers, but, as a result of the Ratana-Labour alliance, all instances of lower benefits and expenditures for Maoris were eliminated, and, in some fields, higher per capita expenditures were made to compensate for past disadvantages. In addition, in 1947 the word 'Maori' was substituted for the word 'Native' in the Native Department and in all official usage.

Integration, 1960-
In 1960, J.K. Hunn provided a report that evaluated the results of the work of the Department of Maori Affairs since 1861.[15] His report officially recognized that the policy of assimilation had not achieved its expected goals and that the Maori culture was an ongoing part of New Zealand life. According to this report, the official policy of the day was no longer assimilation – it was now integration. The purpose of integration was 'to combine (not fuse) the Maori and pakeha elements to form one nation in which Maori culture remains distinct.' The former objective of assimilation (i.e., the complete absorption of the Maori into white culture) was not forgotten, but its achievement was officially deferred to the indefinite future:

> The Swiss (French, Italians, Germans) appear to be an integrated society; the British (Celts, Britons, Hibernians, Danes, Anglo-Saxons, Normans) are an assimilated society. In the course of centuries, Britain passed through integration to assimilation. Signs are not wanting that that too may be the destiny of the two races in New Zealand in the distant future.

Integration implied a tolerance, albeit unenthusiastic, for a distinct Maori presence in New Zealand:

> Integration ... implies some continuation of Maori culture. Much of it, though, has already departed and only the fittest elements (worthiest

of preservation) have survived the onset of civilization ... Only the Maori themselves can decide whether these features of their ancient life (language, arts, and crafts) are, in fact, to be kept alive; and in the final analysis, it is entirely a matter of individual choice.

The report concludes that 'differentiation between Maoris and Europeans in statute law should be reviewed at intervals and gradually eliminated.' The future role of the Department of Maori Affairs was to be in the field of interdepartmental policy rather than in the field of policy administration for special Maori programs. New measures, including the establishment of district Maori councils and of the New Zealand Maori Council, were advocated in order to facilitate Maori contributions to policy formulation.

At the same time, services to Maori were gradually merged with general services. This was accomplished by disbanding the distinct Native Schools Division of the Department of Education, repealing the power of the Maori Land Court to recognize Maori adoption practices, and extending all general social services to Maori people. In addition, measures were introduced to complete the process of bringing remaining Maori land within the land title system.

This last measure was seen as an assault on the final bastions of Maori tribal identity and a final rejection of the Treaty of Waitangi. The imposition of these measures in 1967, despite Maori opposition, was deeply resented and led to united Maori opposition to the loss of any further land. This determined opposition resulted in the 1973 repeal of the 1967 legislation, and, in 1975, Matiu Rata (the first Maori minister of Maori affairs since Apirana Ngata) introduced the Treaty of Waitangi Act. The passing of this act led to renewed attention to the Treaty of Waitangi as a founding document of New Zealand society.

Although integration is no longer official policy, many of its features persist. Maori people are served through the mainline services of government rather than by specialized agencies. There is now greater recognition of Maori culture, but the power to decide changes remains vested in the institutions of the unified, and Pakeha-dominated, state.

Maori Resurgence, 1975-
There is more uncertainty over the future course of Maori-Pakeha relations now than in any period since the 1860s. Four major courses

of action indicate the character of the Maori resurgence: (1) the return to the Treaty of Waitangi; (2) Maori control of the Department of Maori Affairs; (3) a language and cultural renaissance; and (4) social policy based on partnership.

Return to the Treaty of Waitangi
In the entire period since the 1860s, the Treaty of Waitangi has been regarded by the government of New Zealand as an important symbolic document of cession, providing the basis for the country's alleged unitary citizenship. However, it has not been regarded by the European majority as a relevant or living document vis-à-vis the continuing conduct of government. This position was reinforced on those occasions when Maori tried to use the treaty in the courts, where it was judged to be a nullity.[16] Nevertheless, to the Maori, the Treaty of Waitangi continued to represent the contract under which they had agreed to settlement, albeit on terms that had not been honoured.

The passage of the Treaty of Waitangi Act, 1975, signalled the first clear step towards correcting this longstanding lack of recognition. The act established the Waitangi Tribunal to hear Maori grievances, to inquire into claims under the treaty, and to make recommendations to Parliament for resolving disputes. Initially, the tribunal was limited to hearing claims on grievances initiated after the act came into effect – a limitation which meant that few claims were presented to it. Nevertheless, some of those claims had a major impact on New Zealand public opinion. For example, in 1981 a claim was presented in which the tribunal ruled in favour of the Maori claimant but the government rejected its recommendation. This drew attention to the continuing injustice constituted by the government's disregard of Maori claims and their historic contract.[17] In 1985, Maori leaders were successful in lobbying a newly elected Labour government to amend the Treaty of Waitangi Act so that the tribunal could receive claims based on acts dating back to 1840. The amendment was passed, and within months the tribunal was deluged with more than 150 claims, all of which dealt with substantial acreages. In addition, claims were presented dealing with the loss of social rights, particularly language rights, resulting from the policy of assimilation.

Maori Control of the Department of Maori Affairs
The Department of Maori Affairs no longer has as its objective the governance of the Maori people; instead, it has become a Maori-run

department, the purpose of which is to assert a Maori presence within the New Zealand government. The transformed department has taken a revised and invigorated view of its responsibilities, as expressed through the philosophical concept 'tu tangata.' Tu tangata, meaning 'standing tall like a man,' was embraced as both a departmental philosophy and as a commitment to the interests of the Maori people. Being Maori and being first committed to one's Maori identity was recognized as a source of pride and as a basis for collective action. A practical outcome of this philosophy was the development of the Kokiri Centre, where departmental decisionmaking was placed in community hands. The word 'partnership' was increasingly used to express the relationship between the New Zealand government and the Maori people.

Language and Cultural Renaissance
Another indication of the renewed commitment to Maori culture was seen in the establishment of the Kohanga Reo program. Kohanga Reo, meaning 'language nests,' is a program designed to ensure the survival and vigour of the Maori language and culture. It is designed to correct three generations of language and cultural loss, which have resulted from the assimilation policies of native schools and daily exposure to monocultural media. Kohanga Reo will be discussed in more detail in the next chapter.

Social Policy Based on Partnership
The Royal Commission on Social Policy, which reported in 1988, used the Treaty of Waitangi as a foundation document and embraced a 'partnership' concept for social policy:

> For its part the Commission is strongly of the opinion that the Treaty in its entirety should be entrenched as a constitutional document and recommends that purposeful and deliberate discussions proceed, in accord with the principle of partnership ...[18]
>
> The Commission believes that the Treaty is always speaking and that it has relevance to all economic and social policies. Not only must the past be reviewed in the light of its principles, but the Treaty's promise must also be seen as fundamental to those principles which will underlie social well being in years to come.[19]

At the departmental level, Maori influence can be seen in the Puao-te-Ata-tu Report. Puao-te-Ata-tu, meaning 'daybreak,' was the report of a review which had been conducted during 1985-6 and which examined the Department of Social Welfare from a Maori perspective. Sixty-nine community meetings were held, thirty-nine of which took place in local Maori meeting areas (marae). In total, 267 written submissions were received and 1,424 oral presentations were delivered. The report provides an account of the racism with which the department was riddled, and it concluded with thirteen major recommendations, most of which have been acted upon.

Summary

The present period of Maori resurgence has already produced fundamental challenges to New Zealand social policy. These challenges have, unfortunately, incurred a reaction against the Maori people and against the use of the Treaty of Waitangi in contemporary social policy. One form of this reaction recognizes the inequalities faced by the Maori people but rejects any preferred status based on their being the tangata whenua (indigenous people) recognized in the treaty. The following extract from Richard Mulgan's *Maori, Pakeha and Democracy*, published in 1989, illustrates this point of view:

> However, if genuine equality rules out monocultural blindness to the difficulties faced by the Maori, it also rejects special measures for the Maori which go beyond rectifying disadvantages. There can be no first- and second-class citizens ... If Maori leaders wish the Pakeha to accept biculturalism, they must be prepared to renounce unequivocally the agenda of the radical Maori who wish to establish a separate Maori state.[20]

Robin Mitchell, *The Treaty and the Act*, goes further, attacking the Treaty of Waitanga on the grounds of reverse racism:

> Throughout this book, legislation favouring Maoris against others has been referred to as racist – sometimes 'brown' racist, though the adjective is unnecessary. Racism is racism, whether those practising it are brown, white or any other skin colour ...
> In today's New Zealand, there is an official racial bias which is almost entirely in favour of Maoris ... In the opposite direction, racial bias against Maoris – almost non-existent only a few years ago – seems to have been stirred up enormously through this official pro-Maori racial bias, as well as by interpretations which are being placed

on the Treaty of Waitangi by the Waitangi Tribunal, and the largely unjustified Maori expectations aroused as a result.

The appalling social statistics showing Maoris as underachievers suggest strongly that the present policy of 'positive discrimination' in their favour is doing them no good at all. It could well be that the Maoris' general lack of performance is because of – not in spite of – all the special provisions that are made for them.[21]

Obviously, there is no clear consensus in New Zealand society regarding the moral necessity of respecting the Treaty of Waitangi.

New Zealand Social Policy and the Maori

Unlike Australia's and Canada's experiences with respect to defining aboriginal peoples, the administrative definition of who is Maori has not resulted in major problems in New Zealand – largely because access to services specific to Maori was open to whoever defined themselves as Maori. The Treaty of Waitangi provided a sound base for New Zealand social policy by extending to all its citizens – irrespective of race – the status of British subjects. This meant that there was no necessity to construct administrative definitions in order to determine eligibility or ineligibility for basic human rights. Maori were never prohibited, on the grounds of race, from voting, visiting a pub, or living outside a reserve. The few distinctions which were based on race stand out as unusual and were withdrawn early. For example, until the actions of the Ratana Movement in the early 1940s, pension legislation had resulted in Maori receiving lower payments than did Pakehas.

In 1962, J.K. Hunn identified all the statutory definitions of Maori in Appendix C of his report. There were two approaches then in effect: one (used in the Electoral Act, 1956, the Adoption Act, 1955, the Maori Affairs Act, 1953, the Births and Deaths Registration Act, 1951, the Education Act, 1914, and a number of other minor statutes) defined 'Maori' as persons who belonged to the aboriginal race of New Zealand, including half-castes and persons who fell somewhere in between half-castes and persons of pure descent; the second approach (used in the Maori Housing Act, 1935, the Maori Purposes Fund Act, 1934-5, and the Maori Soldiers Trust Act, 1957) defined 'Maori' as persons belonging to the aboriginal race of New Zealand and any persons descended from them. In practice, by 1962, more than three generations after first settlement, the administration of who could and could not be defined as Maori was permissive – one could claim Maori status if one wished to be recognized as a Maori and had at least one Maori ancestor. On the other hand, no one, however complete their Maori ancestry, was compelled to define themselves as a Maori; for, as will be recalled, every New Zealander had the right to define him or herself as a British subject.

Most services which affected Maori operated without having to be formally defined. Native schools were established in rural areas, where Maori predominated. As they were frequently the only schools in those areas, Maori had to attend them, as did non-Maori living in the same areas. Access to the Maori Land Court is restricted to the holders of Maori land interests and, hence, to people of Maori descent. Similarly, access to the Waitangi Tribunal is only open to people who wish to claim that, as descendants of Maori covered by the Treaty of Waitangi, they are entitled to rights which are not currently being honoured. Affirmative action programs need to define who has Maori status, and critics attempt to discredit such programs by dwelling at length on how difficult it is to determine who should and should not so qualify.[22] However, in practice, who is and is not qualified to receive the benefits of affirmative action programs appears to be easily determined through self-definition and Maori peer evaluation.

Number and Distribution of Maori

The earliest source of data on the Maori is Captain Cook's estimate that there were 100,000 of them. Cook's estimate arose from his charting of the New Zealand coastline. As he did not attempt to survey the interior, he had no direct knowledge of the Maori people living there. Ian Pool, in his contemporary study of the Maori population of New Zealand,[23] reports a number of early estimates varying from 70,000 to 180,000, but he reaches no firm conclusion as to which is accurate.

By the time of the Treaty of Waitangi, it was the opinion of the missionaries who had been in New Zealand for about twenty years that the Maori population had declined by about 25 per cent since their arrival. Loss of life to epidemic disease arising from initial contact appears to have continued, for at the time of the first official attempt to count the number of Maori in 1851 (by visiting all the known Maori villages), a total of 56,049 was recorded, along with the cautionary phrase 'as far as can be ascertained.'[24] The scale of European immigration which followed the conclusion of the Treaty of Waitangi can be seen from the fact that, by 1851, from a mere 2,000 settlers in

1840, the non-Maori population had expanded until it was approximately the same size as the Maori population.

No census of the Maori was possible in 1861 (due to the war between the Maori and the colonial government), and an attempt at a census in 1871 was not sufficient to record the total Maori population. By 1881, the Maori total is given as 46,161, a loss of a further 20 per cent since 1851, while the non-Maori had grown to 489,933. The Maori thus comprised only 8 per cent of the population by 1881, whereas forty years earlier they comprised 98 per cent of it.

To provide a continuing picture of the relationship between the Maori and non-Maori populations, Table 6.1 has been compiled from census data. It also shows the number and percentage of Maori and non-Maori children. The year 1891 was selected for the commencement of this table, as that was the occasion of the first census in which children were distinguished in the Maori totals. The Department of Maori Affairs was responsible for collecting data, and this led to some variability in the receipt of information. It was not until the 1926 census that both populations were counted on the same day, using the same procedures. This was also the first occasion when the ethnic origin of Maori residents of northern towns was recorded. The full integration of all statistics was not achieved until 1951.

The Maori population was at its lowest in 1891, when only 44,177 were counted. However, as a proportion of the New Zealand population, it was lowest in 1921, when Maori made up only 4.5 per cent of the overall figure. By 1986, Maori totalled 295,314, representing 9 per cent of the population of New Zealand. Furthermore, Maori young people represent 13 per cent of the next generation of New Zealand citizens.

The 1951 census, in an attempt to give an accurate presentation of the extent of those claiming Maori descent, includes a table which records Maori and non-Maori ethnic origin in eighths. In practice, this was a difficult determination to make, and, after 1956, the use of proportions based on descent was abandoned in favour of a fuller use of the policy of self-declaration. This was achieved through a question in the 1961 census that enabled people who said they were of Maori descent to be recorded regardless of the fraction of that descent. Table 6.2 shows the number of people counted as both Maori and of 'Maori descent' since 1961.

The view that being a Maori is not simply a matter of proportion of descent is now common and is used in such current legislation as the

Table 6.1

Maori and non-Maori population and children, aged 0-14, 1891-1986

Year	Maori (000s)	Maori, 0-14	Maori, % 0-14	Pakeha (000s)	Pakeha, 1-14	Pakeha % 0-14
1891	42.0	15.1	34.2	626.7	250.6	40.0
1901	43.1	16.7	36.8	772.7	258.1	33.4
1911	49.8	19.9	40.0	1,008.5	315.6	31.5
1921	52.7	21.1	40.0	1,218.9	382.7	31.4
1936	82.3	37.0	45.0	1,491.5	367.5	24.6
1951	115.7	53.8	46.4	1,823.8	517.9	28.3
1956	137.1	64.5	47.0	2,037.4	618.8	30.4
1961	167.1	82.2	49.2	2,247.9	717.1	31.9
1966	201.2	101.3	50.3	2,475.7	771.1	31.3
1971	227.4	111.7	49.1	2,735.2	797.9	29.1
1976	270.0	122.4	45.3	2,847.7	805.4	28.2
1981	279.2	111.4	39.8	2,896.4	738.6	25.5
1986	295.3	101.5	34.4	2,969.0	693.5	23.3

Source: Census of New Zealand, 1891-1986

Table 6.2

Maori and Maori descent populations, 1961-86

Year	Total population	Maori descent (000s)	Maori descent (%)	Maori (000s)	Maori (%)
1961	2,414.9	202.5	8.4	167.1	6.9
1971	2,862.6	290.5	10.1	227.4	7.9
1981	3,175.7	385.5	12.1	279.2	8.8
1986	3,273.3	404.7	12.4	295.3	9.0

Source: Census of New Zealand, 1961, 1971, 1981, 1986

Electoral Act and the Maori Affairs Act. The wider definition based on those who claim Maori descent led the Royal Commission on Social Policy to its conclusion that, in a few years, between 20 and 25 per cent of the New Zealand population will be of Maori descent.[25]

The Maori population has always been predominantly a North Island population (95 per cent of Maori live there). Until the Second World War, Maori were overwhelmingly a rural population. This is no longer the case. Tables 6.3 and 6.4 show that, whereas the Maori population was approximately equally divided between rural and urban communities in 1961, today 80 per cent live in communities of more than 1,000 people.

Table 6.3

Rural, urban, and metropolitan distribution of Maori, 1926-61

Year	Country, district	Cities, boroughs	Islands	Total
1926	57,937	5,515	218	63,370
1936	74,419	7,731	176	82,326
1945	82,762	15,758	224	98,744
1951	93,863	21,852	231	115,671
1956	104,545	32,351	255	137,151
1961	111,188	55,681	217	167,086

Source: Census of New Zealand, 1961

Table 6.4

Percentage of Maori and non-Maori population in centres under and over 1,000, 1961-81

Year	Maori, in centres under 1,000	Maori, in centres over 1,000	Non-Maori, in centres under 1,000	Non-Maori, in centres over 1,000
1961	54.0	46.0	21.4	78.7
1971	29.8	70.2	17.5	82.5
1981	21.4	78.6	15.9	84.1

Source: Department of Statistics, *Maori Statistical Profile, 1961-86* (Wellington: Government Printer 1986).

Although the data reported in Tables 6.3 and 6.4 are based on different definitions, the movement of Maori from rural to urban areas in the postwar period is clear. The effect of this movement was to bring Maori into increasing contact with social services which had been established to meet the needs of the Pakeha population. It was also assumed that the movement to urban areas represented the Maori abandonment of their distinct culture and institutions, and that Pakeha institutions were most appropriate to urban living conditions. As a result, no attempt was made to support the Maori connection to extended family still living in rural areas.

Administration of Maori Affairs

The major institutions established to govern the Maori after the Pakeha Wars were identified earlier in this chapter. Three of these institutions – (1) the Maori Land Court, (2) the Native schools, and (3) the Native Affairs Department and, after 1947, the Department of Maori Affairs – have had a significant effect on Maori social policy.[26] In addition, in the period since the 1960s, integrated services has functioned as a fourth such institution.

The Maori Land Court

The Maori Land Court was established in 1865 to rule on the contested matter of Maori land ownership and, hence, on the right to sell Maori land. The operation of the court, as it was open to all manner of manipulation, had an extremely divisive effect upon the Maori community. As long as the members of a hapu (tribe) maintained solidarity in their refusal to sell Maori land, there was nothing that the court could do. However, once one member approached the court with a request to raise a land title in his or her name, the court could do so over the opposition of the rest of the community. The result was that settlers wishing to buy land would resort to pre-payment and other forms of corruption in order to get the process started. Once started, all legal costs incurred by Maori could be charged against the property. The result was that, even if the legal action to prevent the sale were successful, the property could be sold to pay the legal bills incurred in resisting its sale!

The records of the Maori Land Court contain much traditional and tribal history, as they disclose the Maori struggle for title to their land. This history was accumulated as more and more land passed from Maori to Pakeha hands. Ranginui Walker, in *Ka Whawhai Tonu Matou: Struggle Without End*, notes:

> By the turn of the century all the best land had been alienated, and only two million hectares remained in Maori ownership. Pakeha

desire to acquire land was not sated by the 24.4 million hectares they already had. Parliament continued to pass laws to get the rest. Land 'not required or suitable for occupation by Maori owners' was placed under land councils by the Land Settlement Act 1904. Pakeha determined what was 'suitable' as Maori opinion was not represented in the councils. Then came two pieces of legislation designed to mop up the remnants of Maori land ... the Maori Affairs Act 1953 ... and the Maori Affairs Amendment Act 1967.[27]

The importance of this assault on Maori land cannot be underestimated, as their relation to the land was central to their respective tribal identities. The policies proposed in the 1961 Hunn Report would have completed the process of bringing Maori land within the land title system. The Maori Land Court would then have been disbanded, its job finally done. Instead, the determined Maori opposition to the 1967 land legislation resulted in the establishment of the Waitangi Tribunal. The Waitangi Tribunal is presided over by the chief justice of the Maori Land Court. The tribunal now receives claims based on the failure of the New Zealand government to follow the principles of the Treaty of Waitangi. The tribunal has begun the process of re-examining the history of Maori land alienation and of re-opening the records of the land court. This is leading to Maori tribes regaining land that they had lost in the period from 1840 to 1975. Through the work of the tribunal, the Maori Land Court has become a forum in which Maori can obtain a fair hearing. Administratively, the court has been separated from the Department of Maori Affairs and placed under the administration of the Department of Justice as a part of the New Zealand court system.[28]

Despite its origins as an instrument to transfer land from Maori to settlers, the Maori Land Court did develop an understanding of Maori culture. As a result, the court was given a mandate for additional functions related to Maori social affairs. An important example of these functions was its role in providing for the legal recognition of Maori customary adoption.

Native Schools
The Native Schools Act, 1867, was the chosen vehicle for preparing the next generation of Maori children for 'amalgamation.' From 1871 on, the use of English was compulsory as the language of instruction; and, according to Ranginui Walker, from 1905 on

the Inspector of Native Schools instructed teachers to encourage children to speak English in school playgrounds. This instruction was translated into a general prohibition of the Maori language within school precincts. For the next five decades the prohibition was in some instances enforced by corporal punishment.[29]

The 1931 annual report of the superintendent for Native schools, written on the fiftieth anniversary of the Department of Education's assumption of responsibility for Maori education, contains a summary of their objective. There were then 138 Native village schools, 11 Maori mission schools, and 12 Maori secondary schools:

> The school has a larger responsibility for the elevation of the people than any other institution. In many instances it is almost the only influence for Native welfare. Errors or omissions in policy and method in school education are therefore correspondingly more serious.
>
> In this the fiftieth year of Native-schools administration by the Education Department, full credit should be given for the wise provision of those responsible for the original guiding principle upon which the present system functions, and has always functioned.
>
> The three fundamental principles are as follows:
> (1) To give the great mass of the Maori population an elementary but thorough instruction in English and in arithmetic sufficient for simple business transactions.
> (2) To demonstrate to the Maori community, by the unconscious example of the teacher's home and home life, the English mode of living and standards of dress, cleanliness, food, &c.
> (3) To secure secondary and higher instruction for those who are to assume leadership in thought and action.[30]

The second of these objectives was the subject of frequent comment in the *Education Gazette*, under the general heading 'Character Training in the Native School': 'In dealing with the Maori child the problem is made more difficult by reason of the obvious shortcomings in the standards of the Maori home. We must help to remove those shortcomings; raise those standards.'[31]

At the same time as these high-sounding principles were being espoused, the *Education Gazette* was not beyond publishing racist jokes at the expense of the Maori.[32] In fact and in practice, there was a deliberate attempt to make the Maori child reject the values and standards of his or her parents as antiquated and irrelevant.

Native Affairs Department
The Native Affairs Department had the task of displacing independent Maori management of their own affairs. This objective was made quite clear at the department's origin – it was designed to provide a political means of undermining the Maori King Movement. The first Maori king, Potatau the First, was an estalished Waikato chief who in 1858 was given the title king in an attempt by some of the tribes to unify their resistance to European settlement. After the Pakeha wars, Maori interest in self-government was demonstrated by the establishment of a Maori parliament in 1892. This body of government passed laws and resolutions but lacked any administrative authority. Instead the Native Affairs Department, which was reponsible to the New Zealand parliament, provided day-to-day government of the Maori.

In the 1920s, under the leadership of Coates and Ngata, the department brought a series of programs to Maori communities which improved their welfare by providing funds for land development, housing, and local improvement. In 1944, the welfare division was formed, and, in the 1950s and 1960s, the department took on a significant welfare role, leading to the development of paternalistic attitudes towards its Maori clients.

The officers of the Native Affairs Department have also acted as the local representatives of the Maori Trustee. The office of the Maori Trustee was established in 1920 to hold Maori lands in trust for Maori use. In this way, the officers exercised control over a wide range of financial transactions necessary to the development and use of Maori land.

Decisive change came to the Native Affairs Department in 1975, when, under the administration of Secretary Puketapu, the philosophy of tu tangata was introduced. This philosophy had the support of the ruling National Party (Conservative), which saw that it was in keeping with their emphasis on self-reliance.[33] However, tu tangata went far beyond individualism, as it also stressed pride in one's community.

In the most recent period, the Department of Maori Affairs has stressed the importance of strengthening iwi (community) authorities. This is a prelude to the transfer to the community of departmental responsibilities.[34] The change of name from Department of Maori Affairs to Iwi Transition Agency in 1989 symbolized this change of role. However, following the election of the National government in 1990, the minister of Maori affairs, Winston Peters, released a policy paper, *Ka Awatea*,[35] which contains proposals to establish a Maori development agency, offering programmatic support to Maori communities and enterprises. This represents a backing away from the commitment to transfer power to Maori communities embodied in the Iwi Transition Agency; instead, a return to a more traditional approach to government/Maori relationships seems possible.

Integrated Service Agencies
The newest form of administrative structure for the government of the Maori is found in the common service agencies, whose role is based on the philosophy of integration expressed in the Hunn Report. These agencies deal extensively with Maori people but, in their work, give no recognition to them. In the 1960s, 1970s, and 1980s, integrated service agencies became a dominant and pervasive form of government. The specialized agencies established in the 1860s were disbanded following the adoption of the Hunn Report in 1961. That report recommended providing service to Maoris through mainstream government departments and agencies. In theory, this would lead to the social integration of Maori within the Pakeha population. The government intent was that one's individual status as Maori should become an entirely private matter, unrecognized by the state.

The future direction of the New Zealand government's Maori policy requires further clarification. The policies of integration established in the 1960s, following the Hunn Report, remain in effect in the day-to-day operation of New Zealand social and educational services. However, the impact of the Maori resurgence on these services is now substantial. Major adaptations are occurring to give existing services a bicultural character, and separate and distinctive Maori services are being developed.

7
New Zealand: Maori People and Child Welfare Policy

As has been seen, from 1847 to 1960 New Zealand had a policy of assimilation; but it was not accompanied by the major attempts at social engineering which characterized aboriginal family and child welfare policy in Australia and Canada. In most cases, Maori children stayed in their own communities and were raised in extended families. Child welfare was achieved through informal community practices rather than through assimilation, and the impact of assimilation policy was limited to the language policies of the community Native schools. The recognition that this policy of non-intervention gave to the Maori community was strengthened by institutional recognition in the first half of the twentieth century. However, this changed with the introduction of the policy of integration in the 1960s. Large numbers of Maori were then becoming urban dwellers, and the established juvenile justice and child welfare agencies treated them as if they were Pakeha. During the same period, integrated services were also extended to rural areas, and Maori institutions that had been recognized in the period of assimilation were displaced. In the present period, the provision of integrated services to Maori is under review. These services are being overhauled to ensure that they recognize the cultural and social independence of Maori people. In addition, Maori people are developing their own separate institutions. This chapter examines New Zealand family and child welfare policy during each of these periods. The locations referred to in this chapter are all on the North Island where the majority of Maori live. They are marked on Map 3 (p. 137).

Child Welfare Jurisdiction in New Zealand
Unlike Australia and Canada, New Zealand is a unitary state, without a provincial level of government responsible for health, education, and

welfare. In addition, unlike in Great Britain, New Zealand had experienced neither a Poor Law nor its associated local government involvement in social policy. As a result, social policy in New Zealand is centralized to a much greater extent than is the case in other countries of the British Commonwealth. In New Zealand, the field of family and child welfare has not warranted an independent ministerial portfolio at the national level; rather, it was a branch of the Ministry of Education until 1972. Since then, it has been a branch of the Ministry of Social Welfare.

Family and child welfare work in New Zealand began with the establishment of orphanages to care for the children of settlers.[1] These were children who had lost their parents through accident or sickness and/or for whom single mothers could not provide adequate care. Anne Else, a historian of New Zealand adoption policy, writes that the provision of care to the children of single mothers was viewed with suspicion in Victorian New Zealand 'on the grounds that it condoned immorality and made things "especially easy and comfortable for the viciously inclined."'[2] The first orphanage was opened in Christchurch in 1857, and others were established in each of the major centres. By the 1880s, there were five orphanages or children's homes which admitted children on the order of the local magistrate. By 1900, the number of homes had grown to thirty-five, largely as a result of the economic depression of the 1880s and 1890s.

The first child welfare legislation was the Neglected and Criminal Children Act, 1867. This act was aimed at youth and led to the establishment of industrial schools. The Department of Education was made responsible for these schools in 1880; in 1910, it was made responsible for the supervision of orphanages; and, in a further gradual extension of its role, it developed a range of child welfare services which had some mandate to intervene in family matters (e.g., truancy officers, school nurses, protection officers, and probation officers.)[3] The child welfare activities of the Department of Education were reviewed in 1924, and, in 1925, the Child Welfare Act was introduced. This act provided for the appointment of child welfare officers, emphasized foster care, and established a separate Children's Court. Despite the emphasis on foster care, the orphanages (or 'homes') provided the principal form of alternative child care. As late as 1949, there were 75 orphanages containing 2,520 children. Of these children, the 1949 Department of Education's annual report notes that 104 had no parents living, 588 had one parent living, and 1,858 had both parents living – but 'not necessarily together.'

In 1941, the *Education Gazette* devoted a special issue to child welfare. The close integration of child welfare with education is stressed throughout the articles, with child welfare being an extension of the school's responsibility for 'juvenile morals.'[4] Discipline, it is indicated, was an important part of the Department of Education's child welfare responsibilities.

> But it is just as positive as in a well run classroom. There are no bars and few locks in the institutions run by the Branch, and child welfare officers measure their success not by the number of children they get into the Children's Court but by the number they keep out. There are 1,700 'preventative' cases on the books of the Branch, boys and girls who for one reason or another are the better for a little extra supervision by a firm but kindly outsider.[5]

There are two articles in this special edition which indicate the typical day-to-day activities of child welfare officers; one article deals with an urban area and one deals with a rural area. Both stress the monitoring and preventative aspects of child welfare.

Table 7.1 provides an indication of the extent of child welfare work as it applied both to those in care and to those under supervision. The system served several distinct functions. It was an alternative guardianship system for children who were without parents, a child protection system for children whose parent or parents were judged to be negligent or abusive, and a juvenile correctional system for children and youth who were charged with offences. These functions were carried out in an integrated manner.

Between 1920 and 1940, the child welfare system was involved, in any one year, with about one in fifty New Zealand children, of whom the majority were placed in residential institutions. This ratio decreased in the 1950s and 1960s to one in 100, with the majority being under supervision in their own homes. However, beginning in the 1960s, there was a steady increase in the number of children either under supervision or in residential care (this increase is discussed in more detail later in this chapter).

In 1972, the child welfare branch of the Department of Education was transferred to the Social Security Department, and a new Department of Social Welfare was formed. Legislation was also revised with the passage of the Children and Young Persons Act, 1974. This act represented some changes in philosophy, introducing a distinction

Table 7.1
Children in care and under supervision, New Zealand, 1921-86

Year	Protection complaints	Property offences	Offences against persons	Children supervised by branch	Number children sup./1,000 children	Children in care of branch	Children in care/1,000 children
1921	288	443	13	3,839	9.5	5,233	12.9
1931				3,026		4,902	
1936				3,003	7.4	4,269	10.3
1941	576	1,546	81	3,617		4,287	
1946	454	950	56	3,864		4,184	
1951	484	1,161	82	2,856	4.9	3,270	5.7
1956	332	1,754	218	4,147	6.0	3,018	4.4
1961	555	2,776	301	7,884	9.8	3,387	4.2
1966	975	3,289	513	11,278	12.9	3,881	4.4
1971	1,571	6,424	593	10,279	12.3	5,205	5.9
1976	1,721	4,713	512	9,513	10.2	6,838	7.3
1981	2,509	7,502	849	8,821	10.3	6,913	8.1
1988	1,347	6,858	757	4,864	6.1	5,840	7.3

Source: Appendices to the journals of the House of Representatives, 1921-86

between a child under fourteen and a young person between the ages of fourteen and seventeen, and enabling the superintendent of child welfare to take sole guardianship where necessary. A voluntary agreement section was added, through which a child could be brought into care without a court order. The 1974 act remained in force until the passage of the Children, Young Persons and Their Families Act, 1989 (to be discussed later).

Adoptions have always been undertaken in New Zealand under a separate statute administered by the Department of Justice. The first adoption law was passed in 1881 'as a means of encouraging couples to care for children other than their own.' Anne Else, in her history of adoption practice in New Zealand, continues:

> The Bill was at first strongly opposed ... There were two main objections. The first was based on the familiar moralist grounds; the effect would be to legitimise illegitimate children, thus providing an incentive to irresponsibility. The second was that the children might be adopted to provide cheap slave labour or for immoral purposes.[6]

Use of the act was not limited to infants; older children and stepchildren were frequently adopted. Unlike later acts, the 1881 statute contained no requirement not to reveal the birth parent of the child. Adoption in its modern form, with its emphasis on secrecy, adoption by strangers, and adoption of infant children, became the primary means of caring for illegitimate children after the Second World War. The Adoption Act, 1955, was based on the concept that the adoptive parents should completely replace the birth parents. For legal purposes, the child was 'as born to' the adoptive parents. The birth mother was encouraged to get on with her life and to forget this unfortunate mistake, while the adoptive parents were assured that the records of the baby's origin were sealed forever. As is apparent in Table 7.2, adoptions were widespread during the 1960s and 1970s, reaching a peak of 3,500/year in the early 1970s. From that time to the present, the practice of adoption has been in continuing decline; it is now around 1,000/year. The decline is principally the result of effective contraceptive practices and the availability of abortion.

Adoption provides a good example of the different cultural needs of Maori and Pakeha. Until services to Maori were integrated with services to Pakeha in the 1960s, the former had access to a unique form of adoption through the Maori Land Court. These adoptions, which provided official recognition of Maori cultural practices, are recorded separately in Table 7.2.

Table 7.2

Adoption orders, New Zealand, 1956-86

Year	Adoption by strangers	Adoption by relatives	Prior relationship not known	Maori adoptions	Total adoption orders
1956	424	288	175	163	1,051
1961	1,613	501	465	407	2,986
1966	2,230	767	465		3,462
1971	3,176	1,055	745		6,918
1976	1,347	1,207	388		2,942
1981	556	763	328		1,647
1986	n/a	n/a	n/a		1,038

Source: *New Zealand Yearbook*, 1956-86

Child Welfare Practice in the Informal Maori Period

Unlike those in Australia and Canada, the New Zealand authorities did not separate Maori children from their parents in order to enforce the policy of assimilation. In the period up to the 1950s, the Maori community was rural and had little contact with the industrial schools and orphanages which child welfare workers were developing as resources for urban Pakeha communities. As a consequence, the *New Zealand Yearbook, 1990* notes that: 'Until the second half of the century child welfare measures tended to concentrate on the needs of Europeans – Maori were ignored or left to their extended family.'[7]

There is some evidence that this was not entirely the case. In 1930, George Graham wrote to the *Auckland Star*, objecting to the operation of the Child Welfare Act:

> But it is in respect of the application of this law to Maori childhood that I desire to write – for here in particular operate officials who can not speak Maori, know little of nor care less for Maori mentality. They are hence incompetent to allow for those factors; yet they undertake to gather Maori children within their official nets, whence they are relegated to institutions or boarded out to European foster parents whose motives cannot be adjudged as mercenary.[8]

Graham was an advocate of the Maori family and of the 'Native Land Court' (i.e., Maori Land Court), which, in his view, provided a more appropriate means of providing for the welfare of Maori children. His letter continues:

> When cases arise which, in the opinion of the Welfare Department require dealing with, then only the judges of the Native Land Court should act, and make such orders as to trusteeship or guardianship as may be necessary ... For seldom will it be that the next of kin will fail to come forward and claim custody of their own flesh and blood.[9]

There is no doubt but that the Maori extended family provided for the welfare of all but a few children during this period. These informal child welfare practices can be glimpsed in the oral histories of Maori families.[10] The following are extracts from oral historian Judith Binney's account of the life of Putiputi Onekawa, who was born in 1908 and who was sent away to school at Turakina in 1921:

> I started school quite old. And I can't talk English. All we got to do is cry, because 'Don't talk Maori at school!' We can't talk English – so all we got to do is cry. Yes, for a long while. I can't talk English no matter what. I Try. But the only thing I know is 'stomach'! Yes, I know that! Oh, yes, Sister Anne, Sister Dorothy, Sister Jessie, and Mr. Laughnton and Mr. Currie. He's hard, very hard. No bloody humbug! A cousin of mine – we are all sitting on the floor, singing, and she was naughty. She did it on the floor. Because we don't know how to go outside! All we do is go like that [putting her hand up] and point outside! And this girl she didn't like to say anything. She was sitting on her slate. She had put her slate over it. We were just going to sing and I was going like that – pointing to her. Mr. Currie gave me a good hiding, supplejack, eh, across my back. He was a murdering thing! And Mr. Laughton didn't like it. He knew, because I don't know how to say outside. It was awful.
>
> I was there one year. Just one year. Then I took off! Because I didn't want to come home and get married! Because, when I was still there, Mac's grandfather, Temata Kiripa, used to write to me a lot and tell me everything that's going on at home. Temata was living at the pa [a fortified Maori community]. This time he said 'oh well, when you come back – in Maori – we got a house ready for you and Mac.' I thought to myself, 'No way! I'm going to take off!'

Putiputi came home after a year or so, stayed for a while, then took off again. Eventually, in 1928, she married Mac – but only after they had had their first child. 'It took Mac a while to get married! He wouldn't have it! He didn't like a wedding. Just to get together; just a Maori wedding.' Binney continues:

> Puti and Mac brought up six of their own children. Two others died in childhood and three were brought up by different families. But they also brought up ten tamariki whangai [foster children]. The first was Zac whom Puti took in before she had any children of her own. Zac was left ... after his parents separated. Puti commented 'Oh a lot of kids – motherless, fatherless. Zac, he just wanders at the pa ... There's nobody to look after him ... Her youngest whangai [child], Moe, she took at birth to replace her daughter Molly, who had died. Moe herself was a daughter of another of Puti's whangai ... 'I delivered that one', she said, 'but the others they were just wandering kids from Maugapohatu.'

There is some evidence that the official welfare system used the Maori system whenever possible, as is shown in the following extract from Binney's account of Ned and Heni Brown:

> We have one whangai, that's his brother's mokopuna [grandchild], Ned's brother's. She was only a little baby – three months – and her mother didn't want her, so the welfare lady came over here,'You want a baby Mrs. Brown!' 'Where?' 'Over there. They don't want the baby.' 'No.' 'You can have it Mrs. Brown!' Away I go and get the baby. 'You want another one Mrs. Brown?' 'NO!' 'Why?' 'I am getting tired! I already brought up fifteen; that's enough!' The welfare lady look at me and laugh: 'No, have another one!' 'NO!' We could have bought up a lot of welfare kids, but I couldn't take it. Not that I didn't want them – but him and I like to be on our own now and again!'[11]

The responsibility to take in and care for whangai was central to the Maori approach to child care. Responsibility for children extended beyond the nuclear family and was shared between the extended family and the community. Children were not the exclusive possessions of their parents, and taking children away from their community and giving them to strangers to raise was unheard of.

On occasion, the Maori Land Court was used to obtain official recognition of established relationships. This became important in establishing who had the right to receive benefits for caring for a child and who had authority to sign documents needed for school, driving licences, and inheritance purposes. Contrary to the European view that adoption required the separation of ties with birth parents, the Maori view, as explained by the chief judge of the Maori Land Court in 1946, was quite the opposite:

> The fact of an adoption was always widely known among the people; in fact to establish an adoption according to Maori custom, it was generally necessary to show that the adoption had been made public. It would therefore be well known to the child on growing up, and to the people of his hapu [subtribe], that he had been adopted.[12]

These examples of the effectiveness of Maori caring institutions were accepted by government authorities as both convenient and inexpensive. Yet the institution which was providing the care, the whanua (extended family), was under continual attack by the education system. There was no investment in the Maori system of care, and there was neither interest in, nor understanding of, its importance.

Child Welfare in the Integration Period, 1960-

When, in 1960, policy began to integrate services to Maori with services to Pakeha, the role of the extended family was forgotten. The first casualty of this change of policy was the Maori Land Court, which, in 1962, lost its role in Maori customary adoptions. As indicated earlier, Maori adoption practice was much more like informal fostering than was European adoption; yet, in 1962, these practices were forced into the mould created by the Adoption Act, 1955. The Maori Land Court's adoption powers were revoked, and all Maori customary adoptions had to be conducted under this act. As Else noted, the result was that 'in the first two and a half years after the 1962 amendment, Maori adoption orders fell short of their former numbers by about 600 cases.'[13] When questioned in the legislature on the wisdom of replacing the Maori system of adoption, Attorney General Hanan replied:

> Since when is a Maori child not as good as a European? Since when is a Maori child worth only $2 and a European $25 for adoption? I say that a Maori child is entitled to all the rights and to nothing less than a European child, and I know that every Maori man and woman adopting a child realises the necessity for the formalities to be com-

pleted for the change of status and they will willingly pay for the adoption in the same way as is done for a European adoption.[14]

As Maori people moved to urban areas, the lack of support given to Maori extended families showed the same cultural misunderstanding as was apparent in the area of adoption. It was not until the 1988 Royal Commission on Social Policy that official recognition was given to the importance of the extended family:

> The most serious effect of urbanization has been the loss of confidence and self-esteem that comes from knowing who you are and where you come from. The Maori Women's Welfare League study of Maori Women's health graphically explained [that until] recent times a Maori sense of security was related, in large measure, to tribal identity. Understanding social, spiritual and cultural responsibilities and the practice of these responsibilities gave confidence and self-esteem. Community contact was immediate and close if one lived within tribal boundaries. Outside the tribal region it was distant and difficult to sustain, for trips back [for] the turangawaewae [standing in the tribe] were essential to give support to whanua [extended family] and hapu [subtribe] and tangihanga [funerals], and other hui [gathering] associated with the protection of tribal land and food resource areas.[15]

The lack of recognition of Maori institutions and the attempt to replace them by Pakeha social services contributed to a growing involvement of the child protection and juvenile justice systems with Maori families and youth. This growth can be seen from the Children's Court statistics provided in Table 7.3.

In 1956, Maori youth constituted 9.4 per cent of the youth population, but they were involved in 21 per cent of cases brought before the court. In 1986, when Maori youth constituted 12.7 per cent of the juvenile population, they were involved in 54 per cent of the cases brought before the court. In 1956, 3 per cent of Maori youth between the ages of twelve and seventeen were brought before the court annually; by 1986, that proportion had risen to 16 per cent.

A similar growth in the number and proportion of Maori children considered by authorities to need protection seems to have occurred. Data on child welfare complaints with respect to Maori children are only available after 1981. Statistics for 1981 show that, in that year, 49.2 per cent of children in need of care were from Maori families,

Table 7.3
Juvenile offences, total and Maori cases, 1956-86

Year	Total offences against people	Maori offences	Maori offences (%)	Total property offences	Maori offences	Maori offences (%)	Maori as % of youth, 12-17
1956	126	29	23.0	1,867	498	26.6	9.4
1961	210	68	32.3	2,826	854	30.2	10.2
1966	347	85	24.4	3,951	1,334	33.7	11.6
1971	820	357	43.5	7,961	3,687	46.3	12.8
1976	896	427	47.6	6,660	2,932	44.0	13.2
1981	740	395	53.3	7,314	3,960	54.1	13.1
1986	1,410	739	52.4	7,892	4,066	51.5	12.7

Source: Department of Justice, annual statistics, 1956-86

and that the court decided that 1,246 Maori children (representing 11/1,000) were in need of protection. The comparable figures were 1,285 non-Maori children, representing 2 children per 1,000. Unfortunately, New Zealand does not publish a report showing the ethnic origin of children under child welfare supervision, nor is a report available showing the ethnic origin of children in care. However, from the justice statistics on cases before the Children's Court, it would be reasonable to assume that approximately half the children in care in 1981 were Maori. Based on this assumption, an estimate can be made of the number of Maori children in care and of the ratio of children in care per 1,000 Maori children (see Table 7.4).

Table 7.4

Estimate of Maori and non-Maori children in care, per 1,000, 1981

Total children in care	=	6,913
Assume 50 per cent Maori	=	3,456
Total Maori children, aged 1-14	=	111,400
Maori children in care per 1,000	=	31.0
Total non-Maori children, aged 0-14	=	738,600
Non-Maori children in care per 1,000	=	4.7

The figure of 4.7/1,000 children in care for non-Maori children is very similar to the ratio of children in care in the 1950s, before the child welfare system began to work extensively with Maori. Most of the increase in the number and proportion of children in care would seem to result from the extension of Pakeha services to Maori children as Maori people moved to urban areas.

It was the belief of the day that the Pakeha system of child welfare was modern and incorporated the highest standards of both professional knowledge and legal practice. The juvenile justice, child protection, and adoption systems were called European as opposed to Maori, and this was seen as conferring on them an unquestionable advantage. It was the intention of those providing services that the Maori change from their rural and 'backward' ways to urban, Pakeha ways.

Thus, although from 1840 to 1960 Maori had not been subject to the oppressive family and child welfare measures that were used as part of the policies of assimilation in Australia and Canada, from 1960 onward, similar policies were followed in all three countries. In these policies, mainstream social services, developed to meet the needs of the settler majorities, were imposed on the aboriginal peoples.

In their 1990 discussion of the effect of changes in child welfare measures on Maori life, Maori staff of the Department of Social Welfare observed:

> The Children and Young Persons Act of 1974, followed on from the Adoption Act [1955] in promoting the interests of the child as paramount. This effectively cut across the Maori philosophies and practices of seeing the child within the parameters of whanau, not as an isolated individual in need. Most often Maori concepts of child care were ignored but additionally they were regularly denigrated because they did not fit the view espoused by the legislation and the Pakeha practitioners.[16]

By the early 1980s, it was clear that the attempt to impose a service system on the Maori 'for their own good' was unacceptable. An important challenge was initiated by a Women Against Racism Action Group (WARAG) report. In 1984, WARAG members working in government offices produced a report on what they termed 'institutional racism' in the Auckland district office of the Department of Social Welfare.

> The report found from a survey of staff ... that Pakeha outnumbered Maori fifteen to one whereas the national ratio was nine to one ... This imbalance in ethnic composition of staff meant that those delivering service did not match the client group. For instance, only 22% of inmates in residential institutions were Pakeha, against 62% Maori and 16% of Pacific Island origin. But 71% of the staff were Pakeha, only 22% were Maori and 5% Pacific Islander ... The report recommended that the department take steps to eliminate institutional racism [and] become bicultural by handing over power and resources to the Maori to enable their vision to be realised of how social welfare should be implemented.[17]

Initially, the Department of Social Welfare was shocked by the findings and by the charge of racism. The WARAG group was told to disband, and their leader, Tanya Cumberland, was admonished. These actions served to draw more attention to their report. To address the issues raised by WARAG, the Maori Perspective Advisory Committee, chaired by John Rangihau, was established by the Department of Social Welfare in 1985. The committee was asked

> to advise the Minister of Social Welfare on the most appropriate means to achieve the goal of an approach which would meet the needs of Maori in policy, planning and service delivery in the Department of Social Welfare. The Advisory Committee ... is to:
> 1. Assess the current capability of the department in relation to the declared goal [of meeting the needs of Maori];
> 2. Identify those aspects (including for example current practices in staffing, recruitment, staff training and development and public relations) which militate against attainment of the goal;
> 3. Propose a strategy for overcoming problems and deficiencies identified; and,
> 4. Report with recommendations to the Minister within 6 months from the commencement of the task.

The report of the committee was issued in 1986 as the Puao-te-Ata-tu (Daybreak) Report.

Child Welfare and the Maori Resurgence

The Puao-te-Ata-tu Report was a product of the Maori resurgence, but it was neither the first nor necessarily the most significant such product in the field of social policy. In this final section on family and child welfare measures, six initiatives, changes, or programs are considered in order to illustrate the principal social policy changes taking place in New Zealand. The first three are direct initiatives of the Maori community, while the last three indicate some of the changes which are taking place in mainstream services.

Te Kohanga Reo (Language Nests) Movement
Te Kohanga Reo is a movement based on the Maori community's ability to care for its own children in a culturally appropriate manner. The program of activities which constitutes Te Kohanga Reo is designed both to use and to strengthen Maori whanau (extended families), hapu (subtribes), and iwi (communities). Te Kohanga Reo is a uniquely Maori response to the high rates of Maori child neglect and delinquency that are recorded in the mainstream data. It is a response

that recognizes the situations documented as symptoms of the breakdown of traditional family and tribal structures, accompanied by a loss of pride in being Maori.

Te Kohanga Reo is designed to address these problems through offering four interrelated programs/statements. These are:
(1) a pre-school Maori culture and language immersion program which provides the next generation with an introduction to Maori culture and language that their parents often cannot provide
(2) a community intergenerational development program which draws upon grandparents and elders to educate both children and young parents in traditional Maori ways
(3) a response to the alienation of the present generation of teenagers and young people by demonstrating to them the child care capacity of their community
(4) a political statement of the capacity of the Maori community to act and care for its own in the 1990s.

Te Kohanga Reo was proposed by elders of the Maori community in a national hui (gathering) held in 1981. Te Kohanga Reo does not depend on extensive government support and has been developed in a period of financial restraint and ideological conservatism. The Minister of Maori Affairs, Koro Weteve of the National party, noted that 'the ultimate objective of Te Kohanga Reo is nothing less than the rebirth of the Maori nation as an equal but separate element contributing to the common good of New Zealand society.'[18] The first pre-school was opened in April 1982 and was quickly followed by five others. The expansion of centres since then has been extremely rapid and covers all areas of New Zealand. This widespread growth is shown in Table 7.5.

Through these schools, some 11,000 Maori children under five years of age were learning Maori in 1988, representing 30 per cent of Maori pre-school children. The schools receive limited funding from the Te Kohanga Reo Trust, but most of the funding comes from parents. Each parent is expected to make a weekly contribution to program costs. The contribution takes the form of a koha (gift), which is given in accordance with the person's wish. The program operates out of community buildings and has extensive voluntary support. This results in very low operating costs – costs which can be sustained by the Maori community. The Te Kohanga Reo Trust provides a common curriculum, instruction in teaching, and encouragement of new programs. Its ultimate objective is to reach 75 per cent of Maori pre-school children.

Table 7.5

Numbers of Te Kohanga Reo by Maori Affairs District, 1982-8

District	Dec. 1982	Dec. 1984	Dec. 1986	Dec. 1988
Whangarei	9	38	71	75
Auckland	6	24	40	46
Wiri	4	18	26	28
Hamilton	5	27	53	57
Rotorua	5	34	52	59
Gisborne	5	26	47	57
Wanganui	2	26	51	56
Hastings	2	20	28	35
Wellington	9	25	43	48
Turangi				2
South	3	31	55	58
Total	50	269	466	521

Source: Department of Maori Affairs, *Report of the Review of Te Kohanga Reo* (Wellington: Department of Maori Affairs 1988)

Te Kohanga Reo is also a political force. One of the products of its political influence has been increasing pressure on educational authorities to provide primary education on a bilingual or Maori-immersion basis. Change here has been slow, with bilingual primary schools increasing from twelve to twenty between 1987 and 1989, and with Maori immersion schools increasing from one to six in the same time period. The difference in the rate of change between the mainstream school system and the Maori Te Kohanga Reo illustrates a key difference between the systems: mainstream schools have had great difficulty changing during a period of financial restraint, while, because of its financial independence, Te Kohanga Reo has not.

The Waitangi Tribunal Finding Relating to Te Reo Maori (The Maori Language)

The proceedings of the Waitangi Tribunal have principally dealt with issues of land and resource management. However, the tribunal is also prepared to consider social issues, as was seen in the findings relating to Te Reo Maori. The Te Reo Maori claim was lodged with the

Waitangi Tribunal in 1985. The claim was simple: 'Te Reo Maori should be recognized as an official language throughout New Zealand, and for all purposes [3.1.1].'[19] The Waitangi Tribunal considered the history of the Maori language since the Treaty of Waitangi, noting early precedents that included the initial recording of all parliamentary proceedings in both Maori and English when the colonial government was established in 1852. The tribunal received the testimony of elders on the use of the Maori language during this century. It characterized the first twenty-five-year period as one in which Maori was the language the children took to school but, once there, were forbidden to speak. Maori 'had to be left at the school gates [3.2.4].' The next twenty-five-year period was one in which parents were bilingual but in which 'remembering their own experiences at school they brought up their children to speak English from infancy.' As a result, the children tended to lose their fluency, and, while they could still speak Maori to their grandparents, it was clearly a second language (3.2.10). In the third quarter of this century, the process of language loss had accelerated, compounded by the move from rural areas to the city and 'by an official policy of "pepper-potting" homes throughout the suburbs so that Maori people were scattered ... The result was that a whole generation has been reared who know no Maori or who knowing so little of it are unable to use it effectively and with dignity [3.2.11].'

The Te Kohanga Reo Movement is recognized for its achievement in beginning to reverse this trend, but the tribunal noted that Maori families are concerned that their efforts may not be successful. 'They complain that their efforts are nullified by the present education system and that their children lose their Maori fluency after six months or so at primary school where they are swamped with English and never hear so much as one word of Maori [3.3.10].'

The Waitangi Tribunal had to decide whether this unusual claim was within its jurisdiction. Was the loss of language covered by a provision of the Treaty of Waitangi? Article 2 in the Maori version assured the chiefs of their authority over 'all their treasures' or 'valued possessions.' The tribunal concluded that there was evidence that language was a 'valued possession.' It then reviewed the evidence that Maori interests had been damaged by restrictions on the use of Maori in the courts, in education, and in broadcasting; and it concluded that, indeed, Maori interests *had* been massively disregarded. The Waitangi Tribunal recommended that:

- the right be established to use Maori in the courts and in any dealings with government
- a permanent body be set up to supervise and foster the use of the Maori language
- there be an inquiry into Department of Education policies to foster the opportunity to learn Maori
- there be an obligation on the Crown to expand the use of Maori in the field of broadcasting
- there be a provision for an English and Maori bilingual requirement with regard to positions designated by the State Services Commission.

The government accepted these recommendations, despite opposition from those sections of New Zealand society that wanted to continue with the earlier policy of monolingualism.[20]

Maatua Whangi (the Parental, Nurturing Family)
Maatua Whangi was commenced in 1983 as a Maori family development initiative, supported by funding from the Department of Maori Affairs and the Department of Social Welfare. The intention was to strengthen the lines of tribal, cultural, and extended family connection so that each family member would see his or her responsibilities in relation to others. Family members in difficulty were seen as needing to know their roots; they would then know to whom they should turn for help. Conversely, the tribe and extended family needed to know who their members were before they would be able to accept their obligations to them. This method of establishing supportive relationships differs from that used in mainstream organizations (where responsibilities are defined by professional obligation). The concept of Maatua Whangi was supported by the Department of Social Welfare because it was seen as a way of finding placements for some of its most difficult cases and as a diversion program which would obviate the need to take some children into care. As a result, Maatua Whangi workers tended to spend their time tracing family connections which might be 'useful' to the processes of placement and diversion. As was pointed out in a 1988 review, this was not the original intent of the program:

> Firstly, Social Welfare has regarded Maatua Whangi as an optional extra rather than a different way of working. This has meant that some Maatua Whangi officers have been unsure as to their role in the

Department; to whom they were reporting (The Department, the Core Committee, or the iwi); what the focus of their work was to be (developing networks or effecting placements); and with whom placements should be made ... These difficulties arise out of a lack of clear philosophy for Maatua Whangi.[21]

As a result of this review, the government sought a deep commitment on behalf of the Department of Social Welfare to the development of extended family networks, not as a means of securing last-resort placements for difficult children or as a diversion opportunity, but as a primary method of problem prevention. Commitment was sought to a different approach to philosophy, culture, staffing, and practice – a commitment which would provide for 'power and authority sharing, non-ownership of programmes and resources, and an acceptance of Maori cultural norms and ethics as opposed to Social Work professionalism.'[22] Staff was to be recruited through iwi (tribal) authorities, based on criteria of language fluency, knowledge of kitanga (kinship and genealogy), maturity, and other relevant life experiences (e.g., parenthood or work with people who are or were major users of Department of Social Welfare services). Maatua Whangi remains a fundamental attempt to base service on tribal relationships rather than on the legislation, definitions, and thought patterns of the Department of Social Welfare.

Puao-te-Ata-tu (Daybreak): The Report of the Ministerial Advisory Committee on a Maori Perspective for the Department of Social Welfare
The origins of this report, which examined racism in the Department of Social Welfare, were mentioned earlier in this chapter. The advisory committee held 69 public meetings, 39 of which were at marae or community venues. It received 1,424 oral submissions and 267 written submissions. Although the committee recognized the Treaty of Waitangi, its primary mandate was to review departmental racism. Racism was regarded as having three forms: personal racism (i.e., as evidenced by the actions and attitudes of individuals); cultural racism (i.e., as evidenced by the negative and selective attitude of a powerful majority culture towards a less powerful minority culture); and institutional racism (i.e., as evidenced by monocultural institutions which simply ignore alternative cultural institutions). The appendix to the report indicated how institutional racism pervaded the department. The committee's conclusions are summarized in the following extract:

The fact is that New Zealand institutions manifest a monocultural bias and the culture which shapes and directs that bias is Pakehatanga ... Institutional racism is the basic weapon that has driven the Maori into the role of outsiders and strangers in their own land ... Institutional racism can be combatted only by a conscious effort to make our institutions more culturally inclusive in their character, more accommodating of cultural difference. This does not begin and end 'at the counter.' The change must penetrate to the recruitment and qualifications which shape the authority structures themselves ... Affirmative action programmes aimed at reducing the monocultural bias in our institutions are an essential ingredient of change. The first stage of change to a more culturally inclusive New Zealand is the recognition of biculturalism. This involves both the place and status of Maoritanga in our institutional arrangements.[23]

The committee's endorsement of biculturalism as the appropriate direction for race relations was embodied in its thirteen major recommendations. These included recommendations about the Department of Social Welfare's
- mission (advocating an attack on all forms of racism and a commitment to incorporate the values, cultures, and beliefs of the Maori people in all policies developed for the future of New Zealand)
- structure (recommending the establishment of a Social Welfare Commission, containing two Maori representatives and two representatives of women to advise the minister on policy and to consult annually with tribal representatives)
- legislation (proposing making the Social Security Act, 1964, and the Children and Young Persons Act, 1974, more culturally sensitive and appropriate)
- relationships (suggesting ways to develop and maintain relationships with tribal and cultural authorities)
- staffing and training (urging measures to ensure Maori staffing and the appreciation of a Maori perspective).

The report was accepted, and the Department of Social Welfare has worked on implementing its recommendations. Not all of these have survived the 1990 change of government from Labour Party to National Party (in particular, the Social Welfare Commission has been terminated). In addition, staffing objectives have been difficult to fulfil in a period which has seen staff cuts in response to government privatization and restraint policies. The legislative objectives have been fulfilled, and new structures include the Maori extended family, tribe, and community in decisions on the welfare of their children. To assist in ensuring a continued Maori perspective, a Maori-staffed internal research unit has been established.

Children, Young Persons and Their Families Act, 1989
A review of the Children and Young Persons Act, 1974, had begun before the work of the Ministerial Advisory Committee on a Maori Perspective commenced. Drafts of the new legislation showed that the committee had not incorporated a bicultural understanding of practice into its proposals. These drafts were rejected, and a new bill, with two distinctive features to permit more culturally appropriate responses, was proposed. These features were the family group conference and the approval of the functioning of iwi authorities under the act.

Under the Children, Young Persons and Their Families Act, 1989, a family group conference is required before a court hears a child welfare complaint or a juvenile correction case. The function of the conference is not only to ensure that the family is consulted but also, wherever possible, to enable the complaint or juvenile justice matter to be dealt with by the family rather than by the court. The process involves convening extended family members (and paying their expenses to enable them to convene). The family is provided with an opportunity to make alternative provision for the welfare of the child or youth, for which it can obtain assistance from the Department of Social Welfare.

The family group conference was the focus of intense evaluation during the first year of its operation. It was credited with changing placement plans in 30 out of 180 cases that were studied. In each case, as a result of the conference, more use was made of care by the extended family.[24] In addition, the introduction of the family group conference process reinforced a style of practice that was family-centred and diversion-oriented. This, it is thought, has had a significant effect on reducing the number of cases subject to protection actions.[25]

The Competency Certification Project
The Competency Certification Project is the latest example of the change in thinking and practice which is occurring within the Department of Social Welfare. In this project, teams of Pakeha, Maori,

and Pacific Islander social workers are working to establish competency, training, supervision, and assessment procedures appropriate to the members of their respective communities. The Department Corporate Plan, 1990-1, notes: 'Although there will be a great deal of overlap in definitions and procedures, this recognition of difference is an important part of the Department's commitment to the provision of bicultural services consistent with the direction of Puao-te-Atatu.'[26]

The Maori team articulated a philosophy and code of practice based on the concept of tino rangatiratanga, 'control over what is defined as knowledge – ensuring that such knowledge is primarily of benefit to Maori people with regard to effective and competent social work service.'[27] The code of practice based on this principle is characterized by collective responsibility; tribal autonomy; asserting the mana (power) of iwi, hapu, and whanau (traditional tribal and family structures); being consistent with tribal development and delivery; and being consistent with developing and maintaining a flow of information and consultation with tribes and other significant groups.

Neither the Adoption Act, 1955, nor the new Children, Young Persons and Their Families Act, 1989, are consistent with this philosophy. Maori consider the Adoption Act to be totally offensive due to its emphasis on secrecy, private choice by the mother, and unknown genealogy. The Children, Young Persons and Their Families Act is better, as it does provide the means, through the family group conference, to involve the family; but this stops short of the transfer of power necessary to accord with the Treaty of Waitangi. An example of the concern of the competency project's Maori staff is provided in the following extract from their draft report on the subject of private adoptions:

> Inappropriate 'private' adoption placements are being facilitated where couples are put in touch with birth mothers by friends, doctors, hospital staff and the like. Maori practice is – to counsel birth mothers against such placements – to advise prospective adoptive parents that the placement will not be sanctioned in our report to court – to encourage whanau in retrieving these children.
>
> This practice is controversial and unfortunately some Maori babies will slip through the net. However, in order to obtain some equity for Maori people we feel we must continue to advocate for the values and

principles that Maori hold dear until such time as the injustices which impact so greatly on Maori whanau/hapu/iwi are eliminated.[28]

Other examples could be given.

The project staff committee also deal with assessing who is competent to work with Maori people as well as with how to make that assessment. Its proposal is that the prospective social worker should be assessed (on the basis of observation, written work, and oral presentation) by the community with whom he or she will be working. The prospective worker should be presented to the community by people who can speak for him or her and who would attest to whether or not they 'are ... willing for this social worker to be working with "their own" i.e., families in their community, whanau.'[29]

The work of the Competency Certification Project was not yet complete in 1991. These examples are provided to show how the Maori team within the Department of Social Welfare was seeking support for an alternative approach to social welfare practice. Whether or not approval will be given will show the extent to which the department is prepared to recognize a new and different Maori practice based on the principles of the Treaty of Waitangi and of the Puao-te-Ata-tu Report.

Summary

Together, the six changes just mentioned affect the conduct of family and child welfare practice through the two basic strategies of independent Maori development and mainstream agency modification. The first strategy is represented by Te Kohanga Reo, by the Waitangi Tribunal finding on Te Reo Maori, and by the Maatua Whangi initiative. Each of these changes is designed to strengthen Maori culture and institutions. The second strategy is represented by Puao-te-Ata-tu, by the Children, Young Persons and Their Families Act, 1989, and by the Competency Development Project. These changes are aimed at making the behaviour of the mainstream child welfare agencies more culturally appropriate. The first set of strategies is the most fundamental, as it aims at strengthening Maori institutions and is based on the resources and commitment of Maori people. The second set of strategies is more closely related to the statutory requirements, more understandable to Pakeha ways of thinking, and, in the end, is part of an overall strategy in which control remains in Pakeha hands. Both sets of strategies differ considerably from the integrated approach to social welfare policy and practice which was evident up to the mid-1980s.

Since 1981, there has been a significant reduction in the number of child welfare protection cases taken before the New Zealand courts (see Table 7.6).

Table 7.6

Child welfare protection complaints, total and Maori, 1981-6

Year	Total complaints	Complaints concerning Maori	% Maori
1981	2,531	1,246	49.2
1983	2,037	921	45.2
1985	1,374	708	51.5
1986	1,274	501	39.3

Source: Department of Justice, Family Court Statistics

Maori people to whom I spoke while in New Zealand welcomed this evidence of change in the mainstream system but insisted that real change in behaviour could only come from within the Maori community itself. When the Maori community has full control of its affairs, it is held, there will be a real improvement in the care of Maori children. The non-Maori systems can back away from the damage they have done, but they cannot generate the healing that is necessary for the Maori community to recover the collective ability to care for its own.

The changes in child welfare policy and practice in New Zealand fall far short of providing the Maori community with 'full control of its affairs.' Under pressure from the Maori community, the New Zealand government has sought ways to give contemporary meaning to the Treaty of Waitangi while retaining sovereignty and final parliamentary authority. The result is a continuing struggle between two cultures that is evidenced in shared institutions as well as in culturally specific institutions. The Pakeha are no longer in full control of the development of social policy in New Zealand, but the Maori still have a long way to go to gain equal power.

As in Australia and Canada, family and child welfare policy in New Zealand has been carried out within the general framework of social relationships between immigrant and aboriginal peoples. The recognition given to Maori sovereignty in the Treaty of Waitangi provided, and still provides, the Maori with a basis for the recognition of their interests – a basis which the aboriginal peoples of Australia and Canada lack. However, the treaty is only a starting point for a process of dialogue and compromise, and, at times (as in the period of service integration following the Hunn Report), it has been largely disregarded in New Zealand social policy. In the present period, the Treaty of Waitangi gives added force to the cultural and political reality of a Maori community sufficiently organized to assert direct influence on the development of social policy.

8
Similarities and Differences among Australia, Canada, and New Zealand

Chapters 2, 4, and 6 document the main features of aboriginal social policy in Australia, Canada, and New Zealand, respectively. Chapters 3, 5, and 7 focus on those family and child welfare measures which have aimed to mould some or all of the next generation of aboriginal children to the ideals of the European society around them in Australia, Canada, and New Zealand, respectively. The purpose of this chapter is to compare and contrast the similarities and differences between the three countries' policies towards aboriginal peoples. The following subjects have been chosen for examination: (1) the objectives and phases of social policy; (2) the labelling of aboriginal peoples; (3) the principal institutions of government policy; (4) the separation of children from their parents; (5) the effects of regional and demographic differences; and (6) the recovery of Aboriginal, First Nations, and Maori peoples. The first three subjects provide a general comparison of assimilation policies, while the second three subjects provide specifics of the family and child welfare fields in which these policies were applied.

Objectives and Phases of Social Policy

A prominent feature of the comparison of the aboriginal social policies of Australia, Canada, and New Zealand is the similarity of their objectives and of their major policy periods. In each of these countries, policy has been consistent for up to a hundred years and then has changed within ten years. These changes can be understood in the overall context provided by Michael Banton's *Race Relations*.[1] Banton distinguishes six orders of race relations which exist after initial contact. They are: (1) 'institutionalized contact,' which occurs when two peoples first meet and establish some trading relationships between each other; (2) 'acculturation,' which occurs when two peoples intermarry and develop institutions with roots in both societies; (3) 'domination,' which occurs when one society takes control of the other; (4) 'paternalism,' which occurs when one society governs the other in what it views as being the other's best interest; (5) 'integration,' which occurs when single institutions are developed and racial or ethnic origin ceases to be recognized; and (6) 'pluralism,' which occurs when more than one ethnic group is recognized as having a right to continued recognition. The principal race relationship stages used in this examination include all those identified by Banton except acculturation. Of these, domination, paternalism, and integration all occur within the general framework of assimilation. The 1837 House of Commons Select Committee on Aborigines was deeply influenced by its understanding of institutionalized contact and domination. It had a formative influence on paternalism and a major influence on the policy of integration. Only in the present movement towards pluralism are the effects of the committee's views finally being displaced.

Institutionalized Contact
The 1837 House of Commons Select Committee on Aborigines conducted its work at a time when the initial forms of institutionalized contact had been established as European settlements, military relationships, treaties, commercial relationships, and missions. These forms of contact differed in detail in each of the three countries, but the powerful, acquisitive, exploitative, and prosletyzing nature of the European invasion was common to all. Initial contacts between Europeans and aboriginal peoples took place over a period of a hundred years. By 1837, there were still large areas of Australia and Canada that were unexplored by Europeans, and a decision on whether or not to colonize New Zealand had yet to be made. The committee had the task of establishing an appropriate social policy for the continuing process of contact and consolidation as British influence continued to expand. The influence of the committee can be identified in the colonial correspondence of the late 1830s and 1840s and in the social policies towards aboriginal peoples that were established in each country.

Prior to the work of the committee, there had not been a unified set of social policies. Aboriginal peoples were treated as foreign, and policy towards them had been established on an ad hoc military or commercial basis. This policy had, in limited ways, recognized the sovereignty of aboriginal peoples while yet reserving the right to conquer and rule them. Policy in this period was also influenced by the competition between European countries for colonial territory and by how useful aboriginal allies might be to facilitating successful acquisitions. However, the social condition of aboriginal peoples themselves was of no importance to colonial governments.

Missionaries had regarded aboriginal peoples as pagan – as lacking both Christianity and civilization. The first social policies in each of the three countries were introduced by missionaries, as they spread the Gospel of Jesus Christ, the Saviour and Lord. The missionaries travelled widely and contacted aboriginal peoples at the same time as commercial relationships were being developed. They were often appalled by what they found (in modern terms, they experienced profound culture shock). Aboriginal peoples had customs which they considered to be idolatrous and evil; but they were equally appalled by the murder, rape, and pillage carried out by their own countrypeople.

The missionaries believed the answer to these problems was based on a dual strategy. First, the knowledge of the Gospel had to be brought to aboriginal peoples. This was to be accompanied by measures to extend European civilization, beginning with settlement and agriculture and proceeding to education and government. In each country, they saw hopeful early signs that aboriginal peoples could be prosletyzed, but there were also many examples of regression. Second, an integrated set of policies was needed to establish a more managed and orderly world – a world in which aboriginal peoples would be protected from individual abuse and from the worst forms of exploitation. This would provide the opportunity for them to learn and to conform to the ideals of civilization held by the missionaries. They could then be Christians and British subjects who, civilized in the European manner, would be equipped to exercise the full rights of citizenship. In the House of Commons select committee's view, all of this would take some time, perhaps a generation, but young aboriginal peoples were likely to adopt Christian ideals – provided they survived and were not corrupted.

The initial forms of contact established in each of the countries varied. In the case of Australia, the convict settlement had a genocidal set of policies towards Aboriginal peoples, who were scattered and organized in such a way that they could not offer a collective resistance. The select committee provided a clear set of prescriptions for the protection of Australia's Aboriginal peoples. In the case of Canada, there was an early history of commercial and military relationships between settlers and First Nations peoples. These now had to be set aside to give primary consideration to social policy. This was considered possible because the military need for alliances had passed, and because the early forms of commercial relationships were being superseded by large-scale European settlement. In the case of New Zealand, the committee's view was that the country should be a Maori sovereign territory, existing outside the range of European settlement, with contact limited to missionaries.

Domination
In each of the countries there was aboriginal resistance to the introduction of settlers, and, in each country, British domination was established as a prerequisite to the introduction of colonial government and social policy. In Australia, the frontier contact between Aboriginal peoples and settlers was brutal, as the former were considered to be racially inferior. They were dispossessed of their land without recognition or compensation, and the individual settler was aided by the police in enforcing his 'rights.' Land was granted by the Crown to the settlers, with no thought given to the rights of its original inhabitants. Those Aboriginals who were not killed or starved became refugees in their own land, 'saved' by the House of Commons select committee's recommendation for the establishment of protectors.

In Canada, First Nations peoples were believed to require careful management. The process of moving from military and commercial relationships to a relationship grounded in social policy had to be conducted with finesse, as it involved convincing First Nations peoples that it was in their interest to yield established rights in exchange for a European future. Canada was in a silent partnership with the United States in this process. Acts of genocide were more common on the American frontier, and this served as a constant reminder to Canadian First Nations peoples of the nature of European power. Outright warfare was comparatively rare in Canada, and treaties were used to confine First Nations peoples to reserves and to establish the power to dominate and to manage them. The select committee had not recommended the use of treaties, foreseeing that they could become an obstacle to assimilation; but in eastern Canada they were already in place, and on the Prairies they were useful in preparing the way for settlement. In the more remote parts of Canada, including most of British Columbia, the Yukon Territory, and the Northwest Territories, treaties were not used, and dispossession and dominance followed a pattern similar to that found in Australia.

In New Zealand, there was a short-lived attempt to use the principles of the 1837 committee as a guide to policy during the process of settlement. 'There are yet other duties owed to the aborigines of New Zealand which may be all comprised in the comprehensive expression of promoting their civilization, understanding by that term whatever relates to the religious, intellectual and social advancement of mankind.' One of these was

> the establishment of schools for the education of the aborigines in the elements of literature ... And until they can be brought within the pole of civilised life, and trained to the adoption of its habits, they must be defended in the observation of their own customs, so far as they are compatible with universal maxims of humanity and morals.[2]

The Treaty of Waitangi envisaged a social order in which protection would be extended to Maori, permitting them to retain control over their own affairs. This era ended with the commencement of large-scale settlement. The result was the Pakeha Wars of the 1860s and the establishment of British colonial dominance.

Through domination, single societies were created in Australia, Canada, and New Zealand, but they were marked by inequality between aboriginal peoples and settlers. The effectiveness of the select committee's attempt to control the settlers and to protect aboriginal peoples depended on the British government's will to impose rule on the former. This reliance on Britain passed with the establishment of independent settler governments, each of which established their own dominance over aboriginal peoples.

Paternalism
The influence of the 1837 House of Commons Select Committee on Aborigines did not end with the establishment of settler dominance; rather, that dominance enabled the settler governments to introduce the committee's policies. In Australia, these policies were introduced through the 'Protection of Aborigines' statutes which were passed in the period between 1869 and 1909; in Canada, they were introduced within the framework of the Indian Act, 1876, and its successors; and

in New Zealand, they were introduced in legislation establishing the Native Department (1861) and the Native Schools Act, 1867. Settlers, confident of their racial and cultural superiority, introduced these paternalistic policies in the 'best interests' of aboriginal peoples.

The paternalistic period lasted for a hundred years, and it included two phases: a first phase, in which the protection of aboriginal peoples was a dominant objective; and a second phase, in which assimilation was a dominant objective. Both objectives were included in the 1837 select committee's thinking, and both were present in each country's earliest expressions of aboriginal social policy. However, up until the 1920s, all three countries also assumed that their respective aboriginal peoples were dying out.

All aboriginal peoples experienced sharp population declines following contact, and the settler governments assumed that these declines would continue. Racial and eugenic theory during the late nineteenth and early twentieth century was influenced by a popularized version of the Darwinian concept of the survival of the fittest. The Europeans assumed that they were the fittest race, and that other racial groups would disappear – at least in those territories where they constituted a small minority. Table 8.1 shows estimates of the pre-contact population and the size of the known aboriginal populations from the earliest enumerations to 1986.

By the 1920s, it was apparent that the aboriginal minorities were neither dying out nor being absorbed, and, in Australia and Canada, attention shifted from policies to protect to policies to assimilate. It seemed to the administrators of aboriginal policy, and to the missionaries of the day, that a more rigorous application of the policy of assimilation was required.

The Maori people had, by the 1920s, established themselves as a politically viable component of New Zealand society. Although they were not declining in number, they appeared to be accepting European values. New Zealand was seen as a successful example of the operation of aboriginal policy. As a result, New Zealand did not resort to such harsh forms of paternalistic policy as banning traditional aboriginal customs, managing aboriginal communities through government agents, and/or separating aboriginal children from their parents.

Integration

In all three countries, paternalistic policies remained in effect until after the Second World War. In each, there was a major policy shift

Table 8.1

Aboriginal populations, Australia, Canada, and New Zealand, pre-contact to 1986

Year	Australia	Canada	New Zealand
Pre-contact estimate (year)	150,000-1,000,000 (1788)	Unknown (1871)	70-180,000 (1769) 56,049 (1851)
1881	89,659	108,000	
1891		120,000	42,000
1901	93,333	127,000	43,100
1911	80,133	105,000	49,800
1921	71,836	110,000	52,700
1931	80,721 (1933)	122,000	
1941		118,000	82,300 (1936)
1951	75,965 (1947)	136,000	115,700
1961	84,470	179,000	167,100
1971	115,953	244,000	227,400
1981	159,807	318,000	279,200
1986	227,645	711,000	295,300

Note: There are two major qualifications to be noted to the figures cited in this table. The figures given for aboriginal people were obtained in each case by local government agents rather than through direct census. This practice ended in the 1920s in New Zealand but continued until the 1960s in Australia and Canada. The early estimates in this period are all low, as contact with aboriginal peoples was not fully established. The second major qualification arises from change in the procedure through which one is recorded as aboriginal. Since the 1960s, there has been an increasing use of self-declaration as a means of indicating aboriginal descent (earlier definitions were based on proportion of descent). The use of self-declaration has resulted in higher numbers of people declaring themselves to be aboriginal and, hence, in a growing pride in aboriginal descent.
Source: Cited for each country in Chapters 2, 4, and 6

from paternalism to integration in the 1950s and early 1960s. It was then almost a hundred years since the policy of assimilation had been introduced, and it was thirty years since there had been a rigorous attempt in both Australia and Canada to use social engineering in an attempt to achieve it. By the early 1960s, general social services were no longer a matter of private philanthropy; they were now full-fledged public services. This provided each country with the opportunity to integrate aboriginal social policy with mainstream social policy. Although the buzz-word was now 'integration,' the objective was still assimilation.

In Australia, the change was evident in the repeal of the various state aboriginal protection statutes which took place during the 1960s and 1970s. Aboriginal peoples were accorded citizenship rights in 1967 and, at the same time, were incorporated into the Census of Australia. In Canada, the Indian Act, 1951, provided the legal base for the extension of provincial social services to First Nations peoples, and services were expanded as funding agreements were reached between the federal government and the provinces. First Nations peoples were also given the federal vote in 1967 without having to lose their status and rights as Indians through enfranchisement. In New Zealand, the specialized Maori services which had been established were terminated, and mainstream services were expanded to serve Maori people. No new electoral provisions were needed in New Zealand, as the Maori had been British subjects since the Treaty of Waitangi, 1840, and had had electoral rights since the Maori Representation Act, 1867.

The policy of integration marked the removal of racial origin as a base upon which to establish a separate set of social policies. However, the services which were extended to aboriginal peoples recognized neither their distinct cultures nor their endurance of a hundred-year period of paternalistic rule. The assumption of settler superiority was as much present in the extension of common services to aboriginal peoples as it had been in the assimilationst period of separate services. In the 1960s, politicians and administrators assumed that aboriginal peoples would welcome being liberated from having to rely on segregated, distinct services and from separate status. Ideally, it was thought that aboriginal peoples would soon become indistinguishable from settlers with regard to their use of public services, and that aboriginal origin would simply be one more piece of the general cultural mosaic. Assimilation would be achieved, and aboriginal peoples would become invisible in so far as public policy was concerned.

These aspirations for aboriginal peoples were not fulfilled. On the one hand, there are many examples of aboriginal peoples who resisted the use of common social services; on the other hand, once these services had been expanded, the proportion of aboriginal clients tended to be much higher than did the proportion of mainstream clients. Statistics on service use by aboriginal peoples are difficult to obtain for the 1960s and 1970s, as the policy of integration led to ethnic origin not being reflected in the statistical record. As a result, the full facts of disproportionate use only became apparent when pressure was applied by scholars and by aboriginal communities to disclose them.

Pluralism

At first, the policy of integration was rejected by aboriginal peoples because it offered no solution to the issues of land rights and territory. Common services were part of a total social policy framework which was designed to repeal all recognition, including territorial recognition, of aboriginal status as a distinct policy category. There would then be no need for special land tenure, social policy, or political institutions; racial origin and cultural heritage would be an entirely private matter. The First Nations rejection of the Canadian White Paper on Indian policy (1969) was paralleled in New Zealand by the vigorous opposition to the steps taken in 1967 to bring all Maori land within the land title system. In both countries, aboriginal peoples began to reverse the historical process of losing their land to settlers, and new claims were made based either on aboriginal title or on treaties negotiated during the first stages of the settlement process. In Australia, opposition to the loss of Aboriginal land manifested itself in the Commonwealth government preventing Queensland from varying Aboriginal land boundaries in order to facilitate mining and in establishing Aboriginal land councils in the Northern Territory.

At the same time as actions were being taken to maintain land under aboriginal control, a parallel process was under way to establish separate social rights for aboriginal peoples based on treaty obligations and distinct legal status. The establishment of new rights for aboriginal peoples marked the reversal of the policies of assimilation and integration. Whereas for a hundred years the objective of social policy had been to end aboriginal status, it is now being directed towards strengthening that status; whereas for a hundred years aboriginal peoples had their rights reduced, those rights are now being augmented; whereas for a hundred years progress was measured by the proportion of aboriginal peoples who abandoned their traditions, progress is now measured by the proportion of aboriginal peoples who are resurrecting and strengthening those traditions (as well as by governments resuming rights and obligations which had been set aside in earlier periods). Although the movement towards pluralism has begun, there is a continuing conflict between its principles and the principles of integration.

Labelling of Aboriginal Peoples

The conduct of aboriginal social policy required working definitions of aboriginal status. In the early stages of contact between the aboriginal and European societies, there was no need for definitions, as there was no intent to change aboriginal peoples. At this stage, aboriginal societies defined their own memberships and exercised their own governance. The colonial society also knew its own boundaries and was governed, sometimes loosely, from London. The relationships between aboriginal and colonial societies were defined by commerce, war, personal relationships, and missionary work. Each group had some difficulty with behaviour which was acceptable to it but not to the other group, and this led to particular problems for children of mixed marriages.

The two societies could have continued to exist alongside one another for an indefinite period, as happened on the Canadian Prairies in the seventeenth and eighteenth centuries. Here, this period resulted in people of mixed blood, the Métis, developing a society of their own. If this had occurred again in the nineteenth century, it would have accorded with Banton's definition of acculturation. However, in the nineteenth century, the British power to govern 'to the ends of the earth' was interpreted by the House of Commons Select Committee on Aborigines as entailing a responsibility to impose European civilization and Christianity upon other cultures. This imposition required that British administrators define who was and who was not an aboriginal person. This was the first step towards administering different policies and laws for settler societies and aboriginal societies, respectively. Initially, the distinction was simply based on recognition of racial difference, which, in the early nineteenth century, meant colour and lineage (often referred to as 'blood'). Europeans organized the different races of humanity hierarchically according to colour, with the white race being at the top and the darkest races at the bottom. The Australian Aboriginal was seen as lower in this hierarchy than were the lighter coloured Maori and the North American Indian. Table 8.2 provides a summary of the different approaches to defining aboriginal peoples that were used, at varying times, in Australia, Canada, and New Zealand.

In each country, a working definition of aboriginal was introduced at the start of the paternalistic period. These definitions were then modified to give more recognition to lifestyle and to simplify administration. In the integrationist period, the policy was to reduce or to eliminate the use of such definitions, while in the pluralist period, self-declaration and/or an application process have become the dominant means used to identify aboriginal status.

There are some important differences between the approaches to establishing aboriginal status taken by each of the three countries. The designation of Maori as British subjects in the Treaty of Waitangi gave them a position in civil law which prevented their being defined as tightly as were Aboriginal and First Nations peoples. It also meant that the Maori never had to undergo any special process in order to qualify for citizenship or voting rights. The New Zealand government's approach to serving Maori differently from Pakeha had to rely on geography, self-declaration, and culturally acceptable institutions; but it always had to recognize the autonomy of the individual Maori, who at all times (as a British subject) retained the right to use Pakeha services. In both Australia and Canada, the approach to establishing aboriginal status was much more rigid and harsh than was the case in New Zealand. In these countries, aboriginal peoples were defined by colonial governments and could not exercise the civil rights of full citizens until the 1960s.

Canada's use of a register to determine Indian status is in marked contrast to Australia's use of racial recognition and lifestyle to determine Aboriginal status. Both processes were arbitrary and harsh, but the Canadian process has been more durable. A major reason for this is that the register has become the basis of a jurisdictional dispute between the federal and provincial governments. As a consequence, the Canadian federal government faced provincial government opposition to any definitional changes which would have increased the latter's obligations to First Nations peoples. In the latest policy period, being defined as a status Indian has emerged as a positive symbol of cultural continuity and pride.

In the 1980s, a conflict developed between the principles of the integrationist period (in which policy did not favour the use of definitions of aboriginal origin) and the principles of the pluralist period (in which policy does favour the use of definitions of aboriginal origin – if they are the result of an individual so identifying him or herself). This conflict increases when access to particular benefits is determined by whether or not one is defined as aboriginal. In Australia, this conflict centres around access to areas reserved for Aboriginals; in Canada, it centres around the process of registration; and in New Zealand, it centres around disputes as to who has the right to be Maori.

Table 8.2

Definitions of aboriginality, Australia, Canada, and New Zealand

Policy period	Australia	Canada	New Zealand
Early institutionalized contact (pre-1860)	Racial recognition; no formal processes	Informal processes and designation of peoples by treaty to receive collective benefits	Informal process followed by designation of Maori as British subjects by treaty
Paternalism: protection period (1860-1920)	Racial recognition formalized in the power of the protector to designate a person as Aboriginal	Legal definition based on lineage and marriage rules, a register established along with concept of 'enfranchisement'	Basic rules of descent established for voting purposes; services extended for Maori on a geographic basis
Paternalism: assimilation period (1920-60)	Definitions broadened to definition based on a way of life or registration; exempt status established by formal actions	Registration dominant mode of definition; enfranchisement rules changed to remove Indian status without application	Specific Maori services provided by application; political commitment to Maori service development; some special provisions

Policy period	Australia	Canada	New Zealand
Integration period (1960-)	No definition	Registration retained and used for cost-sharing purposes on provincial services	Special provisions repealed, limited use of definition by declaration
Pluralist period (1975-)	Definition established by permissive processes initiated by the Aboriginal person and by territory	Register reopened to persons seeking to re-establish lineage	Self-declaration as 'Maori' or 'of Maori descent'; tribal definition also encouraged

In each of the policy periods, people of mixed racial background have posed many practical problems for administrators. The Australian use of lifestyle to define who is Aboriginal is one approach to this problem; the Canadian use of a register to define who is Indian is a second approach; and the New Zealand use of self-declaration to define who is Maori is a third approach. Despite what appear to be sophisticated definitions of aboriginal peoples, the fact is that police, teachers, health professionals, and social workers tend to apply them on the simplistic and racist grounds of appearance and colour. In any case, the very existence of such definitions gives formal approval to one or both of the forms of racism identified by Colin Tatz in his thesis on Aboriginal administration in Australia. These are:

> First, non-active racism or prejudice: that is, any set of beliefs that genetically transmitted differences between people, real or imagined, are intrinsically associated with the presence or absence of certain socially relevant abilities or characteristics. Secondly, overt or active racism: that is, activity which uses, or depends on, such differences as the legitimate basis for differential treatment of groups socially defined as races.[3]

Principal Institutions of Government Policy

The management of aboriginal social policy has required each of the three countries to develop administrative organizations with the necessary authority and resources to govern. These organizations have taken the form of departments of government, educational systems, specialized courts, and government-supported church organizations. In New Zealand, there was also early recognition of the electoral, political, and representative functions of government.

In Australia, each state developed departments of aboriginal affairs to protect the aboriginal population from complete annihilation. In Canada, the federal government was responsible for representing the British Crown in treaty relationships with First Nations peoples. In New Zealand, there was a brief attempt to honour the Treaty of Waitangi by using the Department of Native affairs as a buffer between the Maori and settler communities. This attempt lasted from 1840 to 1846. After the Pakeha Wars, a new native affairs department was established to ensure a government presence in Maori communities.

The mandate of each aboriginal affairs department was similar: they were the representatives of the settler governments, and they were to effectively manage aboriginal peoples. Each department was circumscribed by both the definition of aboriginal status and by geographic boundaries. Power was exercised through control of land, economic affairs, and daily life (see Tables 8.3 and 8.4).

Tables 8.3 and 8.4 show that, during the paternalistic period, the departments of aboriginal affairs were active in their management of the lives of aboriginal peoples; but, whereas the Australian states and the Canadian government were able to govern their wards by coercion, the New Zealand government had to govern Maori as full citizens.

In the integration period, all three countries' specialized institutions of aboriginal government were replaced by integrated institutions. The government of aboriginal land was a particularly sensitive area. The Australian state governments were able to change Aboriginal land status and boundaries without negotiation, as no tenure had ever been given; but this was not possible in either Canada or New Zealand, and attempts to extinguish residual aboriginal land rights in both countries failed. In the pluralist period, procedures have been introduced in all three countries to expand aboriginal land areas, recognize aboriginal hunting and fishing rights, and respect aboriginal self-government.

The role of organized religious institutions in the government of aboriginal peoples requires special recognition. The ideas of the 1837 House of Commons Select Committee on Aborigines were influenced by the reports of missionaries and by the lobbying of the Church Missionary Society. In each of the countries, missionaries went and lived alongside aboriginal peoples, carrying the dual message of civilization and of salvation through the Gospel. Their influence was massive. Most Aboriginals, First Nations peoples, and Maori became at least nominal Christians early on in the process of assimilation. In Australia, many of the Aboriginal settlements were pioneered by missionaries who also served as local agents of the state protectors. In Canada, the churches divided the First Nations population geographically between the major denominations. Once established, these denominational divisions were preserved and administered by the Department of Indian Affairs. The churches were also contracted by the department to provide residential schools. On the west coast of Canada, the churches established model communities inhabited only by Christianized First Nations peoples and organized as theocracies.

Church organization in both Australia and Canada was centralized

Table 8.3

Government of aboriginal land, Australia, Canada, and New Zealand

Policy period	Australia	Canada	New Zealand
Early institutionalized contact (pre-1860)	No recognition of Aboriginal land use; Australia considered vacant	Treaties used to set the boundary between the settler society and the aboriginal society	Maori sovereignty recognized over all of Aotorea (North Island)
Paternalism: protection period (1860-1920)	Limited land holdings set aside for mission use as refuge areas to which Aboriginals could be sent	Title to reserve land held by federal government; department assumes powers of land owner to control use	Maori land confiscated after land wars; Maori Land Court established to ensure sale of Maori land to settlers
Paternalism: assimilation period (1920-60)	Land in Aboriginal communities retained under state control, boundaries changed by regulation, but some major areas reserved	Land use for institutions for Indians; a record of agricultural use kept as an indicator of progress	Specialized Maori agricultural and community services extended to Maori land areas

Policy period	Australia	Canada	New Zealand
Integration period (1960-)	Major reservation areas created in Northern Territory but arbitrary change in boundaries made; general state services extended	Attempt to abolish all reserves rejected; provincial authority extended to reserves; band administration strengthened	Attempt to bring last of Maori land within land title system rejected; integrated services extended to Maori communities
Pluralist period (1975-)	Recognition of Aboriginal communities and leases; in the Northern Territory land councils established	New major land agreements in North and recognition of some rights of self-government of Indian land and aboriginal resources	Waitangi Tribunal begins process of returning land to Maori control; Maori natural resource rights recognized

Table 8.4

Government of financial affairs and daily life, Australia, Canada, and New Zealand

Policy period	Australia	Canada	New Zealand
Early institutionalized contact (pre-1860)	No legal control; settlers and local police able to kill and disperse on their own authority	No legal control; respect based on mutual benefits, alliances, and ability to govern	No legal control; Treaty of Waitangi signed to permit British to control their subjects
Domination	Domination established by military, police, and settler acts of suppression	Domination established by US example and by suppression and hanging of Riel	Domination established by land wars and confiscation of Maori lands
Paternalism: protection period (1860-1920)	Aboriginal people removed to settlements by police and managed by protectors; marriage and movements subject to permission	Management of community affairs by local Indian agents; permits required for movement, assembly, and ceremonies	Maori community self-government continued, but some powers exercised by Maori Trustee

Policy period	Australia	Canada	New Zealand
Paternalism: assimilation period (1920-60)	Permit controls tightened and focused on assimilation; children raised in dormitories; adult labour contracts used; all funds held in trust	Permit controls and enforcement tightened; increased use of residential schools	Maori benefits expanded, and Maori Land Court assumes some special legal function for Maori community
Integration period (1960-)	Controls abolished and citizenship rights extended to Aboriginal people; integrated services extended to Aboriginal communities	Controls relaxed; residential schools closed; provincial education and welfare services subject to federal funding; voting rights given	Specialized Maori services abolished, and integrated community services extended to Maori areas
Pluralist period (1975-)	Some community self-government rights established and some independent Aboriginal services initiated	Communities take control of their own services under negotiated agreements	Maori community establishes independent services and demands change in mainstream services

and colonial. Aboriginal and First Nations cultures were considered pagan, and their symbols and ceremonies were denounced. Native languages were translated to assist with the task of missionaries, but their use by young people was suppressed. When necessary, the missionaries called upon the power of the state to restrict and prohibit cultural practices considered to be heathen or immoral. The Canadian Department of Indian Affairs and the Australian state protection agencies enforced these religious proscriptions.

In New Zealand, the role of the church developed along different lines. The Maori people preserved their religious autonomy, and a succession of Maori prophets provided Maori people with an alternative to the official colonial churches. Perhaps, as a result, organized churches were much less closely aligned with the state than was the case in Australia and Canada, and the Maori language continued to be used in church services. The church in New Zealand organized secondary schools, and, unlike the state primary schools, they provided the opportunity to study and use the Maori language. Attendance was dependent on the receipt of scholarships, as the churches focused on providing a new generation of Christian Maori leadership. In this, they were successful – the leadership of the Young Maori Party was largely drawn from the graduates of the church-organized secondary schools. There was no comparable achievement in either Canada or Australia.

The Separation of Children from Their Parents

The children of aboriginal peoples have received particular attention in each of the three countries. The 1837 House of Commons Select Committee on Aborigines believed that children offered the best means of ensuring that aboriginal peoples would be prepared for the responsibilities of Christianity, civilization, and British citizenship. However, educational institutions in both Australia and Canada had serious attendance problems – problems which the missionaries proposed to address by separating children from their parents for the duration of their formal education. It was soon found that this requirement would have to be enforced by the state.

In the settler communities, children were also separated from their parents; but this was done only in cases in which parents were no longer able to provide care or in cases of abuse and/or negligence. During the paternalistic period, the institutions for aboriginal children differed from those for settler children, but, in the integration period, the latter expanded to include services to aboriginal children. In each of the countries, this led to a sharp increase in the number of children in care in general and to a disproportionate number of aboriginal children in care in particular (see Table 8.5).

In all policy periods (except the earliest and, in New Zealand, the paternalistic), the proportion of aboriginal children separated from their parents was much higher than is the proportion of non-aboriginal children. Whereas, during the paternalistic period, the rates for Australian and Canadian aboriginal children separated from their parents were 200-400/1,000 (with all children being removed from some communities), the rates for children separated from their parents in the non-aboriginal community were 10-20/1,000. Whereas, during the integration period, the rate of aboriginal children in care varied from 100/1,000 in some areas of Australia and Canada to 30/1,000 in New Zealand, the proportion of non-aboriginal children in care varied from 10/1,000 in some areas of Canada to an estimate of 4.7/1,000 in New Zealand, and between 3 and 4/1,000 in Australia.

In the paternalistic period, aboriginal children were separated from their parents in Australia and Canada as part of deliberate policies of social engineering. This was accomplished through the use of special powers embodied in Aboriginal protection acts and Indian acts, respectively. In both countries, the administration could remove a child from his or her parents without the scrutiny of a court and without any cause, such as abuse, neglect, or truancy. Once removed, children were held captive, and any encouragement from their parents or relatives to return home was treated as a criminal act.

Both countries developed large specialized institutions for maintaining aboriginal children. These institutions, in the form of dormitories (Australia) and residential schools (Canada), segregated the children from their parents, from their peers of the opposite gender, and from their younger and older siblings. The use of English was enforced, and aboriginal languages were suppressed through the extensive use of corporal punishment and various forms of humiliation. The institutions were expected to use the labour of the children to reduce their operating expenses to the lowest possible level. This objective was given precedence over the educational objective, with the result that the children spent most of their time providing manual farm labour, cutting wood, baking bread, cooking, and making clothes. The level of educational achievement was low, and the working knowledge achieved from institutional labour was not transferable to any outside

Table 8.5

Separation of aboriginal children from their parents, Australia, Canada, and New Zealand

Policy period	Australia	Canada	New Zealand
Early institutionalized contact (pre-1860)	Very low numbers; children who had no known relatives cared for by missionaries	Very low numbers; separation limited to voluntary placement of Indian children in residential schools	Very low numbers
Paternalism: protection period (1860-1920)	The Protector became the guardian of all Aboriginal children; proportion of children separated from parents high; no rate data available	Authority to require school attendance in Indian Act; residential schools favoured; rates from 118 (1900) to 281 (1920) per 1,000	Maori informal child care systems remain in place; residential schools limited to voluntary attendance at secondary level
Paternalism: assimilation period (1920-60)	Management of children in dormitories was extensive; estimate of 400/1,000 (NSW, 1940), 600/1,000 (Queensland, 1940s); all known half-caste children removed	Residential schools expanded; rates up to 375/1,000 representing all school-age children in some areas of western Canada	Maori care system remains in effect in rural areas; limited use of Pakeha system in urban areas

Policy period	Australia	Canada	New Zealand
Integration period (1960-)	Dormitories closed; children removed by child welfare authorities; estimates of 100/1,000 (NT, 1970), 65/1,000 (Queensland, 1980)	Residential schools closed; children in care of provincial authorities; rates of 62.9/1,000 (1975), plus 66.5/1,000 adoptions	Rising use of Pakeha child welfare and juvenile justice systems. Estimate 31/1,000 (1980) Maori children in care
Pluralist period (1975-)	Children placed with Aboriginal authorities; adoption less frequent and children-in-care rates falling	Child welfare provided by Indian authorities in some areas; children-in-care rates fall 38.9/1,000 (1990); adoptions restricted	Development of Maori services and change in mainstream policy and legislation reduce use of integrated services

employment (with the possible exceptions of farm labour and domestic service). The children were deprived of the opportunity to learn their own aboriginal culture and its technologies, while learning only a very restricted and partial form of European culture and technology.

The children were also deprived of the influence of their parents and of the opportunity to care for their own siblings and peers. Physical and sexual abuse occurred in many of the institutions, and, thus, patterns of violence between and towards children were introduced into the parenting behaviour of the next generation of aboriginal peoples.

In both Australia and Canada the proportion of aboriginal children in institutional care was decided by the available resources. Ideally, in the view of authorities, all aboriginal children would have been in institutions. Where resources were limited, authorities used a variety of criteria to select aboriginal children for placement. In Australia, those who appeared to be of mixed Aboriginal/non-Aboriginal descent were the first to be placed because they were thought more likely to benefit and more deserving of a chance to enter the non-Aboriginal community than were full-blooded Aboriginals. In some areas of Australia, particularly in the Northern Territory, there were specialized institutions for half-caste children. In both countries, children were also sent to institutions because they were the offspring of single parents; because their parents were in ill health; because their parents asked for, or received, welfare assistance; because they were a nuisance; and/or because their parents drank. Basically, any questionable behaviour on the part of either parent or child which came to the attention of the authorities could result in a childhood being spent in a dormitory or residential school. In fact, authorities could decide to take children from their parents simply to maintain the optimum occupancy level of the institution. Although the formal objective was assimilation, internal institutional operating considerations often precluded its achievement.

In the integration period, these internal contradictions were reduced. There was no assumption that it was desirable to remove all aboriginal children from their parents; instead, in each case social workers and judges had to decide that the welfare or protection of the child required that they be removed from their homes. The proportion of aboriginal children being cared for by authorities fell sharply, but it remained much higher than did the proportion of non-aboriginal children in the same position.

Many problems appear to have contributed to the high rates of aboriginal child removal:
- Workers and courts were unfamiliar with the communities that were being served.
- Non-aboriginal values and expectations were imposed on the aboriginal community.
- Aboriginal peoples moved from their own communities to urban areas, where support for the extended family was not available.
- Alcoholism and substance abuse were common.
- In Australia and Canada, aboriginal parents had often spent their childhoods in institutions.

The major difficulty for child welfare services was neither the identification nor the assessment of problems; the major difficulty was their inappropriate response to these problems. This response was based on a paternalistic 'save the child' philosophy. Children who were removed from their parents were placed in a residential institution or foster home until an alternative long-term plan could be made. For younger children, this plan often entailed adoption by a non-aboriginal family. These responses to perceived problems of parental neglect and abuse contained no recognition of aboriginal cultures, values, extended families, communities, languages, or other relationships. And this is not surprising, for they were designed to provide non-aboriginal children with the kind of parenting that would best prepare them for life as adults in mainstream society. However, applied to aboriginal children, this objective had the same purpose and effect as did assimilation. Indeed, the principal difference between the integrationist policy period and that which preceded it was that the goal of assimilation was no longer formally espoused – it was simply assumed.

During the integrationist period, the child welfare authorities had many problems in reaching their objective of providing aboriginal children with alternative care and parenting. Many of these problems applied to all child welfare work and included: maintaining an adequate supply of foster homes; maintaining sibling and family ties; providing stability of care (most children in care undergo many different placements); preventing abuse of children within the system; developing and achieving long-term goals; providing for emotional needs; and ensuring that there is an effective guardian for the individual child. In addition, there were particular problems in caring for aboriginal children. These included: prejudice against aboriginal children (which made them more difficult to place and resulted in less continuity of placement); prejudice towards aboriginal children on entering community schools and on contacting 'natural' children in foster and adoptive homes; isolation from recognizably similar people; and the fact that the guardians, being non-aboriginal, lacked any real contact with the child's life experience.

There were many attempts to reform the child welfare system to enable it to deal with these problems, but they typically overlooked the fact that an increasing proportion of children in the system were aboriginal. Attempts to deal with the particular problems of aboriginal children by recruiting aboriginal foster parents were limited by foster home standards that catered to the non-aboriginal community. As a result, non-aboriginal parents were specifically recruited to care for aboriginal children. However, their knowledge of aboriginal life was often superficial, and contact with other aboriginal people and, particularly, with families of origin was discouraged. Thus aboriginal children lost their knowledge of their roots.

The Effects of Regional and Demographic Differences

There are three major regional and demographic factors which influenced the application of aboriginal family and child welfare policy in Australia, Canada, and New Zealand. They are: (1) the proportion of children in the aboriginal community, (2) remoteness, and (3) urbanization.

Proportion of Children in the Aboriginal Community

The proportion of children in a community is a composite of the birth rate and the infant and child mortality rates. In each of the countries, the combination of these factors meant that in the nineteenth and early part of the twentieth century the aboriginal communities had a much lower proportion of children than did the mainstream communities. This pattern persisted until the 1930s, but, in the postwar period, the birth rate has been much higher in the aboriginal than in the non-aboriginal communities, and the aboriginal mortality rate has fallen. This has resulted in the proportion of children becoming much higher in the aboriginal communities than in the mainstream communities. Table 8.6 shows this pattern in the different policy periods.

The lower proportions of children in the aboriginal as opposed to the non-aboriginal communities in the protection period contributed to the perception that the former were dying out in Australia and

Table 8.6
Children as a proportion of the aboriginal and general population, Australia, Canada, and New Zealand

Policy period	Australia	Canada	New Zealand
Paternalism: protection period (1860-1920)	Aboriginal children 24/100 (1881); non-Aboriginal children 39/100 (1881)	Indian children 22/100; non-aboriginal children 34/100 (1901)	Maori children 34/100; Pakeha children 40/100 (1891)
Paternalism: assimilation period (1920-60)	Aboriginal children 22/100 (1933); non-Aboriginal children 27/100 (1933)	Indian children 30/100; non-aboriginal children 31/100 (1931)	Maori children 40/100; Pakeha children 31/100 (1936)
Integration period (1960-)	Aboriginal children 48/100 (1971); non-Aboriginal children 29/100 (1971)	Indian children 47/100; non-aboriginal children 29/100 (1971)	Maori children 49/100; Pakeha children 29/100 (1971)
Pluralist period (1975-)	Aboriginal children 41/100 (1986); non-Aboriginal children 19/100 (1986)	Indian children 38/100; non-aboriginal children 22/100 (1981)	Maori children 34/100; Pakeha children 23/100 (1986)

Canada. On the other hand, the higher proportion of children in the aboriginal communities today is contributing to the realization that they should be recognized in the social policy of each of the three countries under study.

Remoteness

Both Australia and Canada had different policies for those areas which Europeans considered to be remote and for those areas which they considered to be worthy of settlement. The policies which have been described and compared so far are those that were applied to settled areas. In Australia and eastern Canada, these areas were defined during the nineteenth century. In the western areas of Canada, they were defined by the first decade of the twentieth century. In each case, this ended the period of initial contact; but, in the remote areas of the central and northern part of Australia and the northern area of Canada, the early phase of social policy lasted well into the middle of the twentieth century. In both cases, there were separate, intermediary forms of inter-racial society which operated during the period before the policies of protection and assimilation were fully applied. In northern Canada, this entailed the continuation of trapping and fur-trading societies (on the Prairies, such societies existed until the end of the nineteenth century). In the interior of Australia, it entailed the pastoral station. In both cases, although the settlers were in control, they needed the aboriginal peoples' labour and their knowledge of the land. While they were needed, aboriginal peoples remained on the land that they had always possessed, but their right to be there was undermined by the introduction of European forms of land tenure.

While these intermediary societies lasted, the policies for those aboriginal peoples who lived in the vicinity of settlements differed from the polices for those who lived in the rest of the territory. These policies were designed to control the aboriginal presence and were directed particularly at people of mixed aboriginal-European descent. In the Northern Territory of Australia, the homes for half-caste children at Darwin and Alice Springs were developed during this period.

During the Second World War, military interests in the remote areas of Australia and Canada led to the establishment of highways. This permitted postwar access both for resource extraction and for the extension of government administration. The termination of remote status resulted in the extension of social policy to the aboriginal peoples living in these areas.

There was a particular zeal and thoroughness to the way in which the assimilation policies of the 1950s were applied to the Northern Territory of Australia and to northern Canada. In Canada, entire communities were deprived of all their children, as they were transported long distances to attend residential institutions. Although the period of exposure to these policies was much shorter in remote areas than was the case in settled areas, the suddenness with which they appeared and the intensity with which they were applied resulted in their having a particularly harsh effect on northern aboriginal communities. This major assault on these communities in both countries continued into the integrationist period, with a higher proportion of aboriginal children being in the care of authorities in northern areas than was the case in more settled areas. As aboriginal peoples made up a high proportion of the general population in these areas, the child welfare systems came to be dominated by the issue of caring for aboriginal children. Yet the aboriginal background of these children was ignored, and the agencies attempted to operate as if they were working in a settled, non-aboriginal urban area. As the northern areas did not provide the foster homes and adoption homes that the system required, the children were sent to other areas. In Canada, this led Canadian child welfare authorities to have children adopted in the United States.

Urbanization

The urbanization of aboriginal peoples has been largely a postwar phenomenon in each of the three countries. Measures of urbanization differ, but Table 8.7 shows the trend.

The steady urbanization of aboriginal people had a significant effect on the care of children in all three countries. The movement to urban areas deprived grandparents of contact with parents and deprived parents of the support of their extended families. In addition, the non-aboriginal child welfare and juvenile justice systems were already well established in urban areas and assumed that aboriginal children should be integrated into mainstream service patterns. In all three countries, both factors contributed to the rising proportion of aboriginal children in care.

The Recovery of Aboriginal, First Nations, and Maori peoples

Aboriginal, First Nations, and Maori peoples are now recovering from the effects of intrusive social policies that were developed according

Table 8.7
Urbanized aboriginal populations, Australia, Canada, and New Zealand

Year	Australia		Canada	New Zealand	
1961	Metro	5%	Records of the Department of Indian and Northern Affairs show the proportion of Indian people living 'off reserve' rising from 15% in 1966 to 27% in 1976. These are low estimates. The records of the department only include status Indians and are incomplete for Indian people once they leave a reserve.	Urban	46%
	Urban	20%		Rural	54%
	Rural	75%			
1971	Metro	15%		Urban	70%
	Urban	29%		Rural	30%
	Rural	56%			
1981	Metro	20%		Urban	84%
	Urban	39%		Rural	16%
	Rural	41%			

Note: As the definitions of urbanization used vary among the three countries, no comparison of urbanizaton rates should be made.

to the dictates of the 1837 House of Commons Select Committee on Aborigines. The turning point came in the 1960s, when aboriginal peoples rejected the introduction of integrated policies. These policies were an attempt at a final solution to the issue of the status of aboriginal peoples – an issue that had been left as unfinished business at the time of initial European settlement.

In the field of social policy, integration meant the repeal of statutes which gave aboriginal peoples a different status from that of non-aboriginal people. The mainstream child welfare services of each country were extended, replacing the specialized statutes and institutions which had preceded them. Aboriginal peoples resisted the attempt to extinguish aboriginal land rights, and this led to their rejection of the child welfare policies that had been imposed on them in the names of both assimilation and integration. Recovery from the effects of these imposed policies entails three main tasks: (1) rebuilding roots and identity, (2) modifying mainstream child welfare policies, and (3) establishing alternative aboriginal policies.

Rebuilding Roots and Identity

In each country, aboriginal child welfare policy affects the life experience of all aboriginals. Only in the northern areas of Australia and Canada are there adults who grew up in their own cultural traditions. However, the severity of the assault on family life which occurred during the paternalist period varied greatly among the three countries. The Australian experience was particularly harsh and arbitrary, and it disrupted the families and lives of most aboriginal adults living today. The Canadian residential schools were also harsh, but the children who attended them retained memories of the families and of the communities from which they came, and most returned to those communities when they were able to do so. The New Zealand Maori were spared the direct assault on parenting that occurred when children were removed from their homes, and they were able to continue to provide for their children in a traditional manner. These differences in the life experience of aboriginal adults has had a considerable effect upon the paths to recovery in each country. In the integration period, the assault on aboriginal roots was great in all three countries.

In Australia, Link-Up is an important Aboriginal organization which assists people in locating their lost roots and in building up their identity. Link-Up provides the means to trace lineages through the maze of removals, placements, and adoption, so that adults can find their relatives and their place in Aboriginal society. Link-Up is informal and non-bureaucratic, relying on personal knowledge, visual recognition, memories, and the telephone. In Canada, the DIAND register remains central to the process of establishing one's First Nations identity. Qualifying for recognition as a status Indian still entails a lengthy bureaucratic process. There are rules as to which First Nations people are entitled to reassume Indian status, procedures to be followed on the filing of applications with DIAND, procedures for the review of applications at the band level, and a large backlog of cases awaiting processing. These policies do not apply to Métis people, who often have their own bureaucratic problems in tracing an identity which has been loosely defined and often unrecorded. In New Zealand, it is less difficult for Maori people to know from which tribe they come, as many remain in touch with their families and communities.

In all three countries, tracing one's lineage is seen by aboriginal peoples as an important step in recovering identity. It is specific ties to land, family, and tribe which determine aboriginal identity, not a general knowledge of aboriginal descent. Shared lineages, once established, require continuing attention – both to re-establish trust and to nurture mutual obligations. The Aboriginal workers at Link-Up are experts at the process of reintroducing Aboriginal people to their families. In New Zealand, Maatua Whangi is an example of another aboriginal program which serves this function.

Modifying Mainstream Child Welfare Policies
All three countries provide examples of the modification of mainstream organizations to accommodate a growing acceptance of aboriginal differences. Table 8.8 shows the major changes in legislation and administration which have been introduced in each country. In all three countries, the recognition by royal commissions of the need to change policy and legislation that affect aboriginal child welfare is an indicator of the commitment to change mainstream agency practices.

Professionals in each country are beginning to understand that the so-called normal professional practices of child welfare agencies are 'normal' only in the cultural context in which they are developed. This understanding is not restricted to dealings with aboriginal peoples and, in New Zealand, is being extended to Pacific Islander peoples. In Australia and Canada, there is a growing understanding of the importance to refugee and immigrant peoples of their respective child care practices. At the same time, there is often ambivalence as to how far one should deviate from the security provided by applying one set of standards. Although aboriginal and immigrant communities are no longer being forced to adopt mainstream standards, the latter have yet to be replaced by those developed by distinct aboriginal communities themselves. New Zealand, through the Competency Certification Project, seems to be leading in this task.

Establishing Alternative Aboriginal Policies

In addition to the aforementioned modifications to mainstream organizations, aboriginal communities are developing new approaches to family and child welfare. These are based on taking charge of the management of child welfare by re-establishing culturally appropriate and traditional forms of care. The best example of a well-established program of this type is Te Kohanga Reo in New Zealand. Te Kohanga Reo is a collective expression of the caring values of the Maori community, and it works in both urban and rural areas. Furthermore, Te Kohanga Reo is designed to be independent of mainstream grants and regulations.

Conclusion

This chapter has examined the many similarities and differences which exist among Australia, Canada, and New Zealand with respect to their aboriginal social policies in general and with respect to their child welfare policies in particular. The similarities in the main policy themes are strong and recurrent, while the differences are more often a matter of emphasis and degree rather than of kind. The aboriginal social policies of all three countries are hierarchical, with the Australian policies during the paternalist period being the most severe; Canadian policies being similar to Australian policies but providing at least some recognition of the First Nations communities from which children were removed; and New Zealand policies being mild by comparison, depending more on administrative measures and incentives than on coercion. In the integrationist period, the same descending hierarchy exists; for, although all three countries followed similar policies, the proportion of aboriginal children removed from their parents was significantly higher in Australia and Canada than it was in New Zealand. Finally, in the emerging pluralist period, New Zealand appears to have proceeded further towards developing social policies and administrative procedures which respect aboriginal values and culture than have either Australia or Canada.

Table 8.8

Modification of child welfare systems, Australia, Canada, and New Zealand

Type of modification	Australia	Canada	New Zealand
Legislative	• Incorporation of the Aboriginal Placement Principle into legislation • Prohibition or restriction of adoption of Aboriginal children • Recognition of Aboriginal Customary Law	• Provision for notice to Indian bands in child welfare legislation • Placement principles included in legislation • Agreement sections in legislation permitting Indian bands to exercise statutory powers and modify policies • Rights for adopted Indian children to obtain information on status	• Introduction of family conference procedures in the Children, Young Persons and Their Families Act 1989
Administrative	• Development of the Aboriginal and Islander care agencies • Publication of data on Aboriginal children in care • Development of the Aboriginal legal service	• Funding of Indian band and tribal councils to develop child welfare services • Publication of data on aboriginal children	• Review of Department of Social Welfare by the Maori Advisory Committee

Type of modification	Australia	Canada	New Zealand
Administrative	• Recognition of the effects of child welfare practice on Aboriginal family life in the Royal Commission on Deaths in Custody • Withdrawal of intrusive investigative policies	• Provincial Ministry, Indian Band negotiation to establish protocol on access to reserves • Development of specialized service units for Indian families • Support for the training of Indian child welfare staff • Recognition of the damage to Indian families in the Manitoba Royal Commission on Aboriginal Justice • Report of the Aboriginal Community Panel 'Liberating Our Children: Liberating Our Nation,' British Columbia, 1993	• Introduction of Maori staff into the department as Maatua Whangi workers • Development of Maori and Pacific Islander policy and evaluation units • Publication of data on Maori children • Maori and Pacific Islander reviews of social work competence • Recognition of the damage to Maori families by the Royal Commission on Social Policy

Note: This is not an exhaustive list of legislative and administrative modifications.

9
Understanding the Policy of Aboriginal Assimilation

It has been shown that Australia, Canada, and New Zealand had, in common, a general policy of aboriginal assimilation. This policy was given coherent expression in 1837, and it has been followed for 150 years. At present, there is more debate about the objectives and administration of this policy than has occurred at any point in its history; but that is not to say that it has finally been decided to replace it. Although there exist some threads of what could constitute an alternative policy paradigm, a coherent statement as to how they might come together has yet to be offered by any of the countries studied.

Family and child welfare policy has formed a coherent part of each country's social welfare system. This may be seen in the major differences between the number of aboriginal children as opposed to the number of non-aboriginal separated from their parents during the different policy periods of each country. There are also important differences between rural and urban areas as well as between the severity with which these policies were applied.

Understanding these patterns requires contributions from four related fields of study: (1) race relations, (2) colonialism, (3) ethnonationalism, and (4) social policy. Race relations provides a perspective on what took place between aboriginal and European peoples; colonialism provides an understanding of how and why first the imperial government and then the colonial governments exercised power over aboriginal peoples; ethnonationalism provides a name for aboriginal peoples' universal search for a land in which their values and cultural identities are given precedence; and social policy provides an analysis of the relationship between (1), (2), and (3) and the rights of the mainstream citizen.

Race Relations
The major phases of race relationships between aboriginal and European peoples have been outlined. However, establishing the existence of these phases constitutes neither an explanation of why they existed in particular forms in particular historical periods nor of why they changed. The literature of race relationships focuses on an understanding of: (1) changes in the concept of race, and (2) changes in the relationship between aboriginal and European peoples.

Changes in the Concept of Race
The concept of a race of people is distinctively European. Banton divides the history of thought on race into three principal phases characterized by three different meanings:

> [The first phase] from the sixteenth to the nineteenth centuries ... was that of race as lineage, to refer to a group of persons, animals, or plants, connected by common descent or origin. In this phase the main dispute was whether all humans descended from Adam and Eve. The beginning of the second phase was signalled by the use of race in the sense of type, in which the word designated one of a limited number of permanent forms. This perspective was destroyed by the discovery of the principles of natural selection which made possible an understanding of the evolutionary nature of species and subspecies ... The third phase began with studies furnishing much better descriptions of black-white relations in the United States and which in their interpretations relied upon the idea of race as an indicator of minority status.[1]

The second phase began in the 1800s but was only expressed in full form after the work of Darwin. This led to the replacement of the early ideas of race as type by the more developed idea of race as subspecies, with each subspecies being characterized by a different genetic pool and involved in a process of competitive natural selection. As a basis for public policy, although discredited due to its application by Nazi Germany, it continued in the segregationist policies of the American South until at least the 1960s and in the apartheid policies of South Africa until the 1990s.

Banton considers the third phase to have begun in the 1930s. In it, attention was paid to the role of race in establishing social divisions and to the way in which those divisions were used to benefit one race at the expense of another. Whereas in the second phase it was assumed that differences in the social positions of various races were determined by genetics, in the third phase they were believed to be determined by economics and sociology.

The changing order of race relationships between aboriginal and European peoples has been influenced by the aforementioned phases in the history of the concept of race. The first phase was essentially egalitarian. The missionaries held this view (as did the 1837 House of Commons Select Committee on Aborigines), and they set about the task of bringing the knowledge of the true God and of European civilization to the members of those races who had been, as they saw it, less fortunate than themselves. European superiority was unquestioned and was ascribed to early exposure to Christianity, education, hard work, technical achievement, and military prowess. Other peoples could and would, it was expected, learn from Europeans and establish similar societies for themselves.

The second phase was non-egalitarian, deterministic, and competitive. Each of the races was seen as distinguished by differences of physical and mental capacity. Furthermore, the process of competition between the races was rationalized as serving the function of improving the overall genetic quality of the species. During this period, it was reasonable to assume that the members of different races should have different relationships to the European race. Europeans placed themselves in the position of being the genetically superior race and assumed that, in the course of time, the process of natural selection would lead to the disappearance of aboriginal peoples, particularly where their numbers were low. These ideas contributed to both the protective phase of paternalistic policy and to the idea that aboriginal peoples were dying out.

The third phase relied on sociology and economics. A race of people was identified as being a recognizable social group which occupied a distinct position in the social structure – a position which could be understood in terms of social and economic roles and group history. This phase was egalitarian in that it provided no normative justification for the existence of racial inequalities. Differences in the social positions of different groups were not ignored, but their origins were ascribed to the functions they performed in society rather than to genetics. This phase has supported several forms of social policy. For example, in the assimilation period, it was assumed that with proper education the next generation of aboriginal children would be equipped for new roles in the mainstream societies and would no longer be confined to a limited social position based on their heritage; in the integration period, it was assumed that if a single set of mainstream services served all people equally, then interest in perpetuating distinctions and differences would wane; and in the pluralist period, it was assumed that all cultures should be treated with respect, that a commitment to equity requires that common policy be built on a consensus, and that each culture should have the opportunity to assert those matters in which differences between it and the mainstream society within which it is located need to be maintained.

Adoption of the sociological view of race eroded earlier notions of superiority (i.e., those based on either culture or genetics). It encouraged the respectful treatment of difference, but it did not address the political process through which earlier views were set aside. Thus, although informed opinion has changed, there is ample evidence of the persistence in popular culture of first- and second-phase views on the nature of race – these are now usually referred to as examples of racial prejudice or racism.

Changes in the Relationship between Aboriginal and European Peoples
Although aboriginal peoples often treated European newcomers as guests, the latter viewed the countries that they entered as territories to be seized and developed. The inevitable consequence was that relationships became competitive. Competition began as soon as there were two or more people, each of whom considered him or herself to have a justified claim on a single object. Typically, both aboriginal and European cultures had laws and conventions which determined those forms of competition which were legitimate and those which were not. However, when these two cultures met, the rules of one were contradicted by the rules of the other. This led to a situation in which the members of both cultures felt able to treat the members of the other as outlaws, and, at that point, violence became inevitable.

Racial differences exacerbate competition because they provide an easily recognized boundary between the members of specific groups. Banton believes that the various orders of race relations (e.g., domination, paternalism, and integration) are the 'end products of relations conducted at the interpersonal level.'

> The central argument can be stated very simply. It is that competition is the critical process shaping patterns of racial and ethnic relations.

Competition varies in both intensity and form, since much depends upon the nature of the units which compete and the kind of market in which they compete. When members of groups encounter one another in new situations the boundaries between them will tend to dissolve if they compete as one individual with another; the boundaries between them will be strengthened if they compete as one group with another.²

For each of the aboriginal peoples, there were several sources of conflict. One occurred as a result of differing religious beliefs, another occurred as a result of differing assumptions about family and sexual relationships, and so on. However, one conflict was so central to both aboriginal and European interests that it has tended to define the relationship between both peoples: the conflict over land. From the European perspective, land was one of the three basic elements essential to all production, the other two being labour and capital. According to this view, there could be no secure economic enterprise unless ownership of land were secured. From the aboriginal perspective, the land was a collective resource which was essential to sustenance, identity, and religion.

In each of the countries there was severe conflict over control of the land. In each case, the settlers established dominance over aboriginal peoples by killing a sufficient number to ensure that those who survived would accept the former's right to sell, hold, and manage land according to their conventions and laws. However, the establishment of European domination did not end the conflict over land: in Australia, the conflict continued on the fringe of European settlements and around the property lines of European holdings, with any Aboriginal presence being defined as trespass; in Canada, First Nations peoples were confined to reserves, where mainstream land laws did not apply; and in New Zealand, although Maori lands remained under Maori control, the Maori Land Court had the power to force its sale, under defined circumstances, to settlers. By the end of the nineteenth century, Aboriginal, First Nations, and Maori peoples had been displaced from nearly all the territory that the settlers wanted; and, in each country, they were reduced to holding less than 5 per cent of the land.

In Australia and Canada, there were large, remote areas which remained under the control of aboriginal peoples until the middle of the twentieth century. There was little pressure on aboriginal peoples in these areas to assimilate, because the settlers were not able to use their land. However, when general access was established after the Second World War, there was a sudden change of social policy: these peoples were now to be prepared for integration into mainstream society.

The lands which remained in their control after settlement were very important to aboriginal peoples, but to the colonial governments they were a nuisance – a reminder that aboriginal peoples still held some land which could neither be bought by normal processes nor used for public purposes without rekindling historic conflicts. Throughout the paternalist period, small parcels of land continued to be transferred to settlers on the grounds that they were needed for public works or that aboriginal peoples were not using them. Until the 1920s, most settlers thought that residual aboriginal lands would be yielded once the people died out. When, in the 1930s, governments finally realized that aboriginal populations were actually growing, the policy of assimilation was intensified in order to extinguish the last aboriginal land holdings by absorbing these populations into the mainstream. In the 1960s, the integration periods in Canada and New Zealand were introduced, with attempts by both governments to transfer all remaining land from the control of aboriginal communities to the control of mainstream society. This would have meant replacing collective tribal ownership of land with its division into public and private property. In both Canada and New Zealand, this attempt at a final solution to the land problem came at a time when aboriginal peoples were increasing in number and confidence. The decisive aboriginal rejection of the land proposals of both governments has been followed by a renewal of aboriginal/mainstream negotiations. In the emerging pluralist period, some land has been returned to aboriginal peoples, and their indigenous rights to hunt, fish, and to have access to all Crown land has been recognized.

The Australian Aboriginal/settler land conflict has differed from those in Canada and New Zealand, as in Australia there was never any recognition of aboriginal land rights. As a result, lands reserved for Aboriginal peoples remained subject to settler control. Where some rights have been accorded to Aboriginal communities, the instrument of recognition is typically a lease or a management agreement. These are European instruments, and they have no meaning in Aboriginal cultures.

The aboriginal/settler conflict over land is not a single conflict between the Aboriginal, First Nations, and/or Maori peoples and

Europeans: it is a series of tribal conflicts, in which each aboriginal group has to advance its own claim. There were many conflicts between tribes before contact, and there are many competing claims for territory and for land rights today. These conflicts make agreement difficult, but they also serve to reinforce the separate and continuing individual identities of various aboriginal groups. The existence of these conflicts also ensures that group membership remains an important and sensitive subject. In each of the three countries, the movement towards a more pluralistic society is being accompanied by a reassertion of tribal identities and by the establishment of means of recognizing and controlling tribal membership.

The aboriginal/settler competition over land has been subject to legal action at each stage of the conflict. In both Canada and New Zealand, early laws attempted to control the transfer of land to settlers by making it legal only when the Crown was the purchaser. This was seen as a way of protecting the interests of both the seller and the purchaser. In practice, the law was frequently breached and sometimes suspended. Nevertheless, the principle that any transfer of aboriginal land to settlers was subject to the due process of law has survived. This principle supports the existence of aboriginal title – title which was recognized in Canada and New Zealand but, until recently, was denied in Australia.[3]

The conflict over land is central to the relationship between aboriginals and non-aboriginals. This conflict, which has occurred in each of the policy periods and which has served to define them, is racial. The division of peoples based on descent and culture, which occurred on contact, has been and is perpetuated and reinforced by the continuing conflict over land. Attempts to end the conflict by waiting for aboriginal peoples to die out, by assimilating them into the mainstream, and by abolishing their separate status through integration have all failed. They have failed whether aboriginals people were accorded no rights to land at all (as in Australia) or whether their rights were extinguished by 'due process of law' (as in Canada and New Zealand). Instead, aboriginal peoples are re-establishing their identities and land claims, thus contributing to a racial backlash which can be found in the public discourses of all three countries.

The conflict over land distinguishes aboriginal peoples from multicultural immigrant peoples. From the aboriginal perspective, these peoples are benefitting from the appropriation of their land. It is for this reason that attempts to treat aboriginal peoples as merely one component of a multicultural mosaic are not acceptable – even though, in some situations (e.g., discrimination in urban housing), they face the same difficulties as are faced by all visible minorities.

Thus, the competition over land provides the framework within which race relationships have been conducted, and these relationships, in turn, have determined the objectives of aboriginal social policy. Of course, the relationship between settlers and aboriginal peoples has also been marked by colonialism.

Colonialism
Race relations between aboriginal and European peoples were not conducted on an equal and respectful basis once the latter gained unquestioned dominance. At that point, they became subsumed within the numerous relationships existing between Britain and its colonies. For the European settlers, the colonial era ended in the nineteenth century, with the establishment of self-government. However, Australia, Canada, and New Zealand have all continued to maintain forms of internal colonial government vis-à-vis aboriginal peoples. It is this internal colonialism, and its links to international colonialism, that is considered in this section.

Colonialism was based on the extension of European military, economic, legislative, administrative, and social control throughout the world. J.E. Goldthorpe identifies two main waves of colonial expansion:

> During the first, from about 1500 to the early nineteenth century, Europeans conquered the Americas and wholly occupied many islands around the world; they remained confined, however, to small enclaves on the coasts of the Asian and African continents [also true of Australia and New Zealand]. From about the middle of the nineteenth century, they occupied the whole of Africa and parcelled out between them most of the continent of Asia.[4]

The first period was mercantilist, and it began with a primary interest in the extraction of wealth. This interest expanded to include the establishment of settlements and the direct exploitation of the resources of the colonial territories. The second wave was acquisitive, and competition among the colonial powers was a major factor. Territory was taken not because it was considered to be valuable but to prevent it being taken by another European power. Commercial exploitation, settlement, and missionary activity followed acquisition. The pre-eminence of British naval power in the nineteenth century ensured that Britain acquired more territory than any other European power.

Colonial administration was an extension of the administration of the mother country, and it was designed to ensure that the latter's interests were served. These interests included the establishment of a military presence sufficient to deter other powers; the establishment of markets for industrial goods; the undertaking of major works to extract mineral or natural resource wealth; the regulation of land and trading relationships so that commerce was both safe and predictable; and the guarantee of missionary access in order to extend Christianity and civilization.

The colonial government needed to know how indigenous peoples thought in order to avoid giving unnecessary offence and in order to conduct its business at the least cost; but it was in no way accountable to these peoples. Stewart MacPherson distinguishes three principal features of colonial administrative systems:

> First ... those systems were essentially bureaucratic ... They were systems of administration designed for control, the policies they administered were externally derived. Second, such bureaucracies produced highly centralised systems of administration. Third, the nature of colonial administration was such that virtually all real power was vested in the bureaucracy, and genuine local political institutions were either impotent or non-existent.[5]

Consider the following account of the purpose of British colonial policy in 1927:

> There can be no room for doubt that it is the mission of Great Britain to work continuously for the training and education of the Africans towards a higher intellectual, moral and economic level than that which they had reached when the Crown assumed responsibility for the administration of this territory.[6]

This description of colonialism is in full accord with the principles of paternalistic aboriginal policy which were followed from the late nineteenth century until after the Second World War.

After the Second World War, there were two waves of independence. In the first, which occurred in the late 1940s, India and some of the countries of Southeast Asia established their independence; in the second, which occurred in the 1960s, the other countries of Southeast Asia as well as those in Africa and the South Pacific established their independence. Each wave of independence was preceded by a period of disorder and/or terrorism which tested the ability of the colonial power to establish military control. The colonial response was strongest in those countries where there was a substantial settled European population (e.g., South Africa and Rhodesia). The result was that colonialism was clearly identified with the maintenance of European interests and with the denial of human rights to non-European peoples.

By the 1960s, Australia's, Canada's, and New Zealand's internal departments of Aboriginal, Indian, and Maori affairs, respectively, were viewed as antiquated remnants of the colonial era. Furthermore, as members of the United Nations and the British Commonwealth, the newly independent former colonies were critical of those countries which maintained a system of internal colonialism vis-à-vis aboriginal people. South Africa provided a particularly offensive example of such policies in the form of apartheid.

Article 9 of the UN's International Convention on the Elimination of all Forms of Racial Discrimination required that signatories provide biannual reports on the measures they were undertaking to eliminate racism. Since 1972, this has included a report on:

A. Information on the legislative, judicial, administrative or other measures which give effect to the condemnation of racial segregation and apartheid and to the undertaking to prevent, prohibit and eradicate all practices of this nature in territories under the jurisdiction of the reporting State.
B. Information on the status of diplomatic, economic and other relations between the reporting State and the racist regime of South Africa, as requested by the committee in its general recommendation III of 18 August 1972.[7]

The effect of these international actions was compounded by domestic political action in Australia, Canada, and New Zealand – action which led to each of them eliminating political, commercial, cultural, and sporting ties with South Africa.

Yet the policies which these three countries had directed towards Aboriginal, First Nations, and Maori peoples had many similarities to the internal colonial policies of South Africa.[8] Nonetheless, it was believed that this potentially embarrassing situation had been averted through the introduction of the policy of integration during the 1960s. (In Australia, the government of Queensland resisted this sudden change of policy and continued to follow the policy of assimilation until 1984, causing considerable embarrassment to the Commonwealth government.) However, a serious objection to the policy of integration was that it was imposed on aboriginal peoples without consultation. In fact, the policy of integration was, itself, a further exercise of internal colonialism, and it was made possible by the development of new forms of social policy administration (under the name of the 'Welfare State') in the postwar period.

The rejection of the policy of integration by the aboriginal peoples of Australia, Canada, and New Zealand came as a great surprise to the respective governments of those countries, as they had believed they were giving aboriginal peoples all the benefits of being just like Europeans, including full membership in a modern welfare-state society – a society characterized by equal opportunity for all. This satisfied early UN formulations, for, in former colonies, such policies were accompanied by the establishment of independent governments. However, for internal aboriginal minorities, there were many problems with this vision of postcolonial society:

- Aboriginal concern for land rights was again being ignored.
- Aboriginal identity as separate, indigenous peoples was being denied.
- The cultural forms of health, education, social welfare, and government being offered were entirely European.
- Positions of power and control in the integrated society were all in the hands of the Europeans.
- Aboriginal peoples could never be more than a small minority interest in the political processes of government.

For all these reasons, the policy of integration failed; and there is now incremental movement towards a policy of accommodating the interests of aboriginal peoples within a pluralistic society. Colin Tatz, writing in Australia in 1972, captured the dilemma of the European settlement governments:

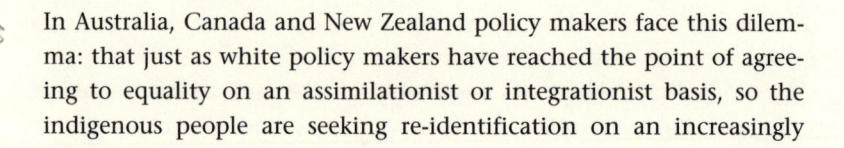

> In Australia, Canada and New Zealand policy makers face this dilemma: that just as white policy makers have reached the point of agreeing to equality on an assimilationist or integrationist basis, so the indigenous people are seeking re-identification on an increasingly

separatist basis ... Separatism is not segregation ... it is the demand that Maoris, Indians, and Aborigines become legitimate participants in the decision making processes and in the institutions of society, and not simply the recipients of what white society determines for them. It is a demand that equal participation is compatible with the retention of cultural forms they see as worthy and valuable, not the souvenir forms that whites perceive as worthy.[9]

Since 1972, each of the three countries has made some progress towards the eradication of internal colonialism. However, each is still a long way from replacing the colonial principle that Europeans have the right to rule with the principle that aboriginal peoples have the right to govern themselves.

Ethnonationalism

Michael Levin defines both the objectives and dilemmas of ethnonationalism as follows:

> The ideal of a state for every people is a prime mover in late twentieth century politics. In uniting in one concept a goal of such apparent simplicity and an ideal of universal application, it has achieved an incomparable capacity to capture the popular imagination and to promise a satisfying national autonomy. This capacity is matched only by the intractability of ethnonational issues and the elusiveness of solutions on the ground ...
>
> The demand of a state for every people is the strong sense of ethnonationalism, the extreme political expression of cultural identity. Reconciling the strong version of this ideal with the institutional realities of a state for every people is, however, a practical impossibility. That there are far fewer states than ethnic groups makes the depth of the attachment to the ideal and the sense of deprivation in its frustration all the more poignant. The politics of ethnonationalism worldwide draws its importance not from this disproportion of numbers, but from the fact that more than half the governments of these independent states must deal with political claims made on an ethnic basis where there are few if any workable solutions ....
>
> Acceptance of the right to self determination – the weak sense of ethnonationalism – also presents problems, since it leaves unattended the question of what forms of institutional autonomy can meet the aspirations of 'people' for autonomy ... New political forms which

offer autonomy without sovereignty are difficult to imagine. Furthermore, any new solution bears the burden of achieving acceptance without a history to give it legitimacy.[10]

Whereas the discussion of race relations indicated some of the underlying conflicts between aboriginal and European peoples during different policy periods, the discussion of colonialism indicates the forms of policy and administration which were used to govern aboriginal peoples. These have changed during the postwar period, following both international pressure and the actions of aboriginal peoples. Each change has also led to modifications in the form of internal colonialism applied to aboriginal peoples within the settler societies of the British Commonwealth.

The direct form of internal colonialism, as administered through a department of native affairs, was discredited by its similarity to rule by the British Colonial Office. It was replaced by a concealed form of colonial rule, using common, mainstream agencies which were based in one culture and which ignored the cultures of aboriginal peoples. Both were solutions based on European ideas of the day. But the problem with all the colonial methods of relating to aboriginal peoples was that they were imposed; they did not and could not satisfy the fundamental aboriginal demand for recognition.

In the postcolonial world, these fundamental demands are accepted as legitimate, but either the means or the will to give substance to them is lacking. The aboriginal peoples of Australia, Canada, and New Zealand watched the aboriginal people of former European colonies take control of their own governments in the 1940s and 1960s. If the people of Fiji and Samoa could govern themselves as independent nations, it was difficult to see why the Maori of New Zealand could not manage their affairs. If the Inuit people of Greenland could be independent of Denmark, then why could the Inuit people of the Canadian arctic not have their own territory and government?

Where an aboriginal nation maintains a dominant position in a separate territory, an ethnonationalistic form of internal decolonization is possible. However, in Australia, Canada, and New Zealand, aboriginal and settler territories and peoples are closely interwoven, and aboriginal peoples are searching for other, not yet clear solutions to their claims. Social policy is one area in which this search is taking place, and, within it, family and child welfare policy provides a specific locus for examination.

Social Policy

The British sociologist T.H. Marshall, in the 1950 essay 'Citizenship and Social Class,'[11] showed that citizenship had three principal components: (1) civil, (2) political, and (3) social. Marshall's view is summarized by Ramesh Mishra:

> The first refers broadly to guarantees of individual liberty and equality before the law; the second to political enfranchisement – the right to vote and to seek political office; the third, a good deal less specific than the other two, comprises a 'modicum of economic welfare and security' and the 'right to share to the full in the social heritage and life of a civilised being according to the standards prevailing in the society.'[12]

Citizenship and, specifically, the extension of social rights through citizenship, links the policy of assimilation with general social policy.

In New Zealand, the Maori were guaranteed the rights of citizenship through the Treaty of Waitangi. Maori were always equal before the law; political rights were made available to them through the Maori Representation Act, 1867; and social rights were made available to them in the 1920s and 1930s through the actions of the Young Maori Party and the Ratana Movement, both of which were able to successfully argue that Maori were entitled to the same level of services as were other New Zealand citizens.

In contrast, the Australian Aboriginal did not have status as a citizen. As a result, equality before the law was not available, and much of the early legal debate in Australia concerned the terms under which the testimony of Aboriginal peoples could be considered as valid in the operation of criminal law. When a form of citizenship was extended to Aboriginal peoples under the terms of the state protection statutes, it was qualified to such an extent by restrictions on residence, employment, and civil rights that they were effectively precluded from enjoying the benefits of Australian society. Even if the Aboriginal person lived outside the Aboriginal community, he or she was subject to a different law than were non-Aboriginal people, and he or she could be 'removed' at the discretion of either the police or the protector.

In Canada, the citizenship status of a First Nations person was defined in the Indian Act, 1876. This act established a series of limits on the citizenship rights of First Nations peoples, including provisions for receiving the 'evidence of non-Christian Indians' and provisions for 'enfranchisement.' Enfranchisement provided a method through which individual First Nations people could become full citizens, but to do so it was necessary for them to renounce their legal identity as Indians and to prove that their lifestyles and educational levels were similar to those of Europeans. Until these steps had been taken, they were subject to a different law than were non-First Nations peoples and did not enjoy full citizenship rights.

In both Australia and Canada, civil rights were restricted, and there was no provision to ensure the political rights of aboriginal peoples. Social rights, when they were created for non-aboriginal peoples, were frequently provided in a form that explicitly excluded their extension to aboriginal peoples. The assumption was that aboriginal peoples were second-class citizens who needed a period of management and tutelage before they would be ready to be full citizens. The form of this tutelage was decided upon by the Australian and Canadian governments without the participation of aboriginal peoples.

For the non-aboriginal population, social rights were developed in all three countries between the late nineteenth century and the 1950s. Although none of the countries adopted the British Poor Law, it and its proposed alternatives were an important source of their respective ideas. Each of the countries tended to look to Britain for advice, and each was attracted to many of the features of the postwar welfare state which Britain had developed as a social contract between the citizen and the state. As a result, the patterns of social security and social welfare established in all three countries had major similarities to one another. By the early 1960s, each country had become a welfare state and had established a set of economic and social policies which provided social security for their citizenry. These policies were seen as essential to modern society – a society in which many traditional forms of personal security had been lost as a result of industrialization, affluence, and urbanization. These social welfare policies were considered to be both desirable and inevitable, as they were believed to provide the best available solution to the social problems caused by industrialism and capitalism. Through the welfare state, every citizen was promised equality of opportunity, insurance against problems of income loss, universal medical care, and services to assist with family and child welfare.

At a theoretical level, the welfare state was viewed both as functionally necessary to a developed industrial society and as an expression of the moral values of fairness, tolerance, and social justice. The welfare state rested on the proposition that it was the role of government to redistribute economic resources from those who were able to participate in the economy to those who were not. Redistribution was based on public policies established by elected governments. Thus, as Marshall observed, the integration of social rights with citizenship rights was a logical conclusion of burgeoning civil and political rights.

In the postwar period, the welfare state was considered to function as a social safeguard against either the reoccurrence of fascism or the further extension of communism. In testimony to royal commissions in both Australia and Canada (which have been cited in earlier chapters) and to the Hunn Report in New Zealand, a coherent argument was made for the full extension of all welfare state benefits and services to aboriginal peoples. MacPherson summarizes the prevailing view of economic and social progress as being characterized by 'an acceptance of the inevitability of traditional organization breaking down, active substitution of organized services for informal support, and the assumption that progress is to be measured in terms of the establishment of more and more organized social services.'[13]

Given this widespread consensus of informed opinion, the expansion of common social services to include aboriginal peoples was seen as beneficial to all. In both Australia and New Zealand, this expansion was completed during the 1970s, and, in Canada, a network of federal/provincial agreements was developed to approximate, in so far as possible, the principle of equality of services with respect to First Nations peoples.

The consensus of informed opinion was not to last. By the time services were being extended to aboriginal peoples, the concept of the welfare state was being challenged. The benign view of the welfare state was criticized by conservative thinkers and politicians who believed that its policies rewarded laziness, lacked foresight, and were inefficient. At the same time, Marxist critics of the welfare state viewed social welfare policy as continuing a framework of social control which prevented a fundamental restructuring of power and wealth. By the 1970s, public opinion was increasingly disenchanted with the welfare state, and, as a result, its development stopped short of the 1960s goals of a guaranteed annual income and a comprehensive set of universal social services. Instead, the social welfare services of each of the three countries are now less confident that they offer a solution to social problems, are under review by conservative critics, and are under pressure to ensure that services are delivered only to those who qualify by meeting very specific criteria.

In each of the countries, the policy of integration led to aboriginal peoples receiving proportionately more services than did non-aboriginal peoples. This could be viewed as progress, since access to service was obviously not being withheld. However, it was also viewed as an indicator of the disadvantaged position of aboriginal peoples and of the extent to which European services were intruding on aboriginal institutions. In all three countries, aboriginal peoples and their representatives adopted the latter view.

The present period of aboriginal social policy development is responding both to the concerns of aboriginal peoples and to the conservative and Marxist criticisms of the welfare state and its services. The development of pluralist views of welfare based on ethnonationalist aspirations is encouraged by the loss of confidence by mainstream agencies and by the conservative reaction against service costs.

Family and Child Welfare Policy and Practice

Family and child welfare policy and practice have been important components of aboriginal social policy in each of the policy periods. Children were and are seen as providing the opportunity to mould the next generation so that it will conform to the ideals of those who are making social policy. In each of the periods, there have been major differences between the theory informing these policies and their actual practice.

In both Australia and Canada, the objective of paternalistic social policy was motivated by 'good intentions.' Aboriginal peoples needed protection, and the argument that they should be prepared for participation in the competitive settler societies seemed reasonable. The forms of social policy which were available to attain this objective consisted of a separate legal status and separate institutions. For families, this meant that officials had the power to take aboriginal children away from their parents and confine them for most of their childhood to either dormitories or residential schools. The model of practice followed was, essentially, industrial (i.e., the workhouse). Aboriginal children were to be educated so that they would forget their origins and become European. The policy was carried out by people, many of them from the organized churches, who believed that they were doing good. In most cases, they did care for 'their native children,' but they had very little cause for satisfaction with the results of their efforts. Upon leaving these institutions, a few aboriginals were assimilated; some lived as fringe-dwellers on the margins of settler society, dependant on mainstream welfare institutions; and most returned eventually to the aboriginal communities from which they came.

A substantial part of the reason for this failure lay in the continuing racist nature of the societies which aboriginal peoples tried to enter. The graduates of the dormitories and/or residential schools were still Aborigines/Indians to mainstream Australian and Canadian society, respectively, and so were treated in accordance with the dictates of mainstream stereotypes. Inevitably, most were drawn to the company of other aboriginal people who had had the same experience. And the residential schools and dormitories themselves were failures, for they did not provide acceptable environments within which to raise children. Mainstream societies used such institutions to deal with juvenile delinquency, loss of parents, and child abuse. These non-aboriginal institutions had all the same problems as did the residential schools/dormitories when it came to transferring institutional experience to the community and attempting to control internal abuses and excessive forms of punishment. Even in mainstream communities, it was recognized that an institutionalized childhood was the least desirable basis upon which to prepare for adult life.

The same problem reappeared in the integrated social services which were introduced in the 1960s. The policy that all citizens should enjoy access to universal services of good quality seemed unassailable to those who argued strenuously for its extension to aboriginal peoples. They were sure that child welfare was possible through the exercise of professional judgement on the part of social workers, teachers, and health officials. And, of course, situations were always subject to court scrutiny in cases where human rights needed to be set aside in a child's best interest. Yet, again, this policy seemed to perpetuate the problems of the aboriginal peoples rather than to solve them. In part, this can again be ascribed to mainstream racism, but this does not explain the failure to provide a secure alternative childhood to non-aboriginal children. Despite much effort, with respect to both aboriginal and non-aboriginal children, professionals were simply unable to replicate a supportive family environment in order to provide them with a sense of security. Unfortunately, with respect to aboriginal children, it was much easier to prevent the transmission of their language and culture than it was to provide them with viable alternatives. The pattern of institutionalized behaviour established in childhood tended to reoccur in adulthood in the form of higher incarceration rates in criminal institutions and in depressive patterns of behaviour characterized by high rates of suicide and substance abuse.

In the 1980s, there were signs that these lessons had finally been learned. The mainstream organizations in all three countries began to listen to aboriginal peoples, who were reasserting their identity and their right to control the upbringing of their children. They were supported in this position by Article 30 of the UN's 1989 Convention on the Rights of the Child, which reads:

> In those States in which ethnic, religious or linguistic minorities exist, a child belonging to such a minority or who is indigenous shall not be denied the right, in community with other members of his or her group, to enjoy his or her own culture, to profess and practise his or her own religion, or to use his or her own language.[14]

In Australia, Canada, and New Zealand, the mainstream social welfare organizations (the primary organs for imposing welfare state services on aboriginal peoples) were modified, in varying degrees, to recognize the continued existence of aboriginal peoples. At the same time, the aboriginal peoples in all three countries developed at least some services of their own. This has entailed a radical redefinition of social policy objectives – objectives which now recognize the right of aboriginal peoples to exist and to prepare their future generations to be proud of their cultures, parents, and status.

Conclusion

The attempt, during the last 150 years, to apply European social policy to aboriginal peoples must be considered a failure. The failure is obvious, as none of the policies achieved any of its primary objectives of protection, assimilation, or integration. The reasons for failure were many, but principal among them were: the assumption of European racial superiority; the colonial attitude, which resulted in the imposition of policy without consultation; and the inability of professional practice to mould aboriginal children. In the place of these failed social policies, an alternative set is being developed. Its principal tenets are:

- Aboriginal cultures are recognized as having integrity and as deserving of respect.
- Aboriginal peoples have the right to change and to adapt European ideas to their cultures.
- Aboriginal peoples have the right to the legal and material resources needed to ensure that alternative social policies will be effective.

Whereas earlier policies had the primary objective of ensuring that the aboriginal person could compete with Europeans, current policies have the primary objective of ensuring the continued existence of aboriginal societies. Two concepts need clarification before this vision can become a reality: (1) the nature of citizenship in aboriginal societies, and (2) the financial and legal relationship between aboriginal and mainstream societies.

Citizenship in Aboriginal Societies

Citizenship in aboriginal societies can be either a private matter determined by individual association or a public matter decided by residence and/or separate legal status. If it is a private matter, the Australian, Canadian, and New Zealand governments will need to develop universal policies and practices which show at least as much respect for aboriginal societies as they do for mainstream societies. If citizenship in aboriginal societies is a public matter, then the mainstream societies of all three countries will need to enact laws which define the right of aboriginal peoples to stay within the boundaries (whether geographic or legal) of their respective societies as well as their right to leave them.

The Financial and Legal Relationship between Aboriginal and Mainstream Societies

The financial relationship between aboriginal and mainstream societies has been conceptualized primarily as a form of welfare, determined by the need of the former. This is too limited as a basis for establishing a long-term relationship; besides, it contains a number of contradictions. One of these arises from seeing the relationship as essentially reparative and as based on compensation for past disadvantage.[15] The problem with this formulation is that its application is determined primarily by the good will of mainstream societies, which have the power to decide when the reparative bills have been paid. Another form of contradiction arises from seeing the relationship between aboriginal and mainstream societies as being based on the welfare principle of equality between people in similar circumstances. The problem with this formulation is that it ties all transfer of resources to the standards of mainstream communities.

A more secure, and certainly more fair, basis for the relationship between aboriginal and mainstream societies can be found in the former's legal right to enjoy specific benefits derived from aboriginal land rights, either in the form of a continuing right to returns from the land or through a collective right to benefits derived from a financial settlement of outstanding claims. These rights, established through the recognition in law of aboriginal status, provide more economic benefit to some aboriginal peoples than to others and may not be available in all situations; however, without the legal recognition of land rights, it would be difficult to distinguish an aboriginal right from that which could be claimed by the members of any minority group.

The use of family and child welfare policy as a means of enforcing aboriginal social policy is one example of the general failure of the latter. The individual missionaries, school teachers, nurses, and social workers who carried out family and child welfare policy were usually sincere and well motivated, but neither the policy which supported their work nor the methods they used were successful. Indeed, as has been pointed out, their methods, while destructive to aboriginal cultures, failed to offer aboriginal children any viable alternative.

Individual missionaries and social workers saw the problems faced by aboriginal peoples in individual terms. They thought that, given the right opportunities, education, and resources, the individual aboriginal person would become like them. They did not recognize the racial discrimination of their own societies, and they did not understand their own colonialism. They misunderstood the nature of cultural change and tried to force it rather than to offer an opportunity to aboriginal peoples to take from it what they chose. The result was a widespread, genocidal form of oppression. Even as applied to mainstream cultures, child welfare policies were full of weaknesses and contradictions; these were increased when they were applied to the families and children of other cultures.

Today's social policy tries to find ways of supporting aboriginal peoples through organizations like Link-Up (Australia), Ma-Mawi-Wi-Chi-Itata (Canada), and Te Kohanga Reo (New Zealand) – organizations through which aboriginal peoples can work on family and child welfare issues within the context of their own cultures. In addition, there are examples of modifications of mainstream agency policy and practice which accommodate aboriginal concerns and which, at the same time, provide non-aboriginal peoples with new ways of working on their own issues. Good examples of these are the family conference procedures in the New Zealand Children, Young Persons and Their Families Act, 1989,[16] and the innovations that are coming from the development of distinct Aboriginal, First Nations, and Maori approaches to social work.

One view of these changes is that they, too, are but another stage of assimilation policy – one in which cultural assimilation has been replaced by institutional assimilation. In this view, aboriginal peoples are permitted to undertake administrative actions only on the condition that they develop policies and programs which mirror those of the mainstream cultures within which they are located. The illusion of self-government exists, but the reality is mainstream control, accomplished by the simple expedient of only funding programs that meet criteria defined by mainstream cultures (e.g., the Canadian child welfare agreements). Thus, assimilation continues under the guise of self-government. As Augie Fleras comments:

> In short, although recent rhetoric about self-determination and self-government suggests a fundamental shift in state policy towards aboriginal people, no such change has occurred. Indeed, far from severing the bonds of dependency and underdevelopment, state initiatives may have had the effect, whether by accident or design, of further incorporating aboriginal people into institutional structures (Cornell 1988). All we have seen are changes in the strategies to achieve policy objectives that do not depart significantly from nineteenth-century assimilationist goals.[17]

In sympathy with this view, some writers encourage a sharp separation between aboriginal and non-aboriginal interests and suggest that aboriginal peoples can and should find their future in their past; that is, they should concentrate on their own traditions and, so far as possible, eliminate European influence.[18]

On Easter day 1991 I was in Ruatoria, New Zealand, as a guest of the Ngati Porou people. We spent the night sleeping on the marae in a communal hall and rose at 4:00 AM to drive to the flank of Mount Hikurangi. Mount Hikurangi stands on the east cape of New Zealand, not far from the international date line, and is reputed to be the first place in the world where the dawn of a new day can be seen. As the first glimpse of dawn lit up the place where we were standing, a thousand Maori voices sang a hymn of praise and thanksgiving for the return to them of their rights to Mount Hikurangi – rights which had been lost through the operation of the Native Land Court. The service of worship was conducted in Maori by a Maori Anglican priest. Later in the day, there was an official ceremony held between the leaders of the Ngati Porou people and the New Zealand minister of Maori affairs, and this completed the return of Mount Hikurangi to the Maori people. As a result of witnessing this ceremony, I find myself standing with those who have faith in the steps which are now being taken towards accommodating, through dialogue and compromise, the self-determination of aboriginal peoples.

This book will have served its purpose if it succeeds in demonstrating that high aspirations lead to discrimination and oppression whenever they take the form of one culture imposing itself upon another. However, if intercultural relationships are conducted in a spirit of open-mindedness, tolerance, and self-criticism, then all cultures may benefit.

Notes

Chapter 1: Introduction

1 British Parliamentary Papers, *Report from His Majesty's Commission for Inquiring into the Administration and Practical Operation of the Poor Laws*, 1834, vol. 27, no. 44, p. 1.
2 British Parliamentary Papers, (House of Commons), *Report of the Select Committee on Aborigines*, 1837, no. 425, 7, 1. The select committee was 'appointed to consider what measures ought to be adopted with regard to the Native Inhabitants of Countries where British Settlements are made, and to the neighbouring Tribes, in order to secure for them the due observance of Justice and the protection of their Rights: to promote the spread of civilization among them, and to lead them to the peaceable and voluntary reception of the Christian religion.'
3 In a section of the report of the Select Committee on Aborigines on the Australian Aborigine, the following duties of protectors were emphasized (a protector was to be a public official):

> The education of the young will be amongst the foremost of the cares of the missionaries: and the Protectors should render every assistance in their power ...
> It should be one branch of the duty of the Protectors to suggest ... such short and simple rules as may form a temporary and provisional code for the regulation of Aborigines, until advancing knowledge and civilization shall have superseded the necessity of any such special laws.
> Each Protector of Aborigines should be invested with the character of a magistrate ...
> Finally, the Protector should be required to make periodical reports to the local government.

4 Sir William Beveridge (chair), *Social Insurance and Allied Services*, HMSO, London, 1942.
5 House of Commons, *Report of the Select Committee on Aborigines*, 44.
6 M.L. McCall, 'An Analysis of Responsibilities in Child Welfare Systems,' *Canadian Journal of Family Law* 8 (1990):345.

7 United Nations, Convention on the Prevention and Punishment of the Crime of Genocide, 1948.
8 Richard Splane, 'Whatever happened to the G.A.I.?' *Social Worker* 48 (1980): 86-8. In this article, Splane examines the fate of the extensive experimentation in negative taxation programming that was undertaken in Manitoba in order to determine the effect of a proposed guaranteed annual income on work incentive. However, the decision not to introduce such a program was made for reasons which have nothing to do with the experiment's results. Usually, there is no such attempt to understand the effects of program change, and new policies are introduced by pragmatic politicians who are responding to timing and opportunity.
9 Joan Higgins, *States of Welfare* (Oxford: Basil Blackwell 1981), 12.
10 Marilyn Callahan and Brian Wharf, *Demystifying the Policy Process: A Case Study in the Development of Child Welfare Legislation in British Columbia* (Victoria: School of Social Work, University of Victoria 1982). Callahan and Wharf trace the origins of reform to practitioner dissatisfaction with available resources and policies; although, in the end, practitioners' concerns are largely lost in senior-level political manoeuvres. In a similar vein, Asa Briggs, in an introductory essay in *Comparative Development in Social Welfare*, ed. E.W. Martin (London: Allen and Unwin 1972), 12, recognizes that 'local action has ... frequently preceded national action in the making of English social policy.'
11 A 'status Indian' is a person whose name is on a list pursuant to the Indian Act.
12 James Frideres, *Native Peoples in Canada: Contemporary Conflicts*, 3rd edition (Scarborough: Prentice Hall 1988).

Chapter 2: General Structure of Aboriginal Policy
1 Robert Hughes, *The Fatal Shore: The Epic of Australia's Founding* (London: Pan Books 1988).
2 Henry Reynolds, 'White Man Came Took Everything,' in *A Most Valuable Acquisition: A Peoples History of Australia* (Victoria: McPhee/Penguin Books 1988).
3 Henry Reynolds, *Dispossession: Black Australians and White Invaders* (Sydney: Allen and Unwin 1989).
4 C.D. Rowley, *The Destruction of Aboriginal Society: Aboriginal Policy and Practice*, vol. 1 (Canberra: Australian National University Press 1970), 88.
5 A.P. Elkin, 'Reaction and Interaction: A Food Gathering People and European Settlement in Australia,' *American Anthropologist* 53, no. 2 (1951):167-9. As cited by C.D. Rowley, *Destruction of Aboriginal Society*, 208.
6 Examples of such legislation include statutes directed to the prohibition of alcohol and firearms as well as statutes such as, in Western Australia, An Act to Prevent the Enticing Away of Girls of the Aboriginal Race from School, or from Any Service in which They Are Employed, 1844, 8 Vict, c. 6.
7 Peter Read, *A Hundred Years War* (Canberra: Australian National University Press 1988).
8 Peter Read, 'The Second Cycle: 1879-1909' and 'The Third Cycle: 1909-1929,' in *A Hundred Years War*.
9 Read, *Hundred Years War*, 98.

10 Australia, *The Policy of Assimilation*, Decisions of Commonwealth and State Ministers at the Native Welfare Conference, Canberra, 26 and 27 January 1961.
11 Governor Lachlan MacQuarrie's Proclamation, '4 May 1816,' *Historical Records of Australia*, ser. 1, vol. 9, pp. 142-3. The proclamation declared that Aboriginals were subject to the protection of the law; however, any infractions of the law which they might commit could render them outlaws.
12 For example, see the definition of Aborigine in South Australia's Aborigines Act, 1934, sec. 4(1):

> Every person who is (a) an Aboriginal native of Australia or of any of the islands adjacent to or belonging thereto: or (b) a half-caste who lives with such an Aboriginal native as wife or husband: or (c) a half-caste who, otherwise than as a wife, or husband of such an Aboriginal native, habitually lives or associates with such Aboriginal natives; or (d) a half-caste child whose age does not apparently exceed 18 years, shall be deemed to be an Aboriginal within the meaning of this Act and of every Act passed before or after this Act, unless a contrary intention appears.

Half-caste is further defined in Section 7(2): 'In this section, the term "half-caste" includes any person either of whose parents is or was an Aboriginal native of Australia ... and any child of any such person.'
13 Exemption clauses applicable to quadroons, with regard to the definition of Aborigine in Western Australia's Aborigines Act Amendment Act, 1936, were subject to the additional qualification that they did not apply where a magistrate ordered that the person be classed as a 'native' under the act. Similarly, in Queensland, the Aboriginals Preservation and Protection Act, 1939, included as an Aborigine 'Any half-blood declared by a judge or police magistrate or two or more justices, after trial, to be in need of the protection of this Act.'
14 Queensland, the Aborigines and Torres Straits Islanders Affairs Act, 1965.
15 Rowley, *Destruction of Aboriginal Society*, 350.
16 Australia, Social Services Act, 1959, sec. 24.
17 Northern Territory, Aboriginals Ordinance Act, 1936, sec. 1.
18 South Australia, Aboriginal Affairs Act, 1962, sec. 17.
19 Rowley, *Destruction of Aboriginal Society*, 358.
20 Western Australia, Aboriginal Affairs Planning and Authority Act, 1972, sec. 1.
21 South Australia, Pitjantjatjara Land Rights Act, 1981, sec. 1.
22 This section of the text draws heavily upon L.R. Smith, *The Aboriginal Population of Australia* (Canberra: Australian National University Press 1980).
23 United Kingdom, Commonwealth of Australia Constitution Act, 1900, 63 and 64 Vict. c. 12, sec. 127. (Repealed by Constitution Alteration [Aboriginals] Act, 1967, sec. 3).
24 Smith, *Aboriginal Population*, 206.
25 The Torres Strait Islanders Act, 1939, resulted in a separate enumeration of the islanders, who had previously been considered as Aboriginal.
26 Smith, *Aboriginal Population*, 8.
27 Concern about the accuracy of the census enumeration of Aboriginal children

has been addressed in these estimates by comparing results from areas where enumeration standards were known to be high (e.g., New South Wales) with other areas of Australia and then adjusting the proportions accordingly. See Smith, *Aboriginal Population*, 226.
28 See, for example, British Parliamentary Papers, 1831, *Papers Relating to the Instruction of the Natives of New South Wales* (Dublin: Irish University Press Series 1970).
29 Rev. Robert Cartwright, Letter to His Excellency Governor MacQuarrie, 6 December 1818. Reproduced in British Parliamentary Papers, *Papers Relating to Instruction*, 156.
30 Cartwright, in British Parliamentary Papers, *Papers Relating to Instruction*, 156.
31 Hughes, *The Fatal Shore*, 168.
32 Rowley, *Destruction of Aboriginal Society*, 231-2.
33 Ibid., 247.
34 Ibid., 248.
35 Ibid., 209.
36 Australia, Aboriginal Development Commission Act, 1980, sec. 3.
38 Northern Territory, Aboriginal Land Act, 1980 (amended 1987). Sir Paul Hasluck, *Shades of Darkness: Aboriginal Affairs 1925-1965* (Melbourne: Melbourne University Press 1988), 145.
39 David Pollard, *Give and Take: The Losing Partnership in Aboriginal Poverty* (Marrickville: Hale and Ironmonger 1988).
40 Colin Tatz, *Race Politics in Australia* (Armidale: University of New England Publishing Unit 1979).

Chapter 3: Aboriginal Peoples and Child Welfare Policy
1 Through the work of Richard Chisolm and Peter Read, child welfare policy and administration in New South Wales is well documented. In the case of Queensland and the Northern Territory, data on child welfare is principally taken from official documents, observations, and direct discussions undertaken while in Australia in 1990. The people interviewed were:
Richard Hall, Director, Queensland, Commission on Aboriginal Deaths in Custody, 1989
Seamus Parker, Investigator, Commission on Aboriginal Deaths in Custody, 1989
Lilla Watson, Instructor, Department of Social Work, University of Queensland
Les Malezar, Director, Community Services, Department of Family and Community Services, Queensland
Elizabeth Hindsen, Supervisor, Community Services, Department of Family and Community Services, Queensland
Graham Zerk, Director of Family Services (1978-88), Queensland
Arthur Anderson, Secretary, Council of Elders, Brisbane
Judy Taylor, Regional Supervisor, Community Support Services, Department of Family and Community Services, Townsville
Bernadine Thornthwaite, Sister, Cherbourg Community
Rory Bone, chairperson, Cherbourg Community Council
Barbara Bartels, Northern Australia Development Unit

Peter Read, Australian National University
Coral Edwards, Link-Up
Harry Geise, Director of Welfare (1952-72), Northern Territory
Peg Havnen, Centre for Aboriginal and Islander Studies, Northern Territory University, Darwin
Josie Crawshaw, consultant, Darwin
Julianne James, Northern Australia Research Unit, Darwin
Ron James, Department of Social Security, Darwin
Barry Smith, Northern Australia Development Unit
Eileen Cummings, Chief Ministers Office, Darwin
Sue Ward, Uniting Church, Darwin
Tim Rowse, Menzies Health Unit, Alice Springs
David Thomas, Community Services and Health, Darwin
Steve Armitage, Family and Community Services, Brisbane
Margaret Allison, Family and Community Services, Brisbane
Richard Chisolm, Associate Dean, Faculty of Law, University of New South Wales, Sydney

Through the support of the Laidlaw Foundation and the courtesy of Allan Halladay and Andrew Jones of the Department of Social Work at the University of Queensland, I was able to spend May and June 1990 in Australia. At that time I visited the Aboriginal Studies Institute of the Australian National University (Canberra), the Northern Australia Research Unit (Darwin), the Menzies Health Centre (Alice Springs), and the University of New South Wales (Sydney).

2 Richard Chisolm, *Black Children: White Welfare* (New South Wales: Social Welfare Research Centre 1985). The work of Richard Chisolm is used throughout this section as a basis for this account of child welfare policy towards Aboriginal people.
3 C.D. Rowley. *The Remote Aborigines* (Harmondsworth: Penguin 1972), cited in Chisolm, *Black Children*, 2.
4 Chisolm, *Black Children*, 17, quoting from Aboriginal Protection Board, *Report*, 1921.
5 Coral Edwards, 'Is the Ward Clean?' in *All That Dirt: Aborigines 1938* (Canberra: History Project Inc., Australian National University, Social Sciences Research School 1982).
6 Peter Read, *The Stolen Generations: The Removal of Aboriginal Children in New South Wales 1883 to 1964*, occasional paper no. 1 (New South Wales: Ministry of Aboriginal Affairs 1982), 11.
7 Paul Hasluck, *Shades of Darkness: Aboriginal Affairs 1925-65* (Melbourne: University of Melbourne Press 1987), 68.
8 Initial conference of Commonwealth and State Aboriginal Authorities, Canberra, 21 to 23 April 1937.
9 Chisolm, *Black Children*, 22, quoting from Aborigines Welfare Board, *Report*, 1956.
10 Read, *Stolen Generations*.
11 Read, *Stolen Generations*, 10.
12 Carla Christine Hankins, 'The Missing Links: Cultural Genocide Through the

Abduction of Female Aboriginal Children from Their Families and Their Training for Domestic Service, 1883-1969,' BA thesis, University of New South Wales, 1982. See the recollections of Matron Hiscocks of the girls home at Cootamundra and Hankins's accounts of the humiliating ways girls were disciplined, often without the matron's knowledge.

13 William C. Langshaw, Director, 'Statement on the Department of Child Welfare and Social Welfare,' Joint Committee of the Legislative Council and Legislative Assembly upon Aborigines Welfare, Sydney, 27 February 1967.
14 Duncan Graham, *Dying Inside* (Sydney: Allen and Unwin 1989), quoting R. Armstrong, *The Kalkadoons* (Brisbane: William Brooks 1980).
15 Queensland, Department of Community Services, *Annual Report*, 1987-8.
16 For an example, see Queensland, *Annual Report of The Chief Protector of Aboriginals for the Year 1916* (Brisbane: Governments Printer 1917).
17 Klaus-Peter Koepping, 'Cultural Patterns on an Aboriginal Settlement in Queensland,' in R. Berndt, ed., *Aborigines and Change* (New York: Random House 1972), 159f.
18 Tennant Kelly, 'Tribes of Cherbourg Settlement,' *Oceania* 5, no. 4 (1935):461-73.
19 A. Chase, 'Land, Law and Aborigines in Queensland,' Aboriginal Land Rights and Justice Conference, Griffith University, 1972, as cited by Lyndall Ryan, in Allan Patience, ed., *The Bjorke-Petersen Premiership 1968-1983* (Melbourne: Longmans 1985).
20 Department of Aboriginal and Islanders Advancement, *Annual Report*, 1982.
21 Australia, *The Policy of Assimilation*, Decisions of Commonwealth and State Ministers at the Native Welfare Conference, Canberra, 26 and 27 January 1961.
22 Lyndall Ryan, 'Aborigines and Torres Strait Islanders,' in Patience, ed., *Bjorke-Petersen Premiership*.
23 Department of Aboriginal and Islander Advancement, *Annual Report, 30 June 1978*, Brisbane, 1979.
24 Matthew Foley. 'From Protectionism to Laissez-Faire,' *Social Alternatives* 2, no. 2 (1981):36.
25 Foley, 'Protectionism,' 40.
26 Department of Family Services, Child Placement Principle Implementation Plan, Queensland, 1985.
27 Northern Territory, *Administrators Report*, Darwin, 1912. The act referred to is the Act to make Provision for the better Protection and Control of the Aboriginal Inhabitants of the Northern Territory, and for other purposes, of the Government of the State of South Australia, 1910.
28 Baldwin Spencer, *Preliminary Report on the Aboriginals of the Northern Territory* (Melbourne: Government Printer for the State of Victoria 1913). This report was commissioned by the Australian Commonwealth government following the separation of the Northern Territory from South Australia in 1911.
29 Spencer, *Preliminary Report*, 47.
30 Northern Territory, *Administrators Report*, 1921.
31 J.W. Bleakley, *The Aboriginals and Half-Castes of Central Australia and Northern*

Australia (Melbourne: Government Printer for the State of Victoria 1928).
32 Australia, Department of the Interior, *Aboriginals: Commonwealth Government's Policy in Respect of the Northern Territory* (Canberra: Government Printer 1933).
33 Ted Evans, 'The Mechanics of Change,' *Nelen Yubu* 12 (1982):3-11.
34 Hasluck, *Shades of Darkness*, 85.
35 Tim Rowse, *White Flour White Power?*, Ph.D thesis, Australian National University, Canberra, devotes much of his thesis to showing how this administration effectively colonized a people.
36 Barbara Bartels was a resident of the Retta Dixon Home and knew many of the children who had been wards in the Hasluck-Geise period. She was interviewed in Darwin in 1990.
37 Northern Territory Administration, Welfare Branch, *Annual Report*, 1970-1.
38 John Tomlinson, 'Fostering and Adoption Territory Style,' *Social Alternatives* 2, no. 2 (1981):46.
39 Richard Chisolm, 'Aboriginal Law in Australia: The Law Reform Commissions Proposals for Recognition,' *University of Hawaii Law Review* 10, no. 1 (Summer 1988):49.
40 Link-Up, Box 93, Bullaburra 2783, New South Wales, Ph. 02-047-591911.
41 For a full statement contact: Secretariat of the National Aboriginal and Islander Child Care, 4, Brunswick Place, Fitzroy, Victoria 3065. Phone 03-417-6744.
42 Important participants in presenting the case for the placement principle were Dr. Peter Read, Australian National University; Dr. Richard Chisolm, University of New South Wales; and Prof. Mathew Foley, University of Queensland.
43 Richard Chisolm, 'Aboriginal Children and the Placement Principle,' *Aboriginal Law Bulletin* 2, no. 31 (April 1988):4-6.
44 New South Wales, Children (Care and Protection) Act (NSW), 1987, sec. 87.
45 Richard Chisolm, 'Aboriginal Children: Political Pawns or Paramount Consideration?' *Child Welfare: Current Issues and Future Directions*, seminar 6 July 1983 (Sydney: University of New South Wales, Social Welfare Research Centre).
46 Read, *Stolen Generations*.

Chapter 4: General Structure of Canadian Indian Policy
1 John Foster Grant, *The Moon of Wintertime* (Toronto: University of Toronto Press 1984), 14.
2 Papal Bull, *Sublimus Deus*, 1537, cited in Grant, *Moon*, 219.
3 David T. McNab, *Research Report on the Royal Proclamation of 1763 and British Indian Policy, 1750-1794* (Ottawa: Ministry of Natural Resources 1979).
4 Jack M. Sosin, *Whitehall and the Wilderness* (Lincoln: University of Nebraska Press 1961), 51, quoting Lord Egremont, Secretary of State, correspondence with General Amherst, Commander in Chief, Northern District.
5 British Parliamentary Papers, House of Commons Select Committee on Aborigines, 1837.
6 British Parliamentary Papers, *Correspondence Returns and Other Papers Relating to*

Canada and the Indian Problem Therein, 1839 (Dublin: Irish University Press 1969), 253-97. Dispatch from the Earl of Gosford, Québec City, to Lord Glenelg, Downing Street, London.

7 British Parliamentary Papers, 'Report of the Committee of the Executive Council ... respecting the Indian Department, Québec City, 13 July 1837,' in *Correspondence Returns*. This report was subsequently forwarded to London with a letter of recommendation and support from the Earl of Gosford, captain general and governor in chief in Lower Canada.

8 British Parliamentary Papers, 'Report of the Committee of the Executive Council,' in *Correspondence Returns*, 215.

9 British Parliamentary Papers, 'Report of the House of Commons Select Committee on Aborigines, 1837,' in *Correspondence Returns*, 44.

10 Grant, *Moon*, 86.

11 J.R. Miller, *Skyscrapers Hide the Heavens: A History of Indian-White Relations in Canada* (Toronto: University of Toronto Press 1989), 108.

12 Jack Woodward, *Native Law* (Toronto: Carswell 1990), 88.

13 Canada, Indian Act, 1876.

14 John L. Tobias, 'Protection, Civilization, Assimilation: An Outline of Canada's Indian Policy,' *Western Canadian Journal of Anthropology* 6, no. 2 (1976):13-30.

15 Tobias, 'Protection,' 24-5.

16 Canada, Indian Affairs Branch, H.B. Hawthorn, ed., *A Survey of the Contemporary Indians of Canada: Economic, Political, Educational Needs and Policies*, 2 vols. (Ottawa: Indian Affairs 1966).

17 S.M. Weaver, *Making Canadian Indian Policy: The Hidden Agenda 1968-70* (Toronto: University of Toronto Press 1981).

18 Jean Chrétien, Minister of Indian Affairs and Northern Development, 'Statement of the Government of Canada on Indian Policy,' first session, twenty-eighth Parliament, Ottawa, 1969.

19 Canada, Constitution Act, 1982.

20 Canada, Canadian Charter of Rights and Freedoms, 1982, section 25.

21 Miller, *Skyscrapers*, 236, indicates three reasons for difficulty with the concept of self-government: (1) a lack of practical experience with the existence of a parallel jurisdiction within the country and, hence, no clear answers to issues of jurisdictional conflict; (2) a lack of commitment by the mainstream population to a concept of civil society in which all people are not treated equally; and (3) a lack of independent economic resources with which to govern a series of independent First Nations societies.

22 Canada, House of Commons, *Report: Special Committee on Indian Self-Government* (Ottawa: Queen's Printer 1983).

23 Miller, *Skyscrapers*, 244.

24 Canada, An Act for the Better Protection of the Lands and Property of Indians in Lower Canada, 1850, as cited in Miller, *Skyscrapers*, 109.

25 Miller, *Skyscrapers*, 109.

26 Woodward, *Native Law*, 20.

27 For a complete set of references, see Woodward, *Native Law*, 4-6. Examples include the use of the term 'aborigine' to indicate entitlement to fishing rights under the Fisheries Act; the use of the term 'people of native origin' to

indicate different rights of land usage under the Park Act; and the term 'North American Indian Race' to define entitlement to benefit from 'the First Citizens Fund' in British Columbia.
28 Miller, *Skyscrapers*, 242.
29 Canada, *1971 Census of Canada: Profile Studies – Ethnic Origins of Canadians*, cat. 99-709, Ottawa.
30 Canada, *1981 Census Dictionary*, cat. 99-901, Ottawa, 1982.
31 Canada, *1986 Census Dictionary*, cat. 99-101E, Ottawa, 1987.
32 James S. Frideres, *Native Peoples in Canada: Contemporary Conflicts* (Scarborough: Prentice Hall 1988).
33 Frideres, *Native Peoples*, 155.
34 Grand Chief Michael Mitchell, 'Akwesasne: An Unbroken Assertion of Sovereignty,' in Boyce Richardson, ed., *Drumbeat: Anger and Renewal in Indian Country* (Toronto: Summerhill Press and Assembly of First Nations 1989).
35 Frideres, *Native Peoples*, 86.
36 Frideres, *Native Peoples*, 72.
37 Indian Commissioner J. Provencher, 31 December 1873, as cited in Frideres, *Native Peoples*, 73.
38 Alexander Morris, PC, *The Treaties of Canada with the Indians of Manitoba and the Northwest Territories* (Toronto: Belfords, Clarke 1880), as cited in Frideres, *Native Peoples*, 76.
39 Frideres, *Native Peoples*, 263.
40 Frideres, *Native Peoples*, 264. The land claims have yet to be settled in British Columbia. In 1990, the BC government gave its first formal indication of its willingness to participate in land-claim discussions, while continuing to refuse recognition of any concept of aboriginal title.
41 Frideres, *Native Peoples*, 244.

Chapter 5: First Nations Family and Child Welfare
1 Although the provinces and territory were chosen in order to illustrate a range of differences in family and child welfare approaches, an additional reason for this choice was the availability of scholarly work on First Nations family and child welfare in each of these jurisdictions. Brian Wharf (University of Victoria) has documented family and child welfare issues in British Columbia, Ken Coates (University of Victoria) has taken a similar interest in the Yukon Territory, and Peter Hudson and Brad McKenzie have studied family and child welfare policy in Manitoba. Finally, the choice reflects the author's field experience in both administration and research in British Columbia and the Yukon.
2 Alan McEachern (Chief Justice, Supreme Court of British Columbia), *Reasons for Judgement between: Delgamuukw, also known as Ken Muldoe (plaintiff) and: Her Majesty the Queen in right of the Province of British Columbia and the Attorney General of Canada (defendants)*, no. 0843, Smithers Registry, 1991.
3 For a full discussion see, Jack Woodward, *Native Law* (Toronto: Carswell 1989).
4 See, for example: (1) Manitoba Métis Federation, *Michif Child and Family Services, Inc.* (Dauphin: North West Métis Council 1989); (2) Manitoba Métis Federation, *Submission to the Aboriginal Justice Inquiry* (Winnipeg: Queen's

Printer 1989); and (3) Native Council of Canada, *Native Child Care* (Ottawa: Native Council of Canada 1990).
5. Frank Cassidy and Robert L. Bish, *Indian Government: Its Meaning in Practice* (Lantzville: Oolichan Books 1989).
6. J.R. Miller, *Skyscrapers Hide the Heavens: A History of Indian-White Relations in Canada* (Toronto: University of Toronto Press 1989), 106.
7. Nicholas Flood Davin, 'Report on Industrial Schools for Indians and Half-breeds,' unpublished report in DIAND library, Ottawa, 1969.
8. Jean Barman, Yvonne Hébert, and Don McCaskill, 'The Legacy of the Past: An Overview,' in Jean Barman, ed., *Indian Education in Canada*, vol. 1, *The Legacy* (Vancouver: University of British Columbia Press 1986).
9. Miller, *Skyscrapers*, 107.
10. Duncan Campbell Scott, 'Indian Affairs 1867-1912,' in Adam Shortt, ed., *Canada and Its Provinces* (Toronto: Edinburgh University Press 1913), as cited in Barman et al. eds., *Legacy*.
11. Miller, *Skyscrapers*, 197-8, quoting Canada, House of Commons, *Debates*, 1904.
12. Barman et al. eds., *Legacy*, 120, citing Duncan Campbell Scott as quoted in Shortt ed., *Canada and Its Provinces*.
13. Harry Assu and Joy Inglis, *Assu of Cape Mudge: Recollections of a Coastal Indian Chief* (Vancouver: University of British Columbia Press 1989), 95-6.
14. Foster Grant, *The Moon of Wintertime* (Toronto: University of Toronto Press 1984), 185f.
15. As cited by Grant, *Moon*, 185.
16. Douglas Cole and Ira Chaikin, *An Iron Hand Upon the People* (Seattle: University of Washington Press 1990), 80, citing Halliday correspondence to Superintendent General, Department of Indian Affairs, V1652, 1 February 1907.
17. A visit to Alert Bay confirms the extent of the assault on First Nations culture. In the 1920s, Alert Bay was a community of 200-300 people. The effect of the trials and imprisonment was doubtless magnified by the building of the school and the effective removal of children from the influence of their parents. Today (1990), the dancing regalia has been returned and can be seen in a museum. The school, still the only brick building in the community, continues to dominate the reserve but is now in a partly derelict state, with some sections being used as offices by the Alert Bay band. A road was also placed along the Alert Bay waterfront in the 1920s, passing directly through the First Nations graveyard.
18. Kenneth Coates, 'Best Left as Indians,' in Robin Fisher and K. Coates, eds., *Out of the Background: Readings on Canadian Native History* (Toronto: Copp Clark Pitman 1988), 248.
19. Richard King, *The School at Mopass* (Stanford: Holt, Reinhart and Winston 1967). King's detailed account of the operation of the school at Carcross, YT, shares many features with other accounts of residential school operation. It is thus provided here as a general model of how such schools went about achieving their objectives.
20. King, *School at Mopass*, 54.
21. Basil Johnston, *Indian School Days* (Toronto: Key Porter Books 1988), 8.
22. King, *School at Mopass*, 52.

23 Johnston, *Indian School Days*, 79, cites a letter received by one of his friends:

> Dear Son,
> This is to let you know we are all fine and hope you are the same. The weather has been real good hear [sic]. We are trying to get you home. I spoke to the priest and the agent and they said they were going help. That's all for now and be a good boy and do what the priest tell you. I pray for you every night for you to come home.
> Love Mom.

Johnston writes, 'Such a letter gave a boy hope and inspiration and the strength to go on from month to month and year to year.'
24 Johnston, *Indian School Days*, 164.
25 See, for example, Jean Barman, 'Indian and White Girls at All Hallows School,' in Barman et al. eds., *Legacy*, 126.
26 *The Residential School Syndrome*, television documentary made for the Canadian Broadcasting Corporation, Northern Network, 1986.
27 Douglas Todd, 'School for Shame,' *Vancouver Sun*, 26 April 1991.
28 Barman et al. eds., *Legacy*, 8.
29 Patrick Johnston, *Native Children and the Child Welfare System* (Toronto: James Lorimer 1983), 3.
30 Canadian Welfare Council and Canadian Association of Social Workers, *Joint Submission to the Special Joint Committee of the Senate and House of Commons Appointed to Examine and Consider the Indian Act* (Ottawa: Canadian Welfare Council 1947), 3.
31 Johnston, *Indian School Days*, 20.
32 H.B. Hawthorn (chair), *A Survey of the Contemporary Indians of Canada: A Report on Economic, Political, Educational Needs and Policies* (Ottawa: Supply and Services 1966).
33 Brad McKenzie and Peter Hudson, 'Native Children, Child Welfare and the Colonization of Native People,' in Ken Levitt and Brian Wharf, eds., *The Challenge of Child Welfare* (Vancouver: University of British Columbia Press 1985).
34 British Columbia, *Report of the Royal Commission on Family Law* (Victoria: Queen's Printer 1976).
35 John McDonald. 'The Spallumcheen Indian Band By-law,' in Levitt and Wharf, eds., *Challenge of Child Welfare*, 255.
36 Technical Assistance and Family Planning Associates, *A Starving Man Doesn't Argue: A Review of Community Social Services to Indians in Canada* (Toronto: Technical Assistance and Family Planning Associates, 1979), 5-7.
37 Manitoba Tripartite Committee, *Manitoba Indian Child Welfare Sub-Committee Report* (Winnipeg: Government of Manitoba 1980).
38 Department of Indian Affairs and Northern Development (DIAND), *Indian Child and Family Services Management Regime: Discussion Paper* (Ottawa: DIAND 1989).
39 Wayne Goreau, *Native Child and Family Services in Manitoba* (Winnipeg: Department of Community Services 1986).

40 Peter Hudson and Sharon Taylor-Henley, *Agreement and Disagreement*, 95-9.
41 Coopers and Lybrand Ltd., *Assessment of Services Delivered Under the Canada-Manitoba-Indian Child Welfare Agreement* (Winnipeg: Department of Community Services, 1990).
42 See, for example: (1) Peter Hudson and Brad McKenzie, *Evaluation of the Dakota Ojibway Child and Family Services* (Winnipeg: Department of Northern and Indian Affairs 1987); and (2) Peter Hudson and Sharon Taylor-Henley, *Agreement and Disagreement: An Evaluation of the Canada-Manitoba Northern Indian Child Welfare Agreement* (Winnipeg: School of Social Work, University of Manitoba 1987).
43 Hudson and Taylor-Henley, *Agreement and Disagreement*, iii.
44 Hon. Justice Brian Giesbrecht, *Report on the Death of Lester Desjarlais* (Winnipeg: Office of the Chief Medical Examiner 1992).
45 Elizabeth Hill, 'Urban Models for Native Child Welfare: Progress and Prospects,' report from the University of Manitoba, School of Social Work, 1987.
46 Ma-Mawi-Wi-Chi-Itata, *First Annual Meeting Report* (Winnipeg: Ma-Mawi-Wi-Chi-Itata Centre 1985).
47 Laidlaw Foundation, *National Report* (Toronto: Ma-Mawi-Wi-Chi-Itata Centre 1991).
48 Laidlaw Foundation, *National Report*.
49 Brian Wharf, *Towards First Nations Control of Child Welfare* (Victoria: School of Social Work, University of Victoria 1987), 16.
50 Wharf, *Towards First Nations Control*, 10.
51 Nuu Chah Nulth Tribal Council (Vancouver Island), Carrier-Sekani Tribal Council (Prince George), Spallumcheen Band (Enderby), McLeod Lake Band (McLeod Lake).
52 Report of the Aboriginal Committee, Community Panel, Family and Children's Services Legislation Review in British Columbia, *Liberating Our Children: Liberating Our Nations* (Victoria: Queen's Printer 1992), viii.
53 Andrew Armitage, Frances Ricks, and Brian Wharf, *The Champagne-Aishihik Child Welfare Pilot Project: Evaluation* (Victoria: School of Social Work, University of Victoria 1988).
54 Assembly of First Nations, *Report of the National Inquiry into First Nation Child Care* (Ottawa: Assembly of First Nations 1989), viii.
55 Assembly of First Nations, *Strengthening the Family, Building the Community: Final Report on the First Canadian Indian-Native Child Welfare Conference* (Ottawa: Assembly of First Nations 1988).
56 Assembly of First Nations, *For Discussion: National Strategy on First Nations Child and Family Services* (Ottawa: Assembly of First Nations 1991).

Chapter 6: The General Structure of Maori Policy

1 The gathering of materials for this and the succeeding chapter was assisted by being able to visit New Zealand in 1991, through a grant provided by the Laidlaw Foundation. During the course of this visit, particular assistance and guidance was given by:
John Angus, Department of Social Welfare, Head Office, Wellington

John Dunlop, Consultant, Christchurch
Mason Durie, Massey University, Palmerston North
Anne Else, Author, Wellington
Vapi Kupenga, Massey University, Palmerston North
Neil Johnstone, Head, Regional Legal Unit, Department of Social Welfare, Christchurch
The Ngati Porou people, whose hospitality, interest, ideas, and determination were of great assistance to me
Roslyn Noonan, Director, New Zealand Educational Institute, Wellington
Rahira Ohia, Manager of Social and Cultural Resources, Ministry of Maori Affairs, Wellington
Ani Pitman, Research Officer, Department of Social Welfare, Wellington
James Rota, Maori Land Court Judge
Ian Shirley, Professor, Massey University, Palmerston North
To'aiga Su'a-Hurua, Research Officer, Department of Social Welfare, Wellington
Mark Tisdall, Massey University, Palmerston North
Harry Walker, University of Victoria, Wellington.

2 The periods into which the history of Maori-Pakeha relations are divided are based on those used by Moana Jackson in *The Treaty of Waitangi*, Whakarongotai Manae, Waikene, February 1989.
3 The Maori people take pride in the possession and use of their language. Maori words are commonly used in New Zealand by both Maori and Pakeha people. They have been used in this account in a similar manner to that in which they are used in New Zealand government documents and scholarly writing.
4 Janet M. Davidson, 'The Polynesian Foundation,' in W.H. Oliver and B.R. Williams, eds., *The Oxford History of New Zealand* (Wellington: Oxford University Press 1981), 6. Note: Maori people do not necessarily agree with this view.
5 Allan Davidson and Peter J. Lineham, *Transplanted Christianity: Documents Illustrating Aspects of New Zealand Church History* (Palmerston North: Dunsmore Press 1987), 21.
6 T. Lindsay Buick, *The Treaty of Waitangi* (New Plymouth: Thomas Avery 1933), 76-8. A quotation from Lord Normanby's instructions to Captain Hobson, 1839.
7 Treaty of Waitangi (English Version):

Article the First
The Chiefs of the Confederation of the United Tribes of New Zealand and the separate and independent Chiefs who have not become members of the Confederation cede to Her Majesty the Queen of England absolutely and without reservation all the rights and powers of Sovereignty which the said Confederation or Individual Chiefs respectively exercise or possess over their respective Territories as the sole sovereigns thereof.
Article the Second
Her Majesty the Queen of England confirms and guarantees to the Chiefs and Tribes of New Zealand and to the respective families and individuals thereof the full exclusive and undisturbed possession of their Lands and

Estates Forests and Fisheries and other properties which they may collectively or individually possess so long as it is their wish and desire to retain the same in their possession; but the Chiefs of the United Tribes and the individual Chiefs yield to her Majesty the exclusive right of Pre-emption over such lands as the proprietors thereof may be disposed to alienate at such prices as may be agreed upon between the prospective Proprietors and persons appointed by her Majesty to treat with them in that behalf.

Article the Third

In consideration thereof Her Majesty the Queen of England extends to the Natives of New Zealand Her royal protection and imparts to them all the Rights and Privileges of British Subjects

Treaty of Waitangi (Maori Version):

The first

The Chiefs of the Confederation and all the Chiefs who have not joined that Confederation give absolutely to the Queen of England for ever the complete government over their land.

The second

The Queen of England agrees to protect the Chiefs, the Subtribes and all the people of New Zealand in the unqualified exercise of their chieftainship over their lands, villages and all their treasures. But on the other hand the Chiefs of the Confederation and all the Chiefs will sell land to the Queen at a price to be agreed to by the person owning it and by the person buying it, the latter being appointed by the Queen as her purchase agent.

The third

For this agreed arrangement therefore concerning the Government of the Queen, the Queen of England will protect all the ordinary people of New Zealand [i.e., the Maori] and will give them the same rights and duties of citizenship as the people of England.

Source: New Zealand, *The Treaty of Waitangi: The Symbol of Our Life Together as a Nation*, pamphlet produced to recognize the 150th anniversary of the Treaty of Waitangi, Wellington, 1990.

8 George Butterworth, *End of an Era: The Departments of Maori Affairs 1840-1989* (Wellington: Department of Maori Affairs 1989), 8.
9 William Williams to the CMS, Turanga, 12 July 1847, as cited by Davidson and Lineham, *Transplanted Christianity*, 62.
10 Maori Land Act, 1862, sec. 5.
11 Michael King, 'Between Two Worlds,' in Oliver and Williams, eds., *Oxford History*, 289.
12 Appendices to the Journals of the House of Representatives, 1906, H-31, p. 67, as cited by Michael King in Oliver and Williams, eds., *Oxford History*, 289.
13 Apirana Ngata, 'Maori Land Settlement,' in Sutherland, *The Maori People Today*, as cited by Michael King in Oliver and Williams, eds., *Oxford History*, 301.
14 Davidson and Lineham, *Transplanted Christianity*, 158.
15 J.K. Hunn, *Report on Department of Maori Affairs* (Wellington: Government Printer 1960).

16 The benchmark case is *Wi Parata* v. *Bishop of Wellington* (1877), in which the Ngai Toa people of Porirua went to court to obtain land conveyed to the bishop on the understanding that a church and school would be built. They argued that under Article 2 of the Treaty of Waitangi they had retained their governance over the land. Chief Justice Prendergast allowed the church to keep the land, ruling that 'Maori people were not capable as a sovereign nation to enter into a treaty, and because there is no statute in New Zealand law to give effect to the Treaty, the Treaty was a *nullity*.'
17 This was the Motuni Outfall claim; for details, see Ranginui Walker, *Ka Whawhai Tonu Matou: Struggle Without End* (New Zealand: Penguin Books 1990), 248f.
18 New Zealand, *Royal Commission on Social Policy*, 5 vols. (Wellington: Government Printer 1988); Summary of Conclusions, vol. 2, 77.
19 New Zealand, *Royal Commission on Social Policy*, vol. 2, 80.
20 Richard Mulgan, *Maori, Pakeha and Democracy* (Auckland: Oxford University Press 1989), 152.
21 Robin Mitchell, *The Treaty and the Act* (Christchurch: Cadsonbury Publications 1990), 148.
22 See, for example, the discussion of race in 'The Billion-Dollar Question: What is a Maori?' in Mitchell, *The Treaty and the Act*.
23 Ian Pool, *The Maori Population of New Zealand, 1769-1971* (Auckland: Auckland University Press/Oxford University Press 1980).
24 New Zealand, *New Zealand Yearbook, 1990* (Wellington: Department of Statistics 1990), 157.
25 New Zealand, *Royal Commission on Social Policy*, vol. 1, 157. Using the definition of Maori based on descent indicates that 19.5 per cent of children were Maori in 1987.
26 The *Maori Land Court*, the *Native Education Department*, and the *Native Affairs Department*; a fourth institution was constituted by the Maori electoral role, but this served a political rather than an administrative function.
27 Walker, *Ka Whawhai*, 139.
28 Maori Affairs Minister Koro T. Were, *Partnership Response* (Wellington: Ministry of Maori Affairs 1988).
29 Walker, *Ka Whawhai*, 147.
30 New Zealand, *Education of Native Children* (Wellington: Department of Education 1931), appendix.
31 Kingsley G. Chapple, 'Character Training in the Native School,' *Education Gazette*, 1 April 1933.
32 Child Welfare Officer: 'What's the child's name?' Maori Mother: 'Brandy.' Officer: 'What name did you say – Brandy?' Maori Mother: 'We call him Brandy because that's the last word his grandfather spoke.' *Education Gazette*, 1 September 1941, 165.
33 Augie Fleras, 'From Social Welfare to Community Development: Maori Policy and the Department of Maori Affairs in New Zealand.' *Community Development Journal* 19 (1984):32-9.
34 Maori Affairs, *Partnership Response*, 23f.
35 Ministry of Maori Affairs, *Ka Awatea* (Wellington: Ministry of Maori Affairs 1991).

Chapter 7: Maori People and Child Welfare Policy

1 *New Zealand Yearbook, 1990* has a special section on the history of orphanages in New Zealand, from which the following comments are principally drawn.
2 Anne Else, 'The Perfect Solution: Adoption in New Zealand,' *International Journal of the Sociology of Law* 15 (1987):239.
3 Department of Social Policy and Social Work, *Social Policy and Social Services: Study Guide 3* (Palmerston North: Massey University 1990).
4 New Zealand, *Education Gazette*, Special edition, *Child Welfare*, 1 September 1941.
5 Department of Education, *Education Gazette*, October 1941.
6 Else, 'Perfect Solution,' 240.
7 *New Zealand Yearbook, 1990*, 217.
8 George Graham, Secretary of Akarana Association, Auckland, 'Maori Childhood,' letter to the editor, *Auckland Star*, 30 October 1930.
9 Ibid.
10 Judith Binney and Gillian Chaplin, *Nga Morenu: The Survivors* (Auckland: Oxford University Press 1983), extracts from pp. 150-65.
11 Binney and Chaplin, *Nga Morenu*, 50.
12 Else, 'Perfect Solution,' 241.
13 Ibid.
14 Ibid., quoting Attorney General Hanan.
15 New Zealand, *Report of the Royal Commission on Social Policy*, vol. 2, 164.
16 Department of Social Welfare, 'Competency Certification Project: Maori Team Report,' draft document of the Department of Social Welfare, 1991.
17 Walker, *Ka Whawhai*, 279.
18 Ministry of Maori Affairs, *Report of the Review of Te Kohanga Reo* (Wellington: Ministry of Maori Affairs 1988).
19 Unless otherwise stated, all quotations on the Te Reo Maori claim are from the *Finding of the Waitangi Tribunal Relating to Te Reo Maori* (Wellington: Department of Justice 1986).
20 Mitchell, 'The Tower of Babel,' in *The Treaty and the Act*.
21 Department of Social Welfare, *Matua Whangi: A New Direction* (Wellington: Department of Social Welfare 1988), 5.
22 Department of Social Welfare, *Matua Whangi: Family Decision Making* (Wellington: Department of Social Welfare 1988), 3.
23 New Zealand, *Puao-te-Ata-tu (Daybreak): The Report of the Ministerial Advisory Committee on a Maori Perspective for the Department Of Social Welfare* (Wellington: Government Printer 1986), 19 and appendix, 26.
24 Michael Harvey, *Interim Report on Findings from the FGC Statistical Information Questionnaires* (Wellington: Evaluation Unit, Department of Social Welfare 1991), 40.
25 J. Renouf, G. Robb, and P. Wells, *Children, Young Persons, and Their Families Act 1989: Report on its First Year of Operation* (Wellington: Department of Social Welfare 1990), sec. 2.37-9.
26 Department of Social Welfare, *Corporate Plan 1990-91* (Wellington: Department of Social Welfare 1990).
27 Department of Social Welfare, 'Competency Certification Project: Maori Team

Report,' draft document of Department of Social Welfare, 1991.
28 Department of Social Welfare, 'Competency.'
29 Department of Social Welfare, 'Competency.'

Chapter 8: Similarities and Differences
1 Michael Banton, *Race Relations* (London: Tavistock 1967), 68-75.
2 T. Lindsay Buick, *The Treaty of Waitangi* (New Plymouth: Thomas Avery 1933), 78, citing Lord Normanby, Colonial Secretary, instructions to Captain Hobson, 1839.
3 Colin Tatz, *Race Relations in Australia* (Armidale: University of New England Publishing Unit 1979), 5.

Chapter 9: Understanding the Policy of Aboriginal Assimilation
1 Michael Banton, *Racial Theories* (Cambridge: Cambridge University Press 1987), xi and xii.
2 Michael Banton, *Racial and Ethnic Competition* (Cambridge: Cambridge University Press 1983), 12.
3 For a full discussion see Gordon Bennett, *Aboriginal Rights in International Law* (London: Royal Anthropological Institute of Great Britain and Ireland 1978). Canadian courts have followed the precedent of the United States Supreme Court, which has held that the legal claim of aboriginal peoples to their ancestral land was established by use and does not require legislative or executive recognition. The position has also been accepted by the New Zealand judiciary. However, in Australia the courts followed, until recently, a feudal doctrine which states that the basis of all land titles is a land grant from the Crown. As the Aboriginal people had never received such a grant, there were no rights to bring before a court. However, in the case of *Mabo v. Queensland, Australian Law Journal Reports* 66 (1993):408-99, the justices of the High Court of Australia ruled that a prior common-law aboriginal right to the land did pre-date settlement. This right could be extinguished by an act of the legislature but not without compensation, for to do so would be to breach the fiduciary responsibility of the Crown. This ruling opens the door to a re-examination of the entire process of dispossession without compensation that has taken place in Australia.
4 J.E. Goldthorpe, *The Sociology of the Third World* (Cambridge: Cambridge University Press 1975), 40-1, as cited by Stewart MacPherson in *Social Policy in the Third World* (Brighton: Wheatsheaf Books 1982).
5 MacPherson, *Social Policy*, 43-4.
6 Great Britain, Secretary of State for the Colonies, 1927. *Future Policy in Regards to Eastern Africa*, Cmd. 6175, HMSO, London, p. 2.
7 United Nations, *Committee on the Elimination of Racial Discrimination*, as cited in Ninth periodic report of New Zealand to the committee. (New York: United Nations 1990).
8 For a full discussion see Tatz, 'Four Kinds of Dominion.'
9 Ibid.
10 Michael D. Levin, ed., *Ethnicity and Aboriginality: Case Studies in Ethnonationalism* (Toronto: University of Toronto Press 1993), 3-4.

11 This essay has been reprinted on several occasions. It can be found in T.H. Marshall, *Class Citizenship and Social Development* (New York: Doubleday 1964), 65-122.
12 Ramesh Mishra, *Society and Social Policy: Theoretical Perspectives on Welfare* (London: Macmillan 1981), 27.
13 MacPherson, *Social Policy*, 147.
14 United Nations, Convention on the Rights of the Child, General Assembly, New York, 20 November 1989.
15 For a good discussion of the limitations of reparative approaches to aboriginal welfare, see Andrew Sharp, *Justice and the Maori* (Auckland: Oxford University Press 1990), especially Part 3, 'Equity, Equalities, and Maori Independence.'
16 For an appraisal of the operation of the act, see Ian B. Hassal, Commissioner for Children, *An Appraisal of the First Year of the Children, Young Persons and Their Families Act* (Wellington: Office of the Commissioner 1991).
17 Augie Fleras and Jean Leonard Elliott, *The Nations Within: Aboriginal-State Relations in Canada, the United States and New Zealand* (Toronto: Oxford University Press 1992), 226, also citing the work of Stephen Cornell, *The Return of the Native: American Indian Political Resurgence* (New York: Oxford University Press 1988).
18 See, for example, Menno Boldt, *Surviving as Indians: The Challenge of Self-Government* (Toronto: University of Toronto Press 1993).

Bibliography

General and International

Books and Articles

Banton, Michael. *Promoting Racial Harmony*. Cambridge: Cambridge University Press 1985
- *Race Relations*. London: Tavistock 1967
- *Racial and Ethnic Competition*. Cambridge: Cambridge University Press 1988
- *Racial Consciousness*. London: Longman 1988

Bennett, Gordon. *Aboriginal Rights in International Law*. London: Royal Anthropological Institute of Great Britain and Ireland 1978

Bienvenue, Rita M. 'Comparative Colonial Systems: The Case of Canadian Indians and Australian Aborigines.' *Australian/Canadian Studies* 1 (1983): 30-43

Brown, Stuart, John Fauvel, and Ruth Finnegan. *Conceptions of Inquiry*. London: Methuen 1981

Donnison, David. *The Government of Housing*. London: Pelican 1967

Finkelhor, David, and Jill Korbin. 'Child Abuse as an International Issue.' *Child Abuse and Neglect* 12 (1988):3-23

Fisher, Robin. 'The Impact of European Settlement on the Indigenous People of Australia, New Zealand and British Columbia.' *Canadian Ethnic Studies* 12, no. 4 (1980):1-14

Fleras, Augie, and Jean Leonard Elliott. *The Nations Within: Aboriginal-State Relations in Canada, the United States and New Zealand*. Toronto: Oxford University Press 1992

Geddes, W.R. 'Maori and Aborigine: A Comparison of Attitudes and Policies.' *Australian Journal of Science* 24, no. 5 (1961):217-25

Guillemine, Jeanne. 'The Politics of National Integration: A Comparison of United States and Canadian Indian Administration.' *Social Problems* 25 (December 1978):320-32

Hall, Phoebe, Hilary Land, Roy Parker, and Adrian Webb. *Change Choice and Conflict in Social Policy*. London: Heinemann 1975

Heidenheimer, Arnold J., Hugh Heclo, and Carolyn Teichadams. *Comparative Public Policy: The Politics of Social Choice in Europe and America*. London:

Macmillan 1978
Higgins, Joan. *States of Welfare*. Oxford: Blackwell 1981
Hocking, Barbara, ed. *International Law and Aboriginal Rights*. Sidney: The Law Book Company 1988
Howe, K.R. *Race Relations: Australia and New Zealand*. Auckland: Longman Paul 1977
Kahn, Alfred, and Sheila Kamerman. *Social Services in International Perspective: The Emergence of a Sixth System*. Washington: US Department of Health, Education, and Welfare 1976
Kamerman, Sheila, and Alfred Kahn. *Family Policy: Government and Families in Fourteen Countries*. New York: Columbia University Press 1978
Kaim-Caudle, P.R. *Comparative Social Policy and Social Security: A Ten-Country Study*. London: Robertson 1973
Korbin, J., ed. *Child Abuse and Neglect: Cross Cultural Perspectives*. Berkeley: University of California Press 1981
Levin, Michael D., ed. *Ethnicity and Aboriginality: Case Studies in Ethnonationalism*. Toronto: University of Toronto Press 1993
MacPherson, Stewart. *Five Hundred Million Children*. Brighton: Wheatsheaf Books 1978
– *Social Policy in the Third World*. Brighton: Wheatsheaf Books 1982
MacPherson, Stewart, and James Midgeley. *Comparative Social Policy and the Third World*. Brighton: Wheatsheaf Books 1987
Martin, E.W. *Comparative Development in Social Welfare*. London: Allen and Unwin 1972
Metge, J. 'Alternative Policy Patterns in Multi-racial Societies.' In *Administration in New Zealand's Multi-racial Society*, Wellington: New Zealand Institute of Public Administration 1967.
Midgeley, James. *Professional Imperialism*, London: Heinemann 1981
Mishra, Ramesh. *Society and Social Policy: Theoretical Perspectives on Welfare*. London: Macmillan 1981
Mohan, Brij. *Toward Comparative Social Welfare*. Cambridge, MA: Schenkman Books 1987
Morse, Bradford. *Aboriginal Self Government in Australia and Canada*. Kingston, ON: Institute of Intergovernmental Relations 1984
– 'Australia and Canada: Indigenous Peoples and the Law.' *Legal Services Bulletin* 8, no. 3 (1983):104-8
Nurcombe, Barry. *Children of the Dispossessed: A Consideration of Intelligence, Cultural Disadvantage, and Educational Programs for Culturally Different People, and of the Development and Expression of a Profile of Competence*. Honolulu: University of Hawaii Press 1976.
Oyen, Else. *Comparing Welfare States and Their Futures*. Hants, England: Gower 1986.
Parker, Roy. 'Comparative Social Policy and the Politics of Comparison.' In *Improving Social Intervention*, edited by John Gandy, Alex Robertson, and Susan Sinclair. New York: Croom Helm 1983
Pittock, A. Barrie. *Australia Aborigines: The Common Struggle for Humanity*. Sydney: International Work Group for Indigenous Affairs 1979

Rodgers, Barbara N., John Crewe, and John S. Morgan. *Comparative Social Administration*. London: Allen and Unwin 1968
Rodgers, Barbara N., with Abraham Doron and Michael Jones. *The Study of Social Policy: A Comparative Approach*. London: Allen and Unwin 1979
Payne, Christopher J., and Keith J. White. *Caring for Deprived Children: International Case Studies of Residential Settings*. London: Croom Helm 1979
Tatz, Colin M. 'Four Kinds of Dominion: Comparative Race Politics in Australia, Canada, New Zealand and South Africa.' Inaugural public lecture delivered in Armidale, New South Wales, 17 July 1972
Winch, Peter. *Ethics and Action*. London: Routledge and Kegan Paul 1972
Wintersberger, Helmut. *Childhood as a Social Phenomenon: Implications for Future Social Policies*. Vienna: European Centre for Social Welfare Training and Research 1987
Young, Crawford, ed. *The Rising Tide of Cultural Pluralism*. Madison: University of Wisconsin Press 1992

Government Documents
British Parliamentary Papers, *Report from His Majesty's Commission for Inquiring into the Administration and Practical Operation of the Poor Laws* 27, no. 44 (1834)
British Parliamentary Papers, House of Commons, *Report of the Select Committee of Aborigines* 425, no. 7 (1837)
United Nations. International Convention on the Elimination of All Forms of Racial Discrimination. Adopted by the General Assembly of the United Nations in Resolution 2106 A (20), New York, 21 December 1965
– Periodic Reports of State Parties under Article 9 of the Convention on the Elimination of All Forms of Racial Discrimination; Australia Reports 5(1985), 6(1989), 8(1991); Canada Reports 9(1987), 10(1989); New Zealand Reports 9(1989)
United Nations Educational, Scientific, and Cultural Organization (UNESCO). *Trends in Ethnic Group Relations in Asia and Oceania*. Paris 1979

Australia: Social Administration

Books and Articles
Baldock, Cora V., ed. *Women, Social Welfare and the State in Australia*. Sydney: Allen and Unwin 1983
Brennan, D., and C. O'Donnell. *Caring for Australia's Children*. Sydney: Allen and Unwin 1986
Brown, Jill W. *Aborigines and Islanders in Brisbane*. Canberra: Australian Government Printing Service 1974
Burgmann, Verity, and Jenny Lee, eds. *A Most Valuable Acquisition*. Australia: McPhee Gribble/Penguin 1988
Graycar, Adam, and Adam Jamrozik. *How Australians Live*. Melbourne: McMillan 1989
Graycar, Adam. *Retreat from the Welfare State: Australian Social Policy in the 1980's*. Sydney: Allen and Unwin 1983

Jayasuria, Laksiri. *Immigration Policies and Ethnic Relations in Australia.* Perth: Department of Social Work and Social Administration, University of Western Australia 1988
Jones, Michael Anthony. *The Australian Welfare State.* Sydney: Allen and Unwin 1980
Kershaw, Jane., ed. *Child Care as a Social Issue.* Sydney: Action for Children 1980
McIntyre, Stuart. *Winners and Losers: The Pursuit of Social Justice in Australian History.* Sydney: Allen and Unwin 1985
Mendlesohn, Ronald. *The Condition of the People: Social Welfare in Australia, 1900-1975.* Sydney: Allen and Unwin 1979
Poad, Doug. *Contact: An Australian History.* Victoria: Heinemann Educational 1985
Sweeney, Tania. *Services for Young Children: Welfare Service or Social Parenthood?* Sydney: University of New South Wales, Social Welfare Research Centre 1982

Government Documents
Australia. *Commission of Inquiry into Poverty, Law and Poverty in Australia.* Canberra: Australian Law Reform Commission 1975
– Family Law Council. *Watson Committee Report.* Canberra: Family Law Council 1982
– Law Reform Commission. *Child Welfare.* Canberra: Australian Law Reform Commission 1981
– Law Reform Commission. *Child Welfare: Child Abuse and Day Care.* Sydney: Australian Law Reform Commission 1980
– Law Reform Commission. *Children in Trouble.* Sydney: Australian Law Reform Commission 1979

Australia: Aboriginal Peoples

Books and Articles
Altman J.C. *The Economic Status of Australian Aborigines.* New York: Cambridge University Press 1979.
Austin, J. 'The Destruction of Aboriginal Families.' *Nunga News,* 2-3 July 1976
Bell, Diane. *Daughters in the Dreaming.* Boston: Allen and Unwin 1983
Berndt, Ronald M., ed. *A Question of Choice.* Perth: University of Western Australia Press 1971
Bernolt, R.W., *Aborigines and Change: Australia in the 1970's.* Canberra: Australian Institute for Aboriginal Studies 1974
Biskup P. 'White – Aboriginal Relations in Western Australia: An Overview.' *Comparative Studies in Society and History* 10 (1967-8):447-57
Chisolm, Richard. 'Aboriginal Law in Australia: The Law Reform Commission's Proposals for Recognition.' *University of Hawaii Law Review* 10, no. 47 (1988):47-80
– 'The Aboriginal Legal Service.' *Justice* (1972):26-33
Gale, Faye, ed. *We Are Bosses Today: The Status and Role of Aboriginal Women*

Today. Canberra: Australian Institute for Aboriginal Studies 1983

Gammage, Bill, and Andrew Markus. *All That Dirt: Aborigines 1938*. Canberra: History Project Inc., Australian National University, Social Sciences Research School 1982

Hill, Kathleen F. *A Study of Aboriginal Poverty in Two Country Towns*. Canberra: Australian National University Press 1975

Howard, Michael C. *Aboriginal Power in Australian Society*. Honolulu: University of Hawaii Press 1982

– *Whitefeller Business: Aborigines in Australian Politics*. Philadelphia: Institute for the Study of Human Issues 1978

Jones, F. Lancaster. *The Structure and Growth of Australia's Aboriginal Population*. Canberra: Australian National University Press 1970

Lippman, Lorna. *Generations of Resistance: the Aboriginal Struggle for Justice*. Melbourne: Longman Cheshire 1981

Lumb R.D. 'Mabo and Aboriginal Title in Queensland.' *Queensland Lawyer* 14, no. 1 (1993):15-18

McCorquodale, John. *Aborigines and the Law: A Digest*. Canberra: Aboriginal Studies Press 1987 (Note: Contains a superb annotated bibliography, listing 800 authors, and an annotated list of 737 references to Aborigines in Australian state and federal statutes.)

Middleton, Margaret. *Yuendumu and Its Children: Life and Health in an Aboriginal Settlement*. Canberra: Australian National University Press 1976

Miller, James. *Koeri: A Will to Win – The Heroic Resistance, Survival and Triumph of Black Australia*. London: Angus and Robertson 1985

Reynolds, Henry. *Dispossession: Black Australians and White Invaders*. Sydney: Allen and Unwin 1989

Rowley, C.D. *Aboriginal Policy and Practice*. Canberra: Australian National University Press 1970

– *The Destruction of Aboriginal Society*. Canberra: Australian National University Press 1970

– *A Matter of Justice*. Canberra: Australian National University Press 1978

– *Outcasts in White Australia*. Canberra: Australian University Press 1971

– *The Politics of Aboriginal Reform*. Victoria: Penguin Books 1986

– *The Remote Aborigines*. Canberra: Australian National University Press 1971

Smith, L.R. *The Aboriginal Population Of Australia*. Canberra: Australian National University Press 1980

Stanner, W.E.H. *White Man Got No Dreaming: Essay 1938-1973*. Canberra: Australian National University Press 1979

Stevens, Frank S. *Black Australia*. Sydney: Alternative Publishing Cooperative 1981

– *Racism: The Australian Experience – A Study of Race Prejudice in Australia* New York: Taplinger 1972

Tatz, C.M. *Race Relations in Australia*. Armidale: University of New England Publishing Unit 1979

Tatz, Colin, ed. *Black Viewpoints: The Aboriginal Experience*. Sydney: Australia and New Zealand Books 1975

Wilson, Paul R. *Black Death, White Hands*. Sydney: Allen and Unwin 1982

World Council of Churches. *Justice for Aboriginal Australians*. Sydney: Australian Council of Churches 1981
Yarwood, A.T., and M.J. Knowling. *Race Relations in Australia: A History*. North Ryde, NSW: Methuen 1982

Government Documents

Australia. Aboriginal Development Commission. *Annual Reports* 1982-90.
– *Australia Yearbook*. 1924, 1930, and 1986
– Department of Aboriginal Affairs. *Annual Reports*.
– Department of Aboriginal Affairs. *Allocation for Government Expenditure on Aboriginal Programs, 1986-7*. Canberra: Budget Branch 1986
– Department of Aboriginal Affairs. *Seven Years On*. Report by Justice Tochey to the Minister for Aboriginal Affairs regarding the Aboriginal Land Rights (Northern Territory) Act, 1976, and related matters. Canberra: Department of Aboriginal Affairs 1984
– High Court. '*Mabo v. Queensland*.' *Australian Law Journal Reports* 66 (1992):408-99
– Law Reform Commission. *Aboriginal Customary Law: Child Custody, Fostering and Adoption*. Sydney: Australian Law Reform Commission 1982

Australia: Aboriginal Peoples and Social Administration

Books and Articles

Bailley, Rebecca J. 'A Comparison of Appearances by Aboriginal and Non-Aboriginal Children before the Children's Court.' Paper delivered at Aborigines and Criminal Justice Seminar, Canberra, 1983
Bonner, Judith. 'Children of Aboriginal Descent in Care and Protection in Brisbane Institutions.' BSW thesis, University of Queensland, 1970
Chisolm, Richard. 'Aboriginal Children: Political Pawns or Paramount Consideration?' Paper delivered at Social Welfare Research Seminar, University of New South Wales, Sidney, 6 July 1983
– 'Aboriginal Law in Australia: The Law Reform Commission's Proposals for Recognition.' *University of Hawaii Law Review* 10, no. 1 (1988):47-80
– *Black Children: White Welfare*. Sydney: Social Welfare Research Centre 1985
– 'Destined Children: Aboriginal Child Welfare in Australia – Directions of Change in Law and Policy.' *Aboriginal Law Bulletin* 14 (1985)
Cole, Keith. 'A Critical Appraisal of Anglican Mission policy and Practice in Arnhem Land 1908-39.' In *Aborigines and Change: Australia in the 70's*. New Jersey: Humanities Press 1977
Collman, Jeffrey Reid. 'Burning Mt. Kelly: Aborigines and the Administration of Social Welfare in Central Australia.' Ph.D. thesis, University of Adelaide, 1979
– *Fringe Dwellers and Welfare: the Aboriginal Response to Bureaucracy*. Brisbane: University of Queensland Press 1988
Davis, Alan, and Janet George. *States of Health: Health and Illness in Australia*. Artarmon: Harper and Row 1988
Downing, Jim. 'Examination and Assessment of the Problem of Juvenile

Deviant Behaviour in Aboriginal Communities in the North West of South Australia.' Alice Springs, 1971 (mimeograph)

Dunn, S.S., and Colin Tatz, eds. *Aborigines and Education*. Melbourne: Sun Books 1969

Edwards, Coral. 'Aboriginal Children in Care in New South Wales: An Historical Overview.' *Proceedings of the Foster Care Association Conference*, Sydney, September 1982

Edwards, R. 'Native Education in the Northern Territory of Australia.' MA thesis, University of Sidney, 1962

Eggleston, Elizabeth M. *Fear, Favour or Affection: Aborigines and the Criminal Law in Victoria, Southern Australia and Western Australia*. Canberra: Australian National University Press 1976

Foley, Matthew. 'From Protectionism to Laissez-Faire.' *Social Alternatives* 2, no. 2 (1981):37-41

– 'Research in Aboriginal and Islander Child Welfare.' Paper delivered at Aboriginal and Islander Child Welfare Seminar, Department of Social Work, University of Queensland, 20 May 1982

Foreman, Lynne. *Children or Families? An Evaluation of the Legislative Basis for Child Protective Statutory Service in the Australian States and Territories*. Queenbeyan: Social Welfare Commission 1975

Gamble, Helen. *Law for Parents and Children*. 2nd edition. Sydney: Law Book Co. 1986

Hankins, Carla Christine. 'The Missing Links: Cultural Genocide through the Abduction of Female Aboriginal Children from Their Families and Their Training for Domestic Service, 1883-1969.' BA thesis, University of New South Wales, 1982

Hasluck, Paul. *Black Australians: A Survey of Native Policies in Western Australia, 1829-97*. Carlton: Melbourne University Press 1970

– *Shades of Darkness: Aboriginal Affairs 1925-65*. Melbourne: Melbourne University Press 1987

Heppell, M., ed. *A Black Reality: Aboriginal Camps and Housing in Remote Australia*. Canberra: Australian Institute of Aboriginal Studies 1987

Kalokennos, Archie. *Every Second Child*. Melbourne: Nelson 1974

Kamien, Max. *The Dark People of Bourke: A Study of Planned Social Change*. Canberra: Australian Institute of Aboriginal Studies 1978

Le Seur, Edwin. 'Aboriginal Assimilation: An Evaluation of Some Ambiguities in Policy and Services.' *Australian Journal of Social Work* 23, no. 2 (1970):6-11

Lickiss, J. Norelle. 'Social Deviance in Aboriginal Boys.' *Medical Journal of Australia* 2, no. 9 (1971):460-70

Martin, Margaret A. *Aboriginal Statistics*. Perth: Western Australia Department of Corrections 1971

Milne, Chris, and Aileen Mongta. *Aboriginal Children in Substitute Care*. Sydney: Aboriginal Children's Research Project 1982

Nettheim, Garth. *Outlawed: Queensland's Aborigines and Islanders and the Rule of Law*. Sydney: Australia and New Zealand Books 1973

– *Victims of the Law: Black Queenslanders Today*. Sydney: Allen and Unwin 1981

Nettheim, Garth, ed. *Aborigines, Human Rights and the Law*. Sydney: Australia and New Zealand Books 1974

Read, Peter. *Link-Up*. Sydney: Link-Up Corporation 1989

– 'The Stolen Generations: The Removal of Aboriginal Children in New South Wales 1883 to 1969.' Occasional paper no. 1. Sydney, New South Wales, Ministry of Aboriginal Affairs, 1982

Schultz, I.M. 'Adopted and Fostered Aboriginal Children in Southern Australia.' In *The Aborigines of Southern Australia*, edited by J.W. Warburton. Adelaide: University of Adelaide Press 1969

Sommerland, Elizabeth-Ann. 'Aboriginal Juveniles in Custody: New Community and Institutional Approaches,' *Australian Child and Family Welfare* 3, nos. 3-4 (1978):43-9

– *Kormilela, the Way to Tomorrow? A Study in Aboriginal Education*. Canberra: Australian National University Press 1976

Stone, Sherman. *Aborigines in White Australia: A Documentary History of the Attitudes Affecting Official Policy and the Australian Aborigine, 1897-1973*. Victoria: Heinemann Education 1974

Tatz, C.M. 'Aboriginal Administration in the Northern Territory of Australia.' PhD thesis, Canberra, Australian National University, 1964

Thorpe, M. 'Queensland Aboriginal and Torres Strait Islander Child Care Agencies Paper.' Sixth International Congress on Child Abuse, Sydney, 11-18 August 1986

Volard, Jill. 'Framing Adoption Legislation in Queensland: Children with Special Needs.' *Legal Services Bulletin* 7, no. 5 (1982):246-8

Government Documents

Australia. Bureau of Statistics. *Children in Care in Australia*. Canberra: Bureau of Statistics 1985

– Law Reform Commission. *Aboriginal Customary Law: Marriage, Children and the Distribution of Property*. Sydney: Australian Law Reform Committee 1982

– Law Reform Commission. *The Recognition of Aboriginal Customary Laws*. Canberra: Australian Law Reform Committee 1986

– Law Reform Commission. *Research Paper No. 4: Child Custody, Fostering and Adoption*. Canberra: Australian Law Reform Committee 1982

Canada: Social Administration

Books and Articles

Armitage, Andrew. *Social Welfare in Canada*. 2nd. edition. Toronto: McClelland and Stewart 1988

Banting, Keith. *The Welfare State and Canadian Federalism*. Montreal: McGill-Queen's University Press 1984

Callahan, Marilyn. *A Prototype for a National Child Welfare Data System*. Ottawa: Welfare Grants Directorate, Health and Welfare Canada 1987

Coates, Kenneth. *Canada's Colonies*. Toronto: James Lorimer 1985

Guest, Dennis. *The Emergence of Social Security in Canada*. 2nd. edition. Vancouver: University of British Columbia Press 1986

Levitt, Kenneth, and Brian Wharf. *The Challenge of Child Welfare*. Vancouver: University of British Columbia Press 1985
Splane, Richard B. 'Whatever Happened to the GAI?' *Social Worker* 48, no. 2 (1980):86-8
Wharf, Brian, ed. *Rethinking Child Welfare in Canada*. Toronto: McClelland and Stewart 1993

Government Documents
British Columbia. *Report of the Royal Commission on Family Law*. Victoria: Queen's Printer 1976

Canada: First Nations Peoples

Books and Articles
Adams, Howard. *Prisoner of Grass*. Saskatoon: Fifth House Publishers 1989
Assu, Harry, and Joy Inglis. *Assu of Cape Mudge: Recollections of a Coastal Indian Chief*. Vancouver: University of British Columbia Press 1989
Boldt, Menno. *Surviving as Indians: The Challenge of Self-Government*. Toronto: University of Toronto Press 1993
Cassidy, Frank, and Robert L. Bish. *Indian Government: Its Meaning in Practice*. Lantzville: Oolichan Books 1989
Cassidy, Frank. *Native Peoples: A Research Agenda*. Ottawa: Institute for Research on Public Policy 1988
Cole, Douglas, and Ira Chaikin. *An Iron Hand Upon the People: The Law against the Potlatch on the Northwest Coast*. Seattle: University of Washington Press 1990
Cumming, Peter, and Neil H. Mickenberg. *Native Rights in Canada*. Toronto: Indian Eskimo Association of Canada 1980
Englestad, Diane, and John Bird, eds. *Nation to Nation: Aboriginal Sovereignty and the Future of Canada*. Concord: House of Anansi Press 1992
Fisher, Robert, and Ken Coates. *Out of the Background*. Toronto: Copp, Clark and Pitman 1989
Frideres, James S. *Native Peoples in Canada: Contemporary Conflicts*. 3rd edition. Toronto: Prentice Hall 1988
Fritz, Linda. *Native Law Bibliography*. Saskatoon: University of Saskatchewan Native Law Centre 1990
Hawthorn, H.B. (chair). *A Survey of the Contemporary Indians of Canada: A Report on Economic, Political, Educational Needs and Policies*. Ottawa: Supply and Services 1966
Haegert, Dorothy. *Children of the First People*. Vancouver: Tillacum Library 1988
Jamieson, Kathleen. *Indian Women and the Law in Canada: Citizen's Minus*. Ottawa: Supply and Services 1978
Kirk, Ruth. *Wisdom of the Elders*. Vancouver: Douglas and McIntyre 1988
Miller, J.R. *Skyscrapers Hide the Heavens: A History of Indian-White Relations in Canada*. Toronto: University of Toronto Press 1989
Morse, Bradford. *Aboriginal Peoples and the Law: Indian, Métis and Inuit Rights*

in Canada. Ottawa: Carleton University Press 1989
Richardson, Boyce. *Drumbeat: Anger and Renewal in Indian Country*. Toronto: Summerhill Press 1989
Salyzn, Vladimir. 'Goals in Indian Affairs.' *Canadian Welfare* 42, no. 2 (1966):79-82
Sheffe, Norman. *Issues for the Seventies: Canada's Indians*. Toronto: McGraw Hill 1970
Tennant, Paul. *Aboriginal People and Politics: The Indian Land Question in British Columbia, 1849-1989*. Vancouver: University of British Columbia Press 1990
Tobias, John. 'Protection, Civilization and Assimilation: An Outline History of Canada's Indian Policy.' *Western Canadian Journal of Anthropology* 6, no. 2 (1976):13-30
Woodward, Jack. *Native Law*. Toronto: Carswell 1989
Yukon Native Brotherhood. *Together Today for Our Children Tomorrow*. Whitehorse: Whitehorse Star 1973

Government Documents

Canada. House of Commons. *Indian Self-Government in Canada*. Ottawa: Queen's Printer 1983
– *Statement of the Government of Canada on Indian Policy*. Ottawa: Queen's Printer 1967
– *Canada Year Book*. Ottawa: Supply and Services 1915-90
– DIAND. *Basic Departmental Data*. Ottawa: Supply and Services 1989
– DIAND. *A Catalogue of Statistical Information Maintained by the Program Reference Centre, Indian and Inuit Program*. Ottawa: Supply and Services 1985
– DIAND. *Implementation of the 1985 Changes to the Indian Act*. Ottawa: Supply and Services 1987
– DIAND. *Indians of British Columbia*. Ottawa: Supply and Services 1969
– DIAND. *Indians of the Prairie Provinces*. Ottawa: Supply and Services 1967
– DIAND. *1986 Census Highlights on Registered Indians*, Ottawa: Supply and Services 1989
– DIAND. *Population Projections of Registered Indians, 1986-2011*. Ottawa: Supply and Services 1990
McEachern, Alan (Chief Justice, Supreme Court of British Columbia). *Reasons for Judgement between: Delgamuukw, also known as Ken Muldoe (plaintiff), and: Her Majesty the Queen in Right of the Province of British Columbia and the Attorney General of Canada (defendants)*. No. 0843, Smithers Registry, 1991

Canada: First Nations Peoples and Social Administration

Books and Articles

Armitage, Andrew, Frances Ricks, and Brian Wharf. *The Champagne-Aishihik Child Welfare Pilot Project: Evaluation*. Victoria: School of Social Work: University of Victoria 1988
Bagley, Chris. 'Child Protection and the Native Child: A Case Study.' *Perception* 8, no. 1 (1987):17-19

Ballard, Kent, Jean Cromwell, and Cathy Cromwell. 'Challenges for Social Work Education North of 60.' *Canadian Social Work Review* 11, no. 1 (1985):249-64

Barman, Jean, Yvonne Hébert, and Don McCaskill, eds. *Indian Education in Canada*. Vol. 1: *The Legacy*. Vancouver: University of British Columbia Press 1988

– *Indian Education in Canada*. Vol. 2: *The Challenge*. Vancouver: University of British Columbia Press 1988

Caldwell, George. *Indian Residential Schools*. Ottawa: Canadian Welfare Council 1967

Canadian Corrections Association. *Indians and the Law*. Ottawa: Canadian Welfare Council 1967

Canadian Welfare Council and Canadian Association of Social Workers. *Joint submission to the Special Senate Committee of the Senate and House of Commons Appointed to Examine and Consider the Indian Act*. Ottawa: Canadian Welfare Council 1947

Carasco, Emily F. 'Canadian Native Children: Have Child Welfare Laws Broken the Circle?' *Canadian Journal of Family Law* 5, no. 1 (1986):111-38

Colorado, Pam, and Don Collins. 'Non-Native to Native Child Care Services: Shifting Paradigms.' Paper delivered at Third National Conference on Provincial Social Welfare Policy, Calgary, University of Calgary, 1987

Giesbrecht, Brian (Hon. Justice). *Report on the Death of Lester Desjarlais*, Winnipeg: Office of the Chief Medical Examiner 1992

Gingrass, Marie. 'The Boarding Home Programme as Experienced by Ten Indian Students in Victoria, B.C.' MA thesis, Faculty of Education, University of Victoria, 1977

Govereau, Wayne. *Native Child and Family Services in Manitoba*. Unpublished. Winnipeg 1986

Hill, Elizabeth. 'Urban Models for Native Child Welfare: Progress and Prospect.' Paper delivered at Third National Conference on Provincial Social Welfare Policy, Calgary, University of Calgary, 1987

Hudson, Peter, and Brad McKenzie. 'Child Welfare and Native Peoples: The Extension of Colonialism.' *The Social Worker* 49, no. 2 (1981):63-7

– *Evaluation of the Dakota Ojibway Child and Family Services*. Winnipeg: DIAND 1987

Hudson, Peter, and Sharon Taylor-Henley. *Agreement and Disagreement: An Evaluation of the Canada-Manitoba Northern Indian Child Welfare Agreement*. Winnipeg: School of Social Work, University of Manitoba 1987

– *Indian Provincial Relationships in Social Welfare: Northern Issues and Future Options*. Winnipeg: Child and Family Services Research Group 1987

Johnston, Basil. *Indian School Days*. Toronto: Key Porter Books 1988

Johnston, Patrick. *Native Children and the Child Welfare System*. Toronto: James Lorimer 1983

King, Richard. *Native Indians and Schooling in British Columbia*. Victoria: Faculty of Education, University of Victoria 1978

– *The School at Mopass*. Stanford: Holt, Reinhart and Winston 1967

McDonald, John. 'The Spallumcheen Indian Band By-law.' In *The Challenge of Child Welfare*, edited by Ken Levitt and Brian Wharf. Vancouver: University of British Columbia Press 1987
McKenzie, Brad, and Peter Hudson. 'Native Children, Child Welfare and the Colonization of Native People.' In *The Challenge of Child Welfare*, edited by Ken Levitt and Brian Wharf. Vancouver: University of British Columbia Press 1985
Manitoba Métis Federation. *Michif Child and Family Services, Inc.* Dauphin: North West Métis Council 1989
– *Submission to the Aboriginal Justice Inquiry*. Winnipeg: North West Métis Council 1989
Native Council of Canada. *Native Child Care: 'The Circle of Care.'* Ottawa: Native Council of Canada 1990
Ryant, Joseph. 'Some Issues in the Adoption of Native Children.' In *Adoption: Current Issues and Trends*, edited by Paul Sachdev. Toronto: Butterworth 1984
Sim, Alex. 'Indian Schools for Indian Children.' *Canadian Welfare* 45, no. 2 (1969):11-14
Stanbury, William. 'Poverty Among B.C. Indians Off Reserve.' *Canadian Welfare* 50, no. 1 (1974):20-2
Tester, Frank. 'Still Not Home: The Indian and Native Child and Family Service Provisions of Ontario's Bill 77.' *Social Worker* 54, no. 4 (1986):160-4
Tester, Frank James and Peter Kulchyski. *Tammarniit (Mistakes): Inuit Relocation in the Eastern Arctic 1939-63*. Vancouver: UBC Press 1994
Timpson, Joyce, B. 'Indian and Native Special Status in Ontario's Child Welfare Legislation.' *Canadian Social Work Review* 7, no. 1 (Winter 1990):49-68
Wharf, Brian. *Towards First Nations Control of Child Welfare*. Victoria: School of Social Work, University of Victoria 1987

Government Documents

Assembly of First Nations (AFN). *For Discussion: National Strategy on First Nations Child and Family Services*. Ottawa: AFN 1991
– *Report of the National Inquiry into First Nations Child Care*. Ottawa: AFN 1989
– *Strengthening the Family, Building the Community: Final Report on the First Canadian Indian-Native Child Welfare Conference*, Fredericton, New Brunswick, 8-10 November 1988
British Columbia. Ministry of Social Services. *Liberating Our Children: Liberating Our Nations*. Report of the Aboriginal Committee, Community Panel, Family and Children's Services Legislation Review in British Columbia. Victoria: Queen's Printer 1992
Canada. Department of Indian Affairs and Northern Development (DIAND). *Indian Child and Family Services Management Regime: Discussion Paper*. Ottawa: DIAND 1989
– DIAND. *Indian Child and Family Services in Canada: Final Report*. Toronto: DIAND 1987
– DIAND. *Indian Child Welfare and Family Services*. Communiqué. Ottawa: DIAND 1988

– DIAND. *Indian Policing Policy.* Ottawa: DIAND 1990
Ministry of Supply and Services. *Report of the Mackenzie Valley Pipeline Inquiry.* Ottawa: Queen's Printer 1977

New Zealand: Social Administration

Books and Articles
Bloomfield, C.T. *A Handbook of Historical Statistics.* Boston: Hall 1984
Campbell, I.D. *The Law of Adoption in New Zealand.* Wellington: Bittenworth 1957
Cendliffe, John Bell. *The Welfare State in New Zealand.* London: Allen and Unwin 1959
Davidson, Allan K., and Peter J. Lineham. *Transplanted Christianity: Documents Illustrating Aspects of New Zealand Church History.* Palmerston North: Dunsmore Press 1987
Easten, B.H. *Social Policy and the Welfare State in New Zealand.* Auckland: Allen and Unwin 1980
Else, Anne. 'The Perfect Solution: Adoption in New Zealand.' *International Journal of the Sociology of Law* 15 (1987):237-57
Mol, Hans. *Religion and Race in New Zealand: A Critical Review of the Policies and Practices of the Churches in New Zealand.* Christchurch: National Council of Churches 1966
New Zealand Planning Council. *Who Gets What? The Distribution of Income and Wealth in New Zealand.* Wellington: New Zealand Planning Council 1990
Oliver, W.H., and B.R. Williams. *The Oxford History of New Zealand.* Wellington: Oxford University Press 1981
Sinclair, Keith. *A History of New Zealand.* Auckland: Penguin Books and Allen Lane 1980
Trlin, A.D., ed. *Social Welfare and New Zealand Society.* Wellington: Methuen 1977

Government Documents
New Zealand. Department of Statistics. *Social Trends in New Zealand.* Wellington: Department of Statistics 1977
– *New Zealand Official Yearbook.* Wellington: Department of Statistics 1990
– *The Royal Commission on Social Policy.* 5 vols. Wellington: Government Printer 1988

New Zealand: Maori

Books and Articles
Auscbel, David P. 'Maoris: A Study in Resistive Acculturation.' *Social Forces* 39 (1961):218-27
Barrington, J.H., and T.H. Beaglehole. *Maori Schools in a Changing Society: An Historical Review.* Wellington: Council for Educational Research 1974
Binney, Judith, and Gillian Chaplin. *Nga Morenu: The Survivors.* Auckland: Oxford Univerity Press 1983

Butterworth, G.V. *End of an Era: The Departments of Maori Affairs 1840-1989*. Wellington: Department of Maori Affairs 1989

Harne, John N. 'Cross-Cultural Problems and the Family.' *New Zealand Social Worker* 4, no. 3 (1968):21-7

Kelsey, Jane. *A Question of Honour? Labour and the Treaty*. Auckland: Allen and Unwin 1990

King, Michael. *Maori: A Photographic and Social History*. Auckland: Heinemann Reed 1983

Levine, Stephen, and Raj Vasil. *Maori Political Perspectives*. Wellington: Hutchinson 1985

Mitchell, Robin. *The Treaty and the Act*. Christchurch: Cadsonbury Publications 1990

Mulgan, Richard. *Maori, Pakeha and Democracy*. Auckland: Oxford University Press 1989

Murchie, Elizabeth. *Rapoura: Health and Maori Women*. Wellington: Maori Women's Welfare League 1984

Pool, Ian. *The Maori Population of New Zealand 1769-1971*. Auckland: Auckland University Press/Oxford University Press 1980

– *Te Iwi Maori*. Auckland: Auckland University Press 1991

Putra, V. 'Planning for Our Children's Future.' *Te Ao Hoi* 53 (1965):17-18

Sharp, Andrew. *Justice and the Maori*. Auckland: Oxford University Press 1990

Spoonley, P., ed. *Tauiwi: Racism and Ethnicity in New Zealand*. Palmerston North: Dunsmore Press 1984

Walker, Ranginui. *Ka Whawhai Tonu Matou: Struggle Without End*. Auckland: Penguin Books 1990

– 'Understanding the Maori Child.' *Te Maori* 2, no. 4 (1971):27-9

Yensen, Helen, Kevin Hague, and Tim McCreanor. *Honouring the Treaty*. Auckland: Penguin Books 1990

Government Documents

– Department of Maori Affairs. *The Integration of Maori and Pakeha in New Zealand*. Wellington: Government Printer 1962

– Department of Statistics. *Maori Statistical Profile 1961-86*. Wellington: Government Printer 1986

– *Education of Native Children*. Annual Report. Wellington: Department of Education 1931

– *Education: Native Schools, 1911*. Annual Report. Wellington: Department of Education 1911

– House of Representatives. *Report on Department of Maori Affairs by J.K. Hunn*. Wellington: Government Printer 1960

Manatu Maori. *A Directory of Maori Statistics*. Wellington: Ministry of Maori Affairs 1991

New Zealand: Maori and Social Administration

Books and Articles
Bennett, C.M. 'Towards a Welfare Programme for the Maori.' *Te Ao Hoi* 18

(1957):6-9
- 'Welfare Division of Department of Maori Affairs.' *New Zealand Child Welfare Workers Bulletin* 3 (1952):18-22

Chapple, Kingsley. 'Character Training in the Native School.' *Education Gazette* (April 1933):53-3

Else, Anne. *A Question of Adoption*. Wellington: Bridget Williams Books 1991

Ferguson, D.M., Jean Fleming, and D.P. O'Neil, *Child Abuse in New Zealand: A Report of a Nation-wide Study of the Physical Ill-Treatment of Children in New Zealand*. Wellington: Department of Social Welfare, Research Division, 1972

Fleras, Augie J. 'From Social Welfare to Community Development: Maori Policy and the Department of Maori Affairs in New Zealand.' *Community Development Journal* 19 (1984):32-9

Harvey, Michael. *Interim Report on Findings from the FGC Statistical Information Questionnaires*. Wellington: Evaluation Unit, Department of Social Welfare 1991

Paterson, Karen. *Evaluation of the Organization and Operation of Care and Protection Family Group Conferences*. Wellington: Department of Social Welfare 1991

Piddington, Ralph. 'Maori Child Welfare: The Cultural Background.' *New Zealand Child Welfare Worker Bulletin* 3 (1952):1-12

Renouf J., G. Robb, and P. Wells. *Children, Young Persons and Their Families Act, 1989: Report on Its First Year of Operation*. Wellington: Department of Social Welfare 1990

Social Work Review. Special Issue. *The Children and Young Persons and Their Families Act (1989): A Review after the First Year of Operation*. February 1991

Tamahere. 'The Native School and The Community.' *National Education* (March 1944):79-84

Government Documents

Education Gazette. Special edition. *Native Education*. Wellington: October 1941
- Special edition. *Child Welfare*. Wellington: September 1941

New Zealand. Adoption Act, 1955
- Children, Young Persons and Their Families Act, 1989
- Department of Justice. *Te Whangai i Te Tika: In Search of Justice*. Report of the Advisory Committee on Legal Services. Wellington: Department of Justice 1987
- Department of Maori Affairs. *Maatua Whangai*. Wellington: Department of Maori Affairs 1986
- Department of Maori Affairs. *Report of the Review of Te Kohanga Reo*. Wellington: Department of Maori Affairs 1988
- Department of Social Welfare. 'Competency Certification Project: Maori Team Report.' Draft Document of the Department of Social Welfare, 1991
- Department of Social Welfare, Maori Unit. *Implementing Puao-te-Ata-tu*. Series 1-5. Wellington: Department of Social Welfare 1989
- House of Representatives. *Education of Native Children*. Appendix to the Journals of the House of Representatives. Wellington: Government Printer 1931

- *Puao-te-Ata-tu (Daybreak): The Report of the Ministerial Advisory Committee on a Maori Perspective for the Department Of Social Welfare.* Wellington: Government Printer 1986
- *Report of the Department of Social Welfare for the Year Ended 31 March 1988.* Wellington: Government Printer 1988
- *Report of the Royal Commission on Social Policy.* Wellington: Government Printer 1988
- *New Zealand Yearbook, 1987-88.* Wellington: Department of Statistics 1988

Waitangi Tribunal. *Finding of the Waitangi Tribunal relating to Te Reo Maori.* Wellington: Waitangi Tribunal 1986

Index

Aboriginal Child Placement Principle (Australia), 54-5, 63, 65, 66-7
Aboriginal Law Bulletin, 66
Aboriginals. *See also* Aboriginals, Australian; First Nations, Canadian; Maori, New Zealand
legislation affecting. *See* Legislation
policy, comparison of Australia, Canada, and New Zealand, 8-10, 185-219
Aboriginals, Australian. *See also* Australia; Organizations, aboriginal
administration of, 33-40, 198-204
assimilation of, attempted, 19-21, 41, 42-7, 53, 59-62, 192, 204-10, 220
and child welfare policy, 41-69, 204-11, 217-19
and citizenship, 25, 192, 233
cultural issues, 19, 64, 204, 215
definition of, 22-7, 67, 195-6, 196-7, 239
education, 42-5, 60
and families, 46, 54, 65, 66-9
half-caste, 20, 23, 44, 57-9, 60, 198, 208
integration of, attempted, 21-2, 190-3
land issues, 37-8, 193, 199, 200-1
legislation affecting. *See* Legislation
and missionaries, 33, 35-6, 42
as 'outlaws,' 22, 24
as pastoral station workers, 17, 21, 36-7
population, 27-33, 190, 191
protected status, 18-19
religion, aboriginal, 204
and self-government, 21-2, 62
settlements, 18, 33-4, 35
and settlers, 16-18, 19, 48, 188, 224
urbanization of, 29, 32-3, 213-14
Aboriginals, Canadian. *See* First Nations, Canadian
Aboriginals, New Zealand. *See* Maori, New Zealand
Adoption, of aboriginal children. *See* Children, aboriginal
Alberta (Canada), aboriginal child welfare policy, 121-2, 123
Assimilation attempts, of aboriginals
Australia, 42-7, 53, 59-62, 192, 204-10
Canada, 75-80, 82, 100, 103-13, 135, 190, 204-10, 220
New Zealand, 141-5, 156-8, 190, 220
policy, comparison of Australia, Canada, and New Zealand, 220-42
'Assisted Aborigine' status (Australia), 24
Assu, Chief, 105
Auckland Star, 165
Australia. *See also* Aboriginals, Australian; names of states and territories
aboriginal child welfare policy, 41-69, 204-11, 217-19, 236-8. *See*

also Children, aboriginal; names of states
aboriginal social policy, 14-39, 202-3, 239-40
delivery of social services, 14, 21, 63
departments governing aboriginals' affairs. *See* Government departments and commissions; Reports and studies
labour laws, and aboriginals, 21, 36-7
legislation affecting aboriginals. *See* Legislation
settlement of, 14-18
Australian Child Endowment, 52

Banton, Michael, 185
Barambah (Australia), 49
Barman, Jean, 103, 104-5, 112
Berger, Thomas, 122
Binney, Judith, 166
Britain. *See also* Government departments and commissions; Legislation; Reports and studies
child welfare policy, and Poor Law, 5-6
colonial administration, and relations with aboriginals, 227-31
colonial empire, settlement of, 3-4
social reforms of 19th century, 4
British Columbia (Canada)
aboriginal child welfare policy, 101, 129-32
lack of treaties with First Nations, 95
Brown, Ned and Heni, 167
Buck, Peter, 143
Butterworth, George, 141

Canada. *See also* First Nations, Canadian; Indian bands (Canada); Métis (Canada)
aboriginal child welfare policy, 100-35, 204-11, 217-19, 236-8. *See also* Children, aboriginal
aboriginal social policy, 70-99, 202-3, 239-40
British conquest of, 73
delivery of aboriginal social services, 82, 98, 101, 102, 113-14
departments governing aboriginals' affairs. *See* Government departments and commissions
human rights legislation, 10, 81, 82, 86
and land claims, recognition of, 81, 201
legislation affecting aboriginals. *See* Legislation
Canadian Association of Social Workers (CASW), 113
Canadian Welfare Council (CWC), 113
Caribbean, extermination of aboriginals, 5
Cartier, Jacques, 70, 72
Champagne-Aishihik band, 132, 133
Cherbourg (Australia), 49, 50
Children, aboriginal. *See also* Residential schools, for aboriginals
adoption of
Australia, 51-2, 66-7
Canada, 114-16, 132, 213
New Zealand, 164-5, 168-9, 181-2
education
Australia, 42-5, 60
Canada, 75-7, 96-7, 106-13
New Zealand, 143, 146, 151, 156-8, 173-5
foster homes
Australia, 46, 61-2, 65-7
Canada, 114, 115, 120, 121
New Zealand, 161, 167-8, 178, 180
juvenile offences, New Zealand, 162, 163, 169, 170, 180
orphanages, New Zealand, 161
overrepresented in child care system
Australia, 47, 204-5
Canada, 117, 119-20, 135, 205
New Zealand, 169, 170-1
population
Australia, 27-9, 211
Canada, 92, 211
New Zealand, 152-3, 211
removal from parents
Australia, 7, 20, 43, 45-6, 51-2, 60-1, 204-10

Canada, 7, 110, 113-22, 204-10
  as form of genocide, 6-7
  New Zealand, 7
  welfare policy
    Australia, 41-69
    Canada, 100-35
    New Zealand, 160-84
Chisholm, Richard, 66
Christian, Wayne, 130
Churches. *See* Religion and churches
Citizenship, of aboriginals
  Australia, 24-5, 192, 233
  Canada, 78, 95, 105, 192, 233-4
  New Zealand, 141, 142, 150, 192, 196-7, 199, 233
'Citizenship and Social Class,' 233
Clarke, George, 141
Coates, Ken, 108
Colonial empire, British. *See* Britain
Competency Certification Project (New Zealand), 180-2, 217
Convicts, as settlers of Australia, 14, 16
Cook, Captain, 138
Cootamundra Home, 43, 47
Cumberland, Tanya, 172

Davidson, Allan, 144
Desjarlais, Lester, 128

Economic development, aboriginal
  Australia, 37
  Canada, 81
Education. *See* Children, aboriginal; Residential schools, for aboriginals
Edwards, Coral, 43, 64
Elkin, Robert, 17
Else, Anne, 161
'Enfranchised' status (Canada), 78-9, 84
England. *See* Britain
Ethnonationalism, 231-2. *See also* Self-government, aboriginal
Evans, Ted, 26, 59
'Exemption' status (Australia), 19-20, 24-7
Extermination, of aboriginals, 5, 17, 33, 48-9

First Nations, Canadian. *See also* Canada; Indian bands (Canada); Métis (Canada); names of provinces and territories; Organizations, aboriginal
  administration of, 89, 94-7, 198-204
  assimilation of, attempted, 75-80, 82, 100, 103-13, 135, 190, 204-10, 220
  and child welfare agreements, 123-33, 134
  and child welfare policy, 100-35. *See also* Children, aboriginal
  and citizenship, 78, 95, 105, 192, 233-4
  cultural issues, 78-9, 105-6, 120-1, 204, 215
  and definition of 'Indian,' 77, 82, 83-7, 102, 194, 195-6, 196-7, 216, 239
  and education, 75-7, 96-7, 100, 106-13. *See also* Residential schools, for aboriginals
  electoral representation, 192
  and families, 88, 110, 111
  integration of, attempted, 79-80, 190-3
  land issues, 77, 81, 199, 200-1
  legislation affecting. *See* Legislation
  and missionaries, 72-3, 75-7, 78, 96, 103-13, 199, 204
  population, 87-9, 90-3, 190, 191
  religion, aboriginal, 97-8, 204
  and Royal Proclamation (1763), 73-4, 81, 95
  and self-government, 80-3, 97, 135
  and settlers, 70-3, 224
  and treaties, 89, 94-5, 188-9
Fitzroy, Captain, 141
Fleras, Augie, 241
Foley, Matthew, 54
France, loss of Canada to Britain, 73

Geise, Harry, 60
Genocide, of Australian aboriginals, 17, 33, 48-9, 187
Giesbrecht, Brian, 128
Goldthorpe, J.E., 227

Gosford, Lord, 75
Government departments and commissions. *See also* Legislation; Reports and studies
  Australia
    Aboriginal and Torres Strait Islander Commission (ATSIC), 37
    Aboriginal and Torres Strait Islanders Council, 63
    Aboriginal Development Commission, 21, 37
    Aboriginal Development Council, 63
    Aborigines Protection Board (New South Wales), 42-5
    Aborigines Welfare Board (New South Wales), 45-7
    Child Welfare Department (New South Wales), 47
    Commonwealth Department of Aboriginal Affairs, 21, 37, 62, 63
    Commonwealth Department of Community Development, 62-3
    Commonwealth Department of Community Services, 63
    Department of Aboriginal Affairs, 34-5
    Department of Community Development (Northern Territory), 62
    Department of Family and Child Services (Queensland), 54-5
    Law Reform Commission, 63-4
    Protector, 34-5, 48-51
    Royal Commission into Aboriginal Deaths in Custody, 64
  Britain
    House of Commons Select Committee on Aborigines (1837), 4, 8, 17, 18, 22, 34, 35, 74-5, 76-7, 78, 136, 139, 186, 189, 194, 199, 204, 222
  Canada
    Bagot Commission, 103
    Department of Indian Affairs, 77, 199
    Department of Indian Affairs and Northern Development (DIAND), 80, 87, 98, 216
    Family and Children's Services Legislation Review Panel, Aboriginal Committee (British Columbia), 131
    House of Commons Special Committee on Indian Self-Government, 81, 89
    Penner Committee, 81
    Royal Commission on Family and Child Welfare Law (1976), 122
    Superintendent of Indian Affairs, 78, 95
  New Zealand
    Children's Court, 161
    Department of Maori Affairs, 145, 146, 147-8, 158, 177
    Department of Social Welfare, 149, 162, 172, 177-8, 179, 180-2
    Maori Council, 146
    Maori Land Court, 143, 146, 151, 164, 166, 167-8, 224
    Maori Trustee, 158
    Ministry of Education, 161
    Ministry of Maori Affairs, 174
    Ministry of Social Welfare, 161
    Native Affairs Department, 158-9
    Native Department, 143, 190
    Royal Commission on Social Policy, 148, 153, 169
    Social Welfare Commission, 179
    Waitangi Tribunal, 147, 151, 156, 175-7, 182
Graham, George, 165, 166
Grant, Foster, 77
Great Britain. *See* Britain
Grey, George, 141, 142

Hasluck, Paul, 38, 59-60
Higgins, Joan, 7
Hobson, Captain, 139, 140
Housing, funding for aboriginal

Australians, 37
Human rights
  Charter of Rights and Freedoms
    (Canada), 10, 81, 82, 86
  United Nations Declaration of
    Human Rights, 10
Hunn, J.K., 145, 150, 156, 159, 184
Huron people (Canada), 72

Indian Act (Canada), 77-8, 79, 82,
  84, 85, 86, 95, 100, 102, 106,
  113, 134, 189
Indian bands (Canada). *See also* First
    Nations, Canadian; Métis
    (Canada)
  band councils, 97
  and child welfare agreements, 123-
    6, 131-3
  and definition of 'Indian,' 86
  as limited form of self-government,
    96
*Indian Child and Family Services
  Management Regime: Discussion
  Paper*, 126
Indian School Days, 110-11
Indians, Canadian. *See* Canada; First
  Nations, Canadian; Indian bands
  (Canada)
Integration
  attempted, of aboriginals and
    settlers, 223, 230
  and social services, 236
Inuit (Canada), 86, 87

Johnston, Basil, 110-11
Johnston, Patrick, 113, 117

*Ka Whawhai Tonu Matou: Struggle
  Without End*, 155
Ke Awatea, 159
Kelly, Tennant, 49
Kilcoy (Australia), 49
Killoran, P.J., 53
Kinchella Home, 44, 47
King, Jane, 43
King, Richard, 109, 111
Koepping, Klaus-Peter, 50

Land issues
  Australia, 16-17, 37, 38, 193, 199,
    200-1
  Canada, 77, 81, 199, 200-1
  comparison of Australia, Canada,
    and New Zealand, 224-7
  New Zealand, 141, 143, 146, 155-6,
    193, 199, 200-1, 242
  resource extraction, and seizure of
    aboriginal land, 9
Languages, aboriginal
  revival of, New Zealand, 148, 174-7
  suppression of
    Australia, 204
    Canada, 110, 204
    New Zealand, 143, 156-7
Legal system
  Aboriginal Legal Service (Australia),
    63, 66
  courts, support for Canadian First
    Nations land claims, 81
Legislation. *See also* Government
    departments and commissions;
    Reports and studies
  Australia
    Aboriginal Affairs Act (South
      Australia, 1962), 25
    Aboriginal Affairs Act (Victoria,
      1967), 20
    Aboriginal Affairs Planning Act
      (Western Australia, 1972),
      26
    Aboriginal Land Act (Northern
      Territory, 1980), 38
    Aboriginal Ordinance (Northern
      Territory, 1936), 25
    Aboriginal Preservation and
      Protection Act (Queens-
      land, 1939), 51-2, 53
    Aboriginals Affairs Planning and
      Authority Act (Western
      Australia, repeal of 1972),
      20
    Aboriginals Protection and
      Restriction of the Sale of
      Opium Act (1897), 48-9
    Aboriginals Protection and
      Restriction of the Sale of
      Opium Act (Queensland,
      1901), 18

Aborigines Act (Northern Territory, 1910), 18
Aborigines and Torres Strait Islanders Affairs Act (Queensland, 1965), 24, 52-4
Aborigines Protection Act (New South Wales, repeal of, 1969), 20
Aborigines Protection Act (Victoria, 1869), 18
Commonwealth Electoral Act (amendment of 1962), 20
Commonwealth Social Services Consolidation Act (1947), 24
Constitution Act (1900), 27-33
Constitution Act (1967 amendment), 20, 21, 37
Native Welfare Act (Western Australia, 1972), 20
Pitjantjatjara Act (South Australia, 1981), 26
Racial Discrimination Act (Queensland, 1975), 53
Social Services Act (1959), 24
Welfare Ordinance (Northern Territory, 1953), 23-4
Britain
  Poor Law (1834), 4-6, 234
  Royal Proclamation (1763), 73-4, 81, 95
Canada
  Charter of Rights and Freedoms, 10, 81, 82, 86
  Children's Act (Yukon Territory, revised 1984), 132-3
  Constitution Act (1982), 73, 81, 86
  Family and Child Service Act (British Columbia), 131
  Indian Act (1876), 77-8, 84, 100, 102, 189
  Indian Act (1879), 95
  Indian Act (1886), 86
  Indian Act (1922 amendment), 79
  Indian Act (1948 amendment), 79
  Indian Act (1951), 82, 85, 86, 106, 113, 134

New Zealand
  Adoption Act (1955), 150, 164, 168, 181
  Births and Deaths Registration Act (1951), 150
  Child Welfare Act (1925), 161, 165
  Children and Young Persons Act (1974), 164, 172, 179
  Children, Young Persons and Their Families Act (1989), 164, 180, 181, 241
  Education Act (1914), 150
  Electoral Act (1956), 150, 153
  Land Settlement Act (1904), 156
  Maori Affairs Act (1953), 150, 153, 156
  Maori Affairs Amendment Act (1967), 156
  Maori Housing Act (1935), 150
  Maori Land Act (1862), 143
  Maori Purposes Fund Act (1934-35), 150
  Maori Representation Act (1867), 143, 192
  Maori Soldiers Trust Act (1957), 150
  Native Schools Act (1867), 143, 156, 190
  Neglected and Criminal Children Act (1867), 161
  Social Security Act (1964), 179
  Treaty of Waitangi, 140-2, 147, 148, 149, 150, 151, 176, 182, 183, 189, 192. *See also* Waitangi Tribunal
  Treaty of Waitangi Act (1975), 146, 147
and research on social policy, 10
Liberating Our Children: Liberating Our Nations, 131

'Maatua Whangi,' 177-8, 182, 216
MacPherson, Stewart, 228
MacQuarrie, Governor, 17, 22, 33
Manitoba (Canada)
  aboriginal child welfare policy, 101, 123-4, 126-9
  First Nations population, 88

Maori, New Zealand. *See also* New
  Zealand; Organizations,
  aboriginal
 administration of, 139-51, 155-6,
   158-9, 198-204
 assimilation of, attempted, 141-5,
   156-8, 190, 220
 and citizenship, 141, 142, 150,
   192, 196-7, 199, 233
 cultural issues, 148, 169, 173-7,
   178-9
 definition of, 150, 152-3, 195-6,
   198, 216, 239
 education, 143, 146, 151, 156-8
 and electoral representation, 142,
   143, 150, 192
 and families, 164-9, 173-5
 integration of, attempted, 145-6
 and land issues, 141, 143, 146, 147,
   155-6, 193, 199, 200-1, 242
 legislation affecting. *See* Legislation
 Maori King Movement, 158
 and missionaries, 138, 140, 141-2,
   144
 parliament, 143, 158
 political activism, 143-4, 145, 158
 population, 151-5, 190, 191
 religion, aboriginal, 144-5, 204
 and self-government, 146-50
 and settlers, 136-41, 224
 and Treaty of Waitangi, 140-2, 147,
   148, 149, 150, 151, 176, 182,
   183, 189, 192
Maori, Pakeha and Democracy, 149
'Maoritanga,' 144
Marshall, T.H., 233-5. *See also* Social
  policy
McCarthy, Grace, 130
'The Mechanics of Choice,' 26
Métis (Canada), 85-6, 87, 88, 101,
  194, 216
Military force, and control of
  aboriginals, 5
Miller, J.R., 84, 103
Mishra, Ramesh, 233
Missionaries. *See also* Religion and
  churches
 Australia, 33, 35-6, 42
 Canada, 72-3, 75-7, 78, 96, 103-13,
   199, 204
 New Zealand, 138, 140, 141-2, 144,
   204
 view of aboriginal religions, 187
Mitchell, Michael, 89
Mitchell, Robin, 149
Mopass, Yukon Territory (Canada),
  109
Morris, Alexander, 94
Mulgan, Richard, 149

Native Welfare Conference (Australia,
  1961), 52
Neville, A.O., 44
New South Wales (Australia)
 aboriginal child welfare policy,
   42-7
 aboriginal population, 29, 30, 32
New Zealand. *See also* Maori, New
  Zealand
 aboriginal child welfare policy,
   160-84, 204-10, 217-19. *See
   also* Children, aboriginal
 aboriginal social policy, 136-59,
   187-8, 202-3, 211-14
 departments governing aboriginals'
   affairs. *See* Government departments and commissions
 legislation affecting aboriginals. *See*
   Legislation
 settlement of, 138-9, 142
New Zealand Association, 139
New Zealand Yearbook, 165
Newfoundland, extermination of
  aboriginals, 5
Ngata, Apirana, 143, 144, 146
Nielsen, Eric, 82
'Non-treaty' Indian (Canada), 84
Northern Territory (Australia)
 aboriginal child welfare policy, 55-
   63
 aboriginal self-government, 21
 aboriginals as majority, 55-6
 and half-caste aboriginals, 20
 legislation affecting aboriginals. *See*
   Legislation
Northwest Territories (Canada)
 First Nations population, 88
 lack of treaties with First Nations, 95

O'Connor, Hubert, 112
Oliver, Father, 111
Onekawa, Putiputi, 166-7
Ontario (Canada)
   aboriginal child welfare policy, 122-3
   treaties with First Nations, 84
Organizations, aboriginal
   Australia, 215-16
      Aboriginal and Islander Child Care Agencies (AICCA), 65, 66, 68
      Link-Up, 64-5, 215-16, 240
      Secretariat of the National Aboriginal and Islander Child Care (SNAICC), 65, 66
   Canada
      Allied Tribes of British Columbia, 97
      Assembly of First Nations (AFN), 98-9, 133-5
      Dakota Ojibway Child and Family Services Agency (Manitoba), 128
      Four Nations Confederacy, 123
      Grand General Indian Council of Ontario and Quebec, 97
      League of Indians of Canada, 97
      Ma-Mawi-Wi-Chi-Itata (Manitoba), 126, 128-9, 240
      Manitoba Indian Brotherhood (MIB), 126
      National Indian Brotherhood (NIB), 80, 98
      Nishga Land Committee, 97
   New Zealand
      Iwi Transition Agency, 158-9
      Kokiri Centre, 148
      Maori Women's Welfare League, 169
      Ratana Political Party, 145
      Te Kohanga Reo, 173-5, 176, 182, 217, 240
      Women Against Racism Action Group (WARAG), 172-3
      Young Maori Party, 143-4, 145, 204

Orphanages, in New Zealand, 161

'Pakeha Wars,' 142-3, 189
Paul III (Pope). *See* Pope Paul III
Peters, Winston, 159
Poisoning, of aboriginal Australians, 49
Pollard, David, 39
Pomare, Maui, 143
Pontiac's Rebellion (Canada), 73
Pope Paul III, 72
Population, aboriginal
   Australia, 27-33
   Canada, 87-9, 90-3
   and definition of 'aboriginal,' 11
   New Zealand, 151-5, 190, 191
   research, problems with, 11-12
Potatau the First, 142, 158
Potlatch, outlawing of, 105-6
Protector (Department of Aboriginal Affairs, Australia). *See* Government departments and commissions
Protectors, Conference of (Australia, 1937), 51
Provencher, J., 94
Puketapu, 158

Quebec, and Royal Proclamation, 1763, 73-4
Queensland (Australia)
   aboriginal child welfare policy, 47-55
   aboriginal population, 29, 30, 32
   administration of aboriginal people, 20-1, 36
   land issues, 21
   legislation affecting aboriginals. *See* Legislation

Race Politics in Australia, 39-40
Race Relations, 185
Race relations, between aboriginals and settlers, 221-7
Racial discrimination
   Australia, 39-40, 237
   Canada, 121, 237
   New Zealand, 149-50
Rangihau, John, 173

Rata, Matiu, 146
Ratana, Tahpotiki Wiremu, 144
Ratana Church (New Zealand), 144-5
Ratana Movement, 150
Read, Peter, 19, 64, 68
Religion and churches. *See also* Missionaries
　Aboriginal, Australian, 204
　Church Missionary Society, 138, 141, 142, 199
　Church of England, 138
　First Nations, Canadian, 97-8, 204
　Jesuit missionaries, in Canada, 72, 75-6
　Maori, New Zealand, 144-5, 204
　Roman Catholic Church, 138
　Wesleyans, 138
Reports and studies. *See also* Government departments and commissions
　Aboriginal Customary Law (Australia), 63-4
　Beveridge Report (Britain, 1941), 5
　Bleakley Report (Australia, 1928), 56, 58
　Davin Report (Canada, 1879), 103
　Hawthorn Report (Canada, 1966), 114-15, 122
　Hunn Report (New Zealand), 156, 159, 184
　Puao-te-Ata-tu Report (New Zealand), 148-9, 173, 178-80, 182
　White Paper on Indian policy (Canada, 1969), 80, 98, 193
Reserves, aboriginal
　Australia, 35, 43, 49-51
　Canada, 89, 102, 122-3, 224
　New Zealand, non-existent in, 140-1
Residential schools, for aboriginals. *See also* Children, aboriginal
　Australia, 42-4, 236-7
　Canada, 77, 96-7, 106-13, 236-7
Retta Dixon Home, 59, 61, 62
Rowley, C.D., 36
Royal Proclamation (Britain, 1763), 73-4, 81, 95
Rua, 144

Ryan, Lyndall, 53

Saskatchewan (Canada), First Nations population, 88
The School at Mopass, 109
Scott, Duncan Campbell, 104
Self-government, aboriginal. *See also* Ethnonationalism
　as assimilation, 241
　Australia, 21-2, 62
　Canada, 80-3, 134, 135, 195
　New Zealand, 146-50
Sexual abuse, of aboriginal children, 44, 112, 208
Sifton, Clifford, 104
Smith, L.R., 27
Social policy. *See also* Aboriginals, Australian; First Nations, Canadian; Maori, New Zealand
　and aboriginals, comparison of Australia, Canada, and New Zealand, 8-10, 185-219
　reform, in 19th century Britain, 4
　research, 7-8, 10-13
Social workers
　as advisors to government on aboriginal matters, 10
　and Canadian First Nations, 113, 125, 126, 132
Spallumcheen band, 130
Spencer, W. Baldwin, 56, 57

Tasmania
　aboriginal population, 29, 30, 32
　extermination of aboriginals, 5, 17, 33
Tatz, Colin, 39, 198, 230
Tawhiaho, 144
Te Kooti, 144
Te Reo Maori, 175-7, 182
Thonloe, George, 105
'Tino rangatiratanga,' 181
Tobias, John, 78
Treaties, with aboriginals
　Australia, lack of, 14
　Canada, 89, 94-5, 188-9
　New Zealand, Treaty of Waitangi, 140-2, 146, 147, 148, 149, 150, 151, 176, 182, 183, 189, 192.

See also Waitangi Tribunal
United States, Two Row Wampum Treaty, 89
The Treaty and the Act, 149
Treaty of Paris, 73
'Tu tangata' philosophy, 158

United Nations
  Convention on the prevention and punishment of the crime of genocide, 6
  Convention on the rights of the child, 238
  Declaration of human rights, 10
  International convention on the elimination of all forms of racial discrimination, 229
Urbanization, of aboriginals
  Australia, 29, 32-3, 213-14
  Canada, 89, 93, 213-14
  New Zealand, 154-5, 213-14

Victoria (Australia)
  aboriginal population, 29, 30, 32
  legislation affecting aboriginals. *See* Legislation

Waitangi Tribunal, 147, 151, 156, 175-7, 182. *See also* Legislation, Treaty of Waitangi
Walker, Ranginui, 155
'Ward,' definition of, 23-4
Welfare state, 8-9, 234-6
Western Australia
  aboriginal population, 29, 30, 32
  legislation affecting aboriginals. *See* Legislation
Weteve, Koro, 174
Wharf, Brian, 129-30
Williams, William, 140, 142
Women, and Indian Act (Canada), 79, 84, 85, 86

Yukon Territory (Canada)
  aboriginal child welfare policy, 101-2, 108, 123-4, 132-3
  First Nations population, 88
  lack of treaties with First Nations, 95

Set in Stone by Val Speidel

Printed and bound in Canada by D.W. Friesen & Sons Ltd.

Copy-editor: Joanne Richardson

Indexer: Annette Lorek

Proofreader: Nancy Pollak

Cartographer: Eric Leinberger